The Haydn Economy

NEW MATERIAL HISTORIES of MUSIC
a series edited by James Q. Davies *and* Nicholas Mathew

Also published in the series:

The Haydn Economy

Music, Aesthetics, and Commerce
in the Late Eighteenth Century

NICHOLAS MATHEW

The University of Chicago Press

Chicago and London

The University of Chicago Press, Chicago 60637
The University of Chicago Press, Ltd., London
© 2022 by The University of Chicago
Published 2022
Printed in the United States of America

31 30 29 28 27 26 25 24 23 22   1 2 3 4 5

ISBN-13: 978-0-226-81984-6 (cloth)
ISBN-13: 978-0-226-81985-3 (e-book)
DOI: https://doi.org/10.7208/chicago/9780226819853.001.0001

This book has been supported by the Joseph Kerman Fund and the General
Publications Fund of the American Musicological Society, funded in part by the
National Endowment for the Humanities and the Andrew W. Mellon Foundation.

Library of Congress Cataloging-in-Publication Data

Names: Mathew, Nicholas, author.
Title: The Haydn economy : music, aesthetics, and commerce in the late eighteenth
    century / Nicholas Mathew.
Other titles: Music, aesthetics, and commerce in the late eighteenth century |
    New material histories of music.
Description: Chicago ; London : The University of Chicago Press, 2022. |
    Series: New material histories of music | Includes bibliographical references
    and index.
Identifiers: LCCN 2021054596 | ISBN 9780226819846 (cloth) |
    ISBN 9780226819853 (ebook)
Subjects: LCSH: Haydn, Joseph, 1732–1809. | Haydn, Joseph, 1732–1809—Travel—
    England—London. | Composers—Austria—Biography. | Music—Economic
    aspects—History—18th century. | Music—Social aspects—History—18th century. |
    Music—18th century—History and criticism.
Classification: LCC ML410.H4 M24 2022 | DDC 780.92 [B] —dc23
LC record available at https://lccn.loc.gov/2021054596

Contents

To my father,
William Mitchell Mathew

Introduction

With bee-like skill, from flower to flower,
Improving every fleeting hour,
Pleas'd I behold my URBAN rove
Through field and forest, vale and grove.
    "To MR. URBAN" (1783)[1]

Ringing Coins

In the course of a long European tour funded by Gustav III of Sweden, the young composer Joseph Martin Kraus dropped in on his musical hero Haydn at the palace of Eszterháza. He pronounced him a "good soul, except for one thing—money." Haydn—so Kraus reported to his parents—was astonished that his junior colleague had not thought to bring along more of his own music, to hawk to publishers while he was on the road. And Kraus gave a mischievous description of Haydn's response to the composer Johann Sterkel, who had written requesting to swap some new arias: "Haydn shook his head, no ringing coins there."[2]

Kraus's amused account of Haydn's indecently keen ear for ringing coins doubtless owed something to the aristocratic pretentions of a newly appointed court Kapellmeister. In his earlier years, moreover, Kraus had come into regular contact with the musical print economies of North Germany and may have assumed a distinction between merely saleable fare and music of a more exclusive and elevated kind. Whereas this distinction increasingly shaped the professional activity of such contemporaries as Carl Philipp Emanuel Bach, Haydn had encountered North German print commerce only at a distance and mostly via the relatively new genre of published critical commentary (which had not always treated him generously).

As it turns out, Kraus had happened upon Haydn as he embarked on a newly lucrative phase in his career. It was 1783, and changing legal protocols and local media environments had lately presented Haydn with the opportunity to earn income from his music in new ways: the largest Viennese *Kunsthandlung*—an art and print shop—run by Carlo and Francesco Artaria had expanded into selling and making music engravings, while Haydn's revised contracts with the Esterházy court no longer explicitly forbade him from supplying his music to outside parties. Haydn's annual income as Esterházy Kapellmeister, exclusive of princely favors and various chattels, was 782 gulden 30 kreuzer. Selling six string quartets to Artaria had recently earned him more than half that.³ A glimpse of how these ringing coins were passed from hand to hand is revealed in a communication from September 1782, when Haydn, who had just provided Artaria with some opera overtures, asked his publishers to "put the 25 ducats (N.B. full weight [*gewichtige Ducaten*]) into a little box, seal it up, wrap it or sew it in an oil-cloth cover, and write nothing on it except '*à Mons Haydn*'"—an elaborate set of remittance instructions apparently aimed at dampening the ringing of the coins, and perhaps also concealing his growing income from the rest of his household.⁴

But by the time of Haydn's London trips—from January 1791 until July 1792 and from February 1794 until August 1795—his money had become a more virtual substance, speeding across the continent in emerging systems of credit. Thus, when a series of misfortunes and political intrigues prevented Haydn's new opera *L'anima del filosofo* from appearing on the London stage early in 1791, he was able to console himself that at least his Viennese bankers—Fries and Co., now directed by the extravagant, music-loving Moritz von Fries—had already received his substantial payment.⁵ Haydn himself had been pulled toward London in the same transnational channels through which his money traveled. Bankers were among the earliest brokers who sought to entice him there, and he spent a great deal of time with this moneyed class in England: his earliest English summer included two months at the country estate belonging to Nathaniel Brassey of the old banking house of Ayton, Brassey and Co. Toward the end of his London visits, Haydn—the prize asset—was an honored guest in the vaults of the Bank of England, where he reported seeing stacks of gold ingots "most of which are worth £700" and "an enormous amount of Spanish taler." Only weeks before, he had wrapped up the 1795 season with a packed concert in the Opera Rooms of the Haymarket Theatre: "I made four thousand Gulden on this evening. Such a thing is only possible in England," he noted.⁶ Here was a musician newly sensitized to the sounds of commerce, to music and money, who had as yet no Romantic notion that "culture" was the "normal antithesis to the market," as Raymond Williams once put it.⁷

That the artist and the market are, or should be, natural antagonists is one of the more recognizable Romantic beliefs. It has received a fair amount of scholarly attention over the years. There exist many studies of how that intellectual and sensuous domain frequently parsed as *the aesthetic* became resistant and even redemptive within modern market societies;⁸ of how social distinctions have been produced and sustained by the division of this domain into art and entertainment, elite and commercial culture;[9] and of how, especially in its modernist phases, art has announced its apparent rejection of market forces through formal strategies that forestall easy or instant consumption habits. The scholarly strategies of disenchantment—perhaps especially when it comes to the paradigmatically Romantic art of music, with its supposedly minimal traction on the material world—have always been within arm's reach, as if the mere fact that musicians, even Romantic or modernist ones, have needed to subsist should be a permanent embarrassment to their aesthetic aspirations.[10] For all that, as innumerable Hollywood musician biopics and productions of La Bohème demonstrate, the image of the otherworldly artist, impervious to the demands of the market, has by now become a trope more commonly encountered in the form of parody or high camp. Nowadays, if it requires no particular feat of imagination to intuit that the economic is the dirty secret of the aesthetic and that the aesthetic is the alluring secret of the economic, this is mostly because these secrets have been so poorly kept. Marxists of various stripes have for some time unpicked the relationships between the commodity form and the artwork.[11] And recent studies of late twentieth-century style and aesthetics, such as Sianne Ngai's Our Aesthetic Categories, tend to start from Fredric Jameson's premise that the annexation of "culture" by market-driven conceptions of human interaction and attraction is one of the distinguishing features of so-called late capitalist societies.[12]

Inspired in part by the theoretical and ethical nuance of recent ethnomusicological studies of musical livelihoods,[13] this book is concerned neither with a postmodern celebration of the relationship between the aesthetic and the economic nor with its ideological unmasking. Part of the reason is straightforwardly historical. In the late eighteenth-century places that Haydn knew, the discourses of sensation and taste, sympathy and sentiment, government and wealth had yet to be reorganized into the hulking nineteenth-century disciplines of aesthetics and economics. This book examines the implications of this distinctive historical situation through the musical practices of Haydn and his contemporaries. In doing so, it responds to a body of research within literary studies that has not only measured the imaginative impact of the urban commercial world on the printed materials of the eighteenth century but has also showed how these materials were as yet indivisible according to a largely nineteenth-century conception of genre: novels, tracts on political economy, reportage, essays on moral philosophy, and even the legal forms of inscription that constituted credit and paper money—all of these existed in a generic tangle.[14] These studies have illustrated in densely material terms what intellectual historians have long maintained: despite their apparently antithetical relation, aesthetics and economics have a shared origin.[15] Only once economics became a discipline aspiring to the status of a natural science could it be separated from aesthetics once and for all, as fact is divisible from value.[16] Thus did a distinctively modern pattern of thought become available: beauty and justice either arise providentially from a market system blindly obeying its own immutable laws, or these become the "values" that humanity must drape over this system's neutral frame. Still, something of the vestigial connection between these domains can be uncovered in words that nowadays seem to oscillate between incommensurable economic and aesthetic or ethical meanings: *interest, investment, value, credit, work.* Terms such as these organize the main arguments of this book. More than mere aesthetic-economic puns, they function as apertures through which we glimpse another world.

The Viennese generation that followed Haydn's included several musicians—his student Ludwig van Beethoven not least among them—who cleaved, at least in theory, to the market-resisting view of the Romantic artist. But Haydn achieved his unprecedented success just before the discord of music and the ringing of coins.

Haydn and the City

Eighteenth-century musicians experienced the processes of economic change that this book theorizes in radically uneven ways, depending on professional status and local circumstance. Haydn's experience was characterized by a clear change of tack: he was a court Kapellmeister turned entrepreneur. To begin with, he produced his music almost exclusively within the ancient physical structures and legal constructs of his region's courts. But, from the 1780s in particular, Haydn's professional life was gradually altered by his increased access to transcontinental print commerce and, by extension, the concert scenes of several European and colonial centers. By 1788, a short biography of Haydn in the *Allmanach der K. K. National-Schaubühne* proudly observed that the "universality of Haydn's genius can be seen in no other way as clearly as through the large demand for his works that obtains in all of Europe": the motions of printed music and print about music within a transcontinental credit economy had made possible an abstract conception of public demand and its accompanying imaginative geography.[17] The culmination of this change in outlook was Haydn's pair of extended trips to England in the early 1790s. "A new world was opened up to him," wrote Haydn's friend and biographer Georg August Griesinger, "and he was enabled by generous profits at last to pull out of the limited circumstances in which he had grown old and gray."[18] These lucrative expeditions transformed Haydn's professional status, even once he had returned to Vienna, nominally still in the service of the Esterházy court, with his duties much reduced.

For some time, music historians have regarded the shape of Haydn's career as emblematic of the most fundamental social upheavals of the eighteenth century and, for that reason, have frequently been unable to resist imposing upon it historiographies of epochal change, as though Haydn were subject to vast, impersonal historical forces. The premise of this book is indeed that Haydn, in dialogue with the changing economic structures of the late eighteenth century, created new ways to experience and value music—ways that continue to shape our musical experiences and values. But his career nonetheless belies an old historiographical assumption—the principal target of Karl Polanyi's seminal study *The Great Transformation*—that once the "constraints" of feudalism are removed, capitalists inevitably burst forth.[19] Haydn never abandoned the shelter of the Esterházy court, which he served from 1761 until his death, and in the early 1790s he frequently yearned to return from the crowded commercial music scenes he occupied in London to a professional existence that, even in the city of Vienna, remained to a large extent structured by centuries-old court hierarchies.

Historians of eighteenth-century music have tended to invoke the court and the city as conceptual and physical opposites: ancient versus modern, aristocratic versus mercantile, feudalist versus capitalist. In this view, the court, along with its patronage model of musical production, is historically supplanted by the city and its marketplaces.[20] And in urban studies, scholars have frequently treated the city as the very emblem of modernity itself. But Haydn's career reminds us that courts were as much a part of the new urban experiences of the late eighteenth century as were an expanding repertoire of commercial relationships. The Esterházy court amounted to more than the palaces of Eszterháza and Eisenstadt and the grand house on the Wallnerstrasse in Vienna: it was embodied and performed in ritual practices and legal protocols that persisted beside and among the urban milieu. In London, meanwhile, Haydn frequently negotiated the complex rituals of court hierarchy and patronage, not least in his close encounters with the Prince of Wales within weeks of his arrival—at the queen's annual birthday ball and subsequently at a musical evening at Carlton House. "A remarkable occurrence happened this evening [January 18, 1791], in the ball-room at St. James's," the *Lady's Magazine* breathlessly reported in its "home news" section,

Haydn, the celebrated composer, though he has not yet been introduced at our court, was recognized by all the royal family, and paid them his silent respects. Mr. Haydn came into the room with Sir John Gallini, Mr. Willis, and Mr. Salomon. The Prince of Wales first observed him, and, upon bowing to him, the eyes of all the company were on Mr. Haydn, every one paying him respect.[21]

King George and Queen Charlotte were enthusiastic sponsors of the public concerts in the Hanover Square rooms and, during Haydn's years as the main attraction there, supported the venue's lavish tearoom.

Conversely, the city was not only a place in which many people lived close together but also a dense gathering of newly ordered relationships that traversed vast distances—a colossal medium of transmission and storage, as Friedrich Kittler would have it.[22] Leaving aside the old Marxist quarrels about whether capitalism was urban or agrarian in origin,[23] the European city had (and continues to have) a distinctive relationship with commerce[24] and, by the late eighteenth century, had come to perform the function of "absorbing the surplus product that capitalists are perpetually producing," as David Harvey puts it.[25] We can think of much of Haydn's music—especially the compositions produced expressly for publication or for ticketed public concerts—as this surplus product. Via the new media forms and new commercial transactions that were generated in Vienna, Paris, or London, Haydn thus came to participate in the musical lives of many urban centers, even when he was resident in faraway Eszterháza, at the southern end of the Neusiedlersee.

None of this is to diminish the importance of Haydn's personal experiences of Vienna and London nor the ways in which these immersive metropolitan experiences shaped and were shaped by his music. Rather, to recognize that cities consisted not only of physical geographies and fabrics but also human relationships and imaginative mediascapes is to characterize these urban spaces with greater texture.[26] London was much more populous than Vienna, of course. More than this, however, these were cities with radically contrasting psychogeographies and media environments. The Vienna in which Haydn moved operated according to the gravitational logic of an imperial capital, which drew a huge number of people—including noble families and their dependents—into its orbit from the multiethnic border regions around it. In 1773, the Londoner Charles Burney, who became a close friend of Haydn's in the 1790s following decades of distant admiration, was struck by a city that seemed to be "composed of palaces rather than of common habitations"—a description that contained more than a hint of hypocritical British disapproval at hierarchies made so legible.[27] For the duration of the eighteenth century, there were no ticketed concerts and, aside from concerts in the Augarten, the major concert venues that could fairly be called "public" were the pair of court theaters that stood near to the imperial palace, the city's drill halls and ballrooms, and a handful of multipurpose ceremonial rooms in aristocratic residences and the university.[28] And while the volume of newsprint and printed music was to increase sharply during the Napoleonic Wars, the late eighteenth-century Viennese media environment was modest by comparison with London's, with its copious print shops, circulating libraries, and booksellers. By 1791, London's newspapers included the *Morning Chronicle*, the *Morning Post*, the *General Advertiser*, the *Morning Herald*, the *Daily Universal Register*, *The Times*, *The World and Fashionable Advertiser*, the *Diary*, and *The Observer*—not to mention a range of magazines and periodicals—many of which reported, in varying levels of detail, on the city's musical events.

Haydn was immediately struck by London's density—by its crowds, by noise from street hawkers and nighttime revelers, by displays of mercantile wealth, by ships and ports and the presence of maritime folk, by the expansion of the city westward and northward into new mansions and squares, and southward across the Thames (he recorded many of his reactions to these things in a series of notebooks, which I discuss at length in chapter 2). And Haydn had never before witnessed such a glut of music making. A preview of the major musical events of the 1791 season in the *Morning Chronicle* listed—besides the concerts in Hanover Square led by the violinist and impresario Johann Peter Salomon, at which Haydn was the star attraction—the "professional concert under the able conduct of *Cramer*," "two rival *Opera* houses," the "*Antient concert*," the "*Ladies subscription concert*" on Sunday evenings, "Oratorios twice a week" during Lent, and the "*Academy of Antient Music*." And this did not include the concerts in the main pleasure gardens, the large musical gatherings sponsored by such organizations as the Anacreontic Society, and countless semiprivate musical performances in the houses of the gentry.[29] People showed up in their droves. The socialite Charlotte Papendiek, whose husband was a court musician during the 1790s, noted on her ticket that "1500 people entered the door" at Hanover Square to hear Haydn's concert on May 3, 1792, even though the main performance space reportedly held only 500–800 people, excluding performers.[30]

And yet one should be cautious not to treat Haydn's urban experience as axiomatically about density and noise, with crowded public spaces or bustling streets as its main symbols: this risks indulging a liberal fantasy of urban dynamism and diversity that dates back to the eighteenth century itself—a trope that connects the endlessly roving attention of Mr. Spectator, or Mr. Urban of the *Gentleman's Magazine*, with the ideas-economy utopianism of Richard Florida and his acolytes.[31] Cities meant, and still mean, not only unruly noise but regimes of control and public quietness: in 1792, the *Public*

Advertiser in London delightedly reported that a notice displayed at the latest Viennese performances of Haydn's newest symphonies had enjoined the audience to observe "Profound Silence."[32] And cities promoted, and continue to promote, not only human proximity but also strict lines of separation: the wealthy Yorkshire landowner Godfrey Bosville complained that, even in London's socially promiscuous Vauxhall Gardens, where a range of city dwellers indulged fantasies of pastoral repose, the crowd remained "all together, all distinct"—divided by class and fashion, even as they made a performance of their intermingling.[33]

In this book, the city is thus necessarily a symbolic domain as well as a densely packed physical space—a mediascape as well as a landscape, a relentless producer and absorber of surplus things, a web of economic relationships, and a portal to imaginative geographies of still wider worlds. Haydn's gradual entry into various urban "scenes" was momentous.[34] Scholars have long acknowledged that his encounters with the Viennese print scene or London's concert scene accompanied claims of musical newness: he advertised to several potential subscribers that the op. 33 string quartets of 1781 were "written in a new and special way" and ten years later set about "surprising the public with something new" (as he put it) with the Symphony no. 94.[35] But the story of Haydn and the city is about much more than his most obvious musical or rhetorical responses to the emerging modern attention economy.[36] Haydn lived through a moment in which it made no sense wholly to separate the demands of art from the demands of the market and when the language of aesthetics was not yet separate from the language of economics. In symphonies, songs, solo piano music, chamber music, and oratorios, Haydn repurposed and repackaged old musical materials, encouraged and entrained new kinds of audience investment and critical response, developed techniques to arouse and channel consumer desire, and, ultimately, came to reconceive the very work of the musician. The episodes of musical close reading in this book do not seek only to describe changing musical styles as a response to these changing historical conditions. They aim to articulate the premises upon which Haydn's music newly sought to engage and imagine its listeners, the aesthetic consequences of the media forms that this music inhabited, and the assumptions about music, the composer, and his world that this music came to embody.

Haydn is the main character of this book, yet he and his music will frequently disappear from view—absorbed or swamped by the whirl of sounds and objects that made his world. This book is not unduly concerned with reconstructing the experience of an exceptional person. It is, however, concerned with people and with experience. No book that centers on the music of a major court composer and venerated musical celebrity can be a history from below, of course. Still, I share E. P. Thompson's vision of history "embodied in real people and in a real context" and his belief that historical changes in values and social organization are meaningful only as they were experienced by people.[37] Indeed, one of the hunches that this book seeks to follow up is that the variously posthuman "new materialisms" that have prompted so much vital rethinking in the humanities lately have more in common than we may think with the anthropocentric "old materialisms" that they supposedly supplant—approaches, that is, predicated on the primacy of human-scale economies.[38] One might make this case especially well via eighteenth-century music, which so frequently performed and aestheticized the uncanny reverberations of the nonhuman world—partly in response to its entry into the all-too-human world of commercial exchange. This seems to me a musical instance of the "deep eighteenth century" postulated by Joseph Roach: the persistence and recrudescence of eighteenth-century values, practices, and aporias in the present.[39] One of the aims of this book is to give historical depth to music studies' renewed concern (a welcome one, to my mind) with categories such as political economy and capitalism.[40] Chapters 2 to 4, on interest, objects, and work, in some ways constitute a musicalizing and historicizing response to Ngai's trio of web-age aesthetic categories—the interesting, the cute, and the zany. I argue that the convergence of market and culture diagnosed by Jameson and assumed by Ngai—as well as the powerful fantasies of the posthuman that this convergence has promoted—echoes and replays episodes from Haydn's late eighteenth-century world.

Media, Motion, Connection

Economic surplus can be generated from sound only via particular technological means. How Haydn's music was imported and exported; how it assumed material forms and occupied performance spaces that made it amenable to new sorts of aesthetic appreciation and economic extraction; how this music was stored and updated: these are matters pertaining to media and the processes of mediation. Though historians have long represented the eighteenth century as a period of accelerated social and economic change, only recently have they explicitly proposed that it was also a period of media experimentation—a period in which new formats and genres, new principles of association, new protocols and laws, and new physical infrastructures gradually coalesced into the media environment that would host the major declarations and interventions of Romanticism.[41] This is, to my mind, less a dogmatic claim about the conceptual or historiographical priority of some universal "media concept" than a heuristic, which might encourage new ways of talking about music and the market in this period. There are a good many music histories that have already productively explored when, where, and how music was commoditized, was consumed, or became intellectual property.[42] But I want to emphasize the material forms and protocols that made these things possible.[43] This means not only the usual suspects, such as print commerce or the rise of the public concert, but the many forms of mediation that these categories have tended to summarize and elide: infrastructures, such as concert rooms, booksellers' warehouses, and piano builders' workshops; rules, such as ticketing and music copyright; formats, such as the piano reduction or the music magazine; and music-related genres, such as the concert review or the celebrity portrait.

Consider again Haydn's concert of May 3, 1792, with its 1,500-person crush. The movement of the elaborately engraved tickets in advance of the event not only allowed for relatively anonymous access but also produced a distinctive mode of social connection across London's beau monde: the day before the concert, Haydn's lover, the widow Rebecca Schroeter, wrote to him, trying to wangle an extra six tickets for friends and colleagues (an eye-watering three guineas' worth).[44] The music on the program revisited several existing compositions by Haydn, as well as promoting a roster of well-known singers and instrumentalists. As usual, the evening began with a piece that had been unveiled previously in the season, so that latecomers would not miss the newest fare (in this case, it was probably Haydn's Symphony no. 98). There followed an aria, a new concertante by Haydn, a cantata sung by Sophia Corri, and a violin concerto by Feliks Janiewicz. The second half followed a similar plan: a brand new symphony by Haydn (almost certainly the Symphony no. 97), a song performed by the tenor Giuseppe Simoni, a harp concerto by Anne-Marie Krumpholtz, a song performed by the German soprano Gertrude Mara, and—a conclusion surely guaranteed to bring the house down—the orchestral version of the "Terremoto," or earthquake, from the choral version of Haydn's Seven Last Words.[45] But the event itself was more than just a "concert program"—an especially extravagant instance of the relatively new medium of the ticketed public concert. It was also a nexus of overlapping media forms, requiring the collaboration of instrumentalists, singers, writers, businessmen, and instrument makers, dispersed across space and time: prepublicity and advertising in more than one newspaper; concert reviews and social diaries, which appeared in newspapers and journals over the following days; the published parts of chamber music by Haydn, which Salomon and others sold as "merch" at the concerts themselves; and a range of associated visual props. The Morning Chronicle announced that Thomas

Hardy's dashing new portrait of Haydn was on show on the day of the concert in the gallery of the Royal Academy—a picture that was already circulating as an engraving published by John Bland.[46] And alongside Haydn, one could also admire portraits of the evening's star performers, Krumpholtz and Mara.

With all this in mind, I try in this book to avoid making claims about what "music" is and what "music" does without posing the foundational question of media awareness: *In what?*[47] Music traveled across continents and oceans. People heard and responded to music in new ways. Music became a commodity. My aim is to turn such observations into questions, by adding—*in what?* Answering these questions means paying closer attention to the people and materials that remade music in its eighteenth-century environments, even as we acknowledge that people nowadays know this music only insofar as the processes of mediation that began in the eighteenth century have not yet ended.[48]

Turning our ears toward the hiss and crackle of mediation is a disciplinary shibboleth these days, one of the activities that distinguishes the new political ecologies of sound studies from the old musicologies.[49] And, to be sure, this turn to the medium-as-message reminds us of the bundles of technologies and processes that are required to extract economic value from sound: during Haydn's lifetime, the viable commercial circulation of his orchestral music as printed notation frequently required the format of the piano reduction, which in turn required the widespread presence of various keyboard instruments, which in turn required people with the competency to use these technologies, and so forth: "All amateurs know [the Andante with the Drum Stroke] in the edition for pianoforte," commented Dies.[50] The piano edition may have lacked a drum stroke, but it introduced its own noise. Still, focusing on the noise that any medium inevitably introduces—the things that reveal a medium as a medium—is far from my main concern. In this book, focusing on media does not axiomatically provide the "methodological detour around the aesthetic" that Lisa Gitelman promises.[51] I am more interested in the way that Haydn designed music with an awareness of the things that mediated it— the manuscripts, the pianos, the rooms, the full scores and printed reductions (that is, versions based around keyboard instruments), the concert reports, the clumsy hands of amateurs, and the well-trained hands of professionals— and thus how he and his music helped to create a media culture that was more than the sum of its constituent technologies and techniques.[52] Music was not just the byproduct of certain media ecologies; music also shaped these ecologies.[53] Rupert Ridgewell has written that print gave composers the "potential to insist upon adherence to their intentions" and a "permanent format" that eventually allowed them to assert intellectual property rights—and he is surely not wrong. But, as Kate van Orden and other historians of early music publications have demonstrated, the naturalized link between print and values that Ridgewell parses as "authority and permanence" was by no means obvious or inevitable.[54] It was a link that Haydn and his contemporaries had to forge and maintain. Meanwhile, Haydn's compositions registered many other possible relationships between music and the people and materials that mediated it (including print).[55] To observe this is not only to trot out the routine claim, foundational to any media history—that the transparency and self-evidence of surviving media apparatuses, along with their values and uses, were historically contingent and typically hard-won. This book aims for something more: to unpick the historical complicity of particular musical media apparatuses with particular practices of economic extraction.

Other parts of this book borrow from sound studies' preoccupation with urban soundscapes and seek to position Haydn's music—especially his London music—amid more plural sonic environments.[56] But, once again, it is not my purpose to reexamine how the distinctions between music and sound, voice and noise, were produced and sustained through technologies of inscription and transduction,[57] nor to reargue the important point that these distinctions are always politicized, contested, and mutually constitutive.[58] Rather, I aim to show how music, including Haydn's, helped to construct the idea of the wider soundscape to which it belonged, in part by appearing to harvest, "musicalize," and generate value from environmental sound (as chapter 2 discusses, audiences even heard one of Haydn's London symphonies as an imitation of commercial street cries, which was itself a trope of popular music from the period). Much eighteenth-century music, I claim, promoted a compelling fantasy of boundaryless sonic connectedness, deploying music to aestheticize the distant attachments made possible by the circulation of sound in the form of print commodities. Indeed, I will argue that the triumphalist neo-Cagean absorption of music by sound and of sound by vibration, which has become an ontological premise within some corners of sound studies, was presaged by the liberal moral and economic philosophy of the eighteenth century—a "resonant ethic" that was overtly thematized in some of Haydn's London music (especially saleable print commodities, such as the books of *Original Canzonettas*). Gavin Steingo and Jim Sykes argue that sound studies has all too frequently turned its sensitive ear to the "globe" without calling into question the European, racialized ontologies of sound that it generalizes.[59] This book argues that these ontologies have a history inextricable from European music aesthetics and related European economic models. And this history should give us pause before welcoming the move away from music and toward vibration as somehow freeing or more inclusive.[60]

This book has nonetheless drawn inspiration from historical studies of music that do indeed strive to include a wider range of people and things, and from methodologies in the humanities and social sciences that—rather than reconstruct "contexts" (historical receptacles to contain inert and self-contained objects of knowledge)—seek to elaborate more complex networks arising from the motion and interaction of many actors.[61] That said, I am chary of treating these useful methodologies (which, it must be said, are in some ways all too well adapted to the additive logic of the digital interfaces from which researchers derive so much of their information nowadays) as reliable claims about the way things really are.[62] The skein of perpetually mobile people and things; a dynamic, global interconnectedness: these are, this book argues, distinctively eighteenth-century ideas, and, what is more, the reverberation of music was their master trope. From the ultraliberal "vibrant matter" theorized in Jane Bennett's "political ecology of things" to the Deleuzian "polyphonic assemblage[s]" in Anna Tsing's ruined capitalist landscapes, and the "music of the networks" that Leo Cabranes-Grant proposes by analogy with the music of the spheres—we are surrounded by intellectual expressions of the deep, and deeply musical, eighteenth century.[63] It is all the more important, then, to acknowledge that one cannot easily separate the eighteenth-century idea of virtuous global interconnection from the geographical imaginaries promoted by the spread of new media, discourses of trade and commerce that articulated visions of what the historian J. G. A. Pocock once dubbed the "world of moving objects," and the globalizing fantasies of European colonial violence.[64] Haydn's music, which was, from the 1780s, more widely accessible and dispersed than ever before, gave a sonic reality to these fantasies—rebounding to Vienna and London from colonial centers in India and America, both in print and within connected urban infrastructures of commercial musical performance. Indeed, given European music's long historical relationship with fantasy and illusion, I am in equal parts thrilled and troubled by those who, like Tsing, would advance listening to music as a viable model for the politically urgent project of "noticing" marginalized things[65] or by musicologists who would confer a special ethical status on their own capacity to "listen." There is no evidence that listening to any kind of music makes us better at listening to subaltern voices. My intuition is that—as with the sentimental cultural program of eighteenth-century abolitionists or the Burkean condemnation of British imperialism in India (subjects that are bound up with the arguments of chapters 1 and 3)—the emphasis on how well "we" listen risks putting the feelings of a community of "good listeners" before the more fractured and challenging demands of justice.

And yet scholars might justly ask how truly network oriented a music history can be when it starts from and leads back to one of the places where the discipline has always been, in one way or another—Haydn and his music. Certainly, my intention is not merely to spruce up a traditional object of knowledge by incorporating into the discussion a roster of more obscure actors or references to a wider range of geographical locations—the same old music, but "away from the same old places" and so "without any discomfort about its elite and canonical status," as Benjamin Walton dryly puts it.[66] It seems to me that the many ethical and methodological challenges facing historians of the arts these days are not best summarized in terms of a choice between talking about their disciplines' long-standing objects of knowledge in the same old guises and places or else shrinking these objects down to a scale appropriate to their new (supposedly less important) position in wider (supposedly less hierarchical) networks. I am convinced of the political necessity of provincializing the regimes of our knowledge,[67] even though I suspect that the provincializing perspective comes most easily to those who already pretend to synoptic visions—the globe's many "cultures" (or, these days, "natures") swirling before the all-seeing gaze of intellectuals based mostly in Europe and North America. But this book is, in any case, about changing musical values and changing ideas of music's value.[68] The metaphor of the province may permit an important claim about the relative dimensions of topographically conceived local perspectives, but it is less able to capture the texture and depth of people's values—the attachments and commitments that constantly perform and remake social relations themselves.[69] This book does not describe a bounded epistemological province. Rather, it is a study in peculiarly musical forms of social relation—attachments and commitments that were instigated, mediated, and held in place by Haydn's music.

Commerce, Interest, Objects, Work, Value

The four main chapters and epilogue proceed in loosely chronological order, following in outline the direction of Haydn's career—from the sphere of the Esterházy court to London, through the years spent plying between Vienna and London, to the last decade or so in Vienna.

Chapter 1, "Commerce," retells the story of what one English verse from 1791 lauded as the "Importation of Haydn, or The Commerce of the Arts"— Haydn's route from the palaces of the Esterházy court, via the print markets of Vienna and other European cities, to London's ferociously competitive concert scene. Particularly in his last years, Haydn was given to describing this period of his career as liberation from an otherwise isolated existence in Eszterháza. And generations of Haydn scholars have thus aimed to associate his diverse publics of the 1780s and 1790s with concrete changes in his musical style. This chapter argues, however, that what Haydn experienced during this episode is better understood as a progressive remaking of his world via the materials and relationships of print commerce and transcontinental media distribution, a world in which it became possible to conceive of the Esterházy court—historically, a vibrant cultural hub—as a periphery. While the changes that Haydn's music underwent can occasionally be described in terms of style, these are only the traces of wider changes: during the 1780s, Haydn pursued a grand project of reformatting whereby, with a monetary incentive, he transferred his musical knowledge into new media forms—proliferating printed materials, newly popular genres, and such platforms as the public concert, upon which he had never previously displayed compositions such as string quartets or piano-based chamber music. The chapter follows the old aesthetic-economic idea of "stock music" from its origin in Italianate pedagogical methods—methods premised on the storage and transmission of musical devices in the bodies of musicians within Europe's courts—to the newer environments of distance-traversing print distribution and public concert series. These commercial regimes, I argue, extracted value from this music in part by harnessing its existing principles of iterability to new forms of technological reproduction. One of the aims of the chapter is to bring a fresh perspective to a cluster of present-day approaches to eighteenth-century music—especially partimento analysis and topic theory—that emphasize and even lionize (as a seeming antidote to Romantic idealism) the "stockness" of this music's character and syntax. Haydn's music was composed, I contend, "before the cliché"—a value-laden concept that, not coincidentally, derives from one of several early nineteenth-century print technologies. Stock musical phrases and characters were not yet associated with the debased logic of the market or mechanical reproduction: to Haydn and his contemporaries, "commerce" meant both economic exchange and a Humean conception of agreeable social intercourse—productive musical communication that spanned ever-widening distances. From the 1780s, Haydn began to compose with an increased awareness of how his music addressed ever more anonymous and widely dispersed audiences. What is more, music—as a common trope of human connectedness itself—gave sensuous shape to an emerging fantasy of global connection. In London, Haydn's music contributed to the implicitly colonial vision of a "resonant world," connected by the global reverberations of trade and sympathy (a vision that was pointedly depicted in an engraving that Haydn acquired in London celebrating the 1795 acquittal of the former governor-general of India Warren Hastings). The colonial history of the resonant world should be particularly troublesome to contemplate in the present, when some critics have enlisted music once again as a symbol of desirable, vibrational human connectedness.

Chapter 2, "Interest," focuses on Haydn's London years. Several contemporary commentators described the London music by Haydn, as well as the music by his former student and onetime London competitor Ignaz Pleyel, as "interesting." This chapter argues that the London symphonies, as well as the records of Haydn's English trips contained in his series of notebooks, bear formal traces of a commercial urban mediascape in which the attention of a consumer public was newly conceivable in terms of the psychic-monetary "investment" of interest (as well as the potentially ruinous disinvestments of boredom)—a "psychic economy" of expenditure and profit. The synecdochal nicknames by which several of the symphonies are still known, such as the *Surprise*, the *Military*, and the *Drumroll*, almost all isolate these compositions' most interesting moments: musical devices that, within a clamorous urban environment, existed to be noted—to be discriminated by audiences, newspaper reports, critical commentaries, and consumers of piano reductions and thus to model a certain practice of noting (which, as the word indicates, implies not only attention but also the related practices of writing and discursive elaboration). These compositions were produced amid a distinctively modern relationship between music, attention, money, and media, which Haydn encountered only in London. For this reason, Haydn's interesting music might alert us to the deeper history of methodological paradigms currently popular within the humanities, which aim to resolve discrete objects of knowledge into networks of people and things gathered together by entangled interests.

Chapter 3, "Objects," stays in Haydn's London but turns its attention to small-scale musical genres: chamber pieces and popular songs. The circulation of this diminutive music—between music sellers and respectable homes, the opulent stages of pleasure gardens and the pages of journals and magazines—mapped out a consumer-oriented public domain in which women were unusually prominent: as shoppers and performers, as subjects and objects of new economic practices. Haydn's small-scale music was gathered up into several intimate exchanges with women in his social circle, including the poet Anne Hunter, who produced the texts for the first volume of his *Original Canzonettas*, and the musician Cecilia Barthélemon, who received presentation copies of these songs and, around the same time, dedicated a piano sonata to Haydn. The commercial domain was humming with vocalizing objects—not only the coins, pens, and journals of the period's many it-narratives (that is, stories narrated by inanimate objects) but also the memorials and commemorative prints, musical instruments and sentimental keepsakes, with which fashionable consumers (Haydn included) communicated and communed. Haydn's songs from the 1790s thus belonged to a wider sentimental-commercial landscape of small, talkative things: trinkets and mementos that promoted sympathetic connection, recollection, and contemplation. Popular songs even seemed to musicalize and so emphasize the common trope wherein a consumer object acquired a touching voice. Widespread Hogarthian theories of beauty, which contemporaries invoked in connection with Haydn's music, were in many ways concerned with just these alluring consumer objects, as well as the desire that animated them: the Hogarthian view was preoccupied above all with the enticing contours of small things—including tremulous sonic or vocal boundaries—where desire's unending pursuits seemed simultaneously to encounter and produce beautiful objects. Haydn's songs and chamber pieces, I argue, did not merely cultivate distinctive musical surfaces—that domain of sensuous immediacy valorized by present-day topic theorists, among others—but made plausible the notion of a musical "surface" altogether: the epidermal boundaries of sound, where the desiring ear and desirable musical objects intermingle. The dubious ethical implications of these gendered and consumerist conceptions of beauty and desire were all too clear to contemporary feminists, such as Mary Wollstonecraft, who believed that certain classes of women were complicit in their own transformation into mere objects. Yet another subgenre of late eighteenth-century popular song adds still graver ethical complications: the substantial corpus of antislavery songs that began to appear in the late 1780s, many of which were intended to be sung by women in the home. The best known of these songs, such as settings of William Cowper's 1788 poem "The Negro's Complaint," were predicated, once again, on a principle of envoicing: they conferred voices upon enslaved African people, to inspire pity and supposedly restore a stolen humanity. I argue that the kind of sentimental role play that these abolitionist songs represent gives the strong impression that consumerism and personhood, agency and commoditization, voice and objecthood, may be impossible to separate. Thus the aesthetic of eighteenth-century popular song may provide grounds to be cautious of historiographies premised on the ethic of "giving voice," which has recently been contested by scholars of transatlantic slavery.

Chapter 4, "Work," follows Haydn from London back to Vienna. Even though Haydn had been permitted to sell his compositions to parties outside of the Esterházy court since the late 1770s, until he arrived in London the pace and quantity of his work had never been dictated by the market. In England, then, Haydn came to understand his composerly labor in wholly new ways. Bound to produce a succession of new orchestral compositions, which would subsequently become the legal property of the impresario Salomon, Haydn found his time and labor measurable in monetary terms and conservable as capital. For three decades, he had been a Kapellmeister, much of which had been spent managing the musical side of a major court theater, so Haydn was no stranger to busy work. Yet in London he began to experience work as an alienating source of stress. This chapter argues that the wild comedy of some of the London music registers in aesthetic terms a change in the status of Haydn's work: the affective labors of the court musician now became an almost desperate testing of every ruse to serve a distant and fickle public. Meanwhile, the English culture of Handel veneration taught Haydn that musical labor, once conserved, could continue to generate value, even long after a composer's death. It was from London's Handelian milieu that Haydn received the poem of *The Creation*—the oratorio that, once back in Vienna, cemented Haydn's status as a living classic of European music. Via this Miltonic retelling of the Genesis story, Haydn's musical setting and its rapturous contemporary reception overtly confounded the work of divine and mortal creators, the work of creation and the work that was *The Creation*—especially in monumental Handelian choruses such as "Achieved Is the Glorious Work." These performances of divine musical labor proved awkwardly incompatible with the georgic tropes of work in Haydn's other late oratorio *The Seasons*, which had its own Handelian chorus, "In Praise of Industry." In early nineteenth-century Vienna, this veneration of sublime labor provoked much perplexed analysis. Following Haydn's depiction of work through James Thomson's 1730 poem "The Seasons" (the source, in Barthold Brockes's 1745 translation, of the much-maligned text by Gottfried Baron van Swieten), the chapter reveals the tensions between emerging Romantic ideologies of creativity and the various historical visions of work that accrued in Haydn's late music, where the artist and artisan, aesthetics and economics, works and work, were not so easily separated.

The epilogue, "Value (1808)," centers on two major Viennese musical events of 1808, the year before Haydn's death: the climax of the Liebhaber Concerte on March 27 in the University Hall—Haydn's *Creation* in Giuseppe Carpani's Italian translation, during which Haydn was publicly honored by the artists and eminences of the city—and Beethoven's unusual all-Beethoven marathon in the Theater an der Wien on December 22, which featured premieres of the Fifth and Sixth Symphonies, the old operatic scena "Ah! perfido," movements from the Mass in C Major, the premiere of the Fourth Piano Concerto, and a grand finale in the form of the Choral Fantasy. Beethoven's more or less explicit bid to present himself as Haydn's surrogate during this turbulent wartime moment involved, I argue, appropriating and radicalizing the newly politicized tension, increasingly audible in Haydn's late music and embodied in a fragile collection of Romantic infrastructures, between artistic value and the values of a world conceived on the model of the market.

Haydn never abandoned composition to become a full-time entrepreneur in the manner of Muzio Clementi or Ignaz Pleyel. And though, by the early nineteenth century, his music was widely dispersed through new colonial channels, Haydn never traveled beyond Europe, as his student and Salzburg colleague Sigismond Neukomm did. In his half century as a professional musician, Haydn nevertheless became the most abundantly mediated musician of his age, who had the opportunity to know, on radically changed terms, his world, his audience, his musical works, and his own musical labor. His music bears the traces of a decades-long encounter with the incipient world of urban capitalism. But it was never entirely at home with the Romantic philosophies that were nurtured there. Indeed, a perceived ambience of worldliness, even ordinariness or self-evidence, marred the reputation of Haydn's music well into the twentieth century.[70] I suspect that this is among the reasons why the literature on Haydn has long been among the more historically nuanced and theoretically creative corners of eighteenth-century music studies, adopting by necessity a sideways relation to the creeping Romantic values that tend to be endemic to neighboring single-composer subdisciplines—whether in analysis, performance studies, or historical criticism.[71] And I would add that this is why Haydn's historical trajectory is especially relevant now, when so many people across the humanities are asking, in so many words, what, if anything, we might usefully retain or repurpose from the cultural and political practices of European modernity, whether we can extract and preserve its moral promise from its moral failures—how we might divide an ethically viable form of value from a crassly materialist one, an ethically viable form of global interconnection from a colonial one, an ethically viable form of mobility from a (neo)liberal one, an ethically viable form of nature from an anthropocentric one, an ethically viable form of desire from an acquisitive one, and an ethically viable form of work from an alienated one. It seems to me that Haydn's music and its inextricably jumbled aesthetic-economic past provide further evidence that these things will ultimately prove impossible to separate. But, inviting neither the suspicion of disenchantment nor a retreat into aestheticism, this music may yet help us to think beyond our present dilemmas.

Commerce

Commerce produces nothing of itself; for it is not of a plastic nature. Its business consists in exchanges. . . . By pervading the earth, by crossing the seas, by raising the obstacles which opposed themselves to the intercourse of nations, by extending the sphere of wants and the thirst of enjoyments, it multiplies labour, it encourages industry, and becomes, in some measure, the moving principle of the world.

GUILLAUME THOMAS RAYNAL, *Histoire philosophique et politique des établissements et du commerce des Européens dans les deux Indes* (1770)[1]

Importation of Haydn

In March 1791, only days after the opening of the Hanover Square concerts that at last presented Haydn and his newest musical works to the London public, the *European Magazine and London Review* contributed to a growing craze by publishing an anonymously composed poem in Haydn's honor, which took its place amid a miscellany of new poetry and a few caustic rhymes by the satirist John Wolcot. Several such celebratory verses were produced around this time and subsequently, but this one uniquely situated the recent arrival of Haydn within the modish conceptual framework of political economy. Announcing its subject as the "Importation of Haydn; or, The Commerce of the Arts," the poem sought to counter long-standing anxieties about the foreign domination of London's most prestigious music scenes with an optimistic vision of international trade (fig. 1.1).[2]

The poem sought to explain how Britain had replenished its native store of music throughout history. The opening lines compare the cultivation of nations with the breeding of racehorses, where improving the natural stock, so the poem maintains, is "more powerful than training, rest, or food." The "Importation of Haydn" subsequently essays a brisk reinterpretation of several centuries of music history in explicitly mercantile terms. Josquin, Lully, and Handel, the poem maintains, were musically important primarily because they were musical importers—men who moved themselves and their music from place to place, from Flanders to Italy, from Italy to France, from Saxony to Britain: "LULLI from Italy to France convey'd / The first rude sketches of the Lyric trade." Haydn was only the latest episode in this unceasing process, an import who would enrich rather than impoverish his British trading partners. The crux of the poem's argument was an image of national

But fo vamp'd up—the fcruples not to
  fhow it ;   [ftring—
For what with varnifh, found-poft, filver
'Tis fo improv'd—he plays before the King
In tone fo fweet—his Godfhip does not
  know it.

By PETER PINDAR, on reading a LITE-
RARY PRODUCTION of Dr. HARRING-
TON's.

" DOCTOR, I much your principles ad-
          " mire.
" Apollo very kindly lent his Lyre !
" And you, the moft retin'd of grateful men,
" To quit the obligation—ftole his Pen."

IMPORTATION OF HAYDN ; OR,
THE COMMERCE OF THE ARTS.

THE Sages of the Turf have long agreed
      To augment the courier's vigour, force,
      and fpeed,
By frequent mixture of *Arabian blood*—
More pow'rful far than training, reft or food.

TUSQUIN, who choral laws from Flanders
      brought,
His polyphonic art Italia taught ;
Mellifluous tones he firft arrang'd, combin'd,
And kindred founds in harmony entwin'd ;
Then bad them mount, and run the facred race
With curling incenfe to the throne of Grace.

LULLI from Italy to France convey'd
The firft rude fketches of the Lyric trade ;
He furnifh'd meafures for each dance and fong,
With which the nation was enraptur'd long.

HANDEL! the mighty Saxon chief fublime,
Britannia's fons fubdu'd a fecond time ;
His name is ftill religion through the land,
Nor had great *Woden* fuch fupreme command.

And now, to eafe us of a ufelefs toil,
And fertilize our cold and barren foil,
HAYDN celeftial fire and *compoft* brings,
And feeds of Genius o'er each fallow flings ;
Plants fruits of fweeteft flavour through the
      land,
Which (if allow'd to thrive and wide expand)
May well enrich us for an age at leaft,
And furnifh out defferts for ev'ry feaft.

Thus in *The Commerce of the Arts* we find
Refources for our wants of ev'ry kind :
If we are furnifh'd with the graceful dance,
And draw Apicius' fenfual art from France ;
If fculpture, architecture, painting come
From Venice, Naples, Tufcany, and Rome ;
If we are indebted to Italian climes
For all the fkill which *vocal found* fublimes ;
If Germany our *inftruments* fupplies,
And HAYDN from all mortals bears the prize ;
Our Bacons, Newtons, Lockes, can Science
      teach,
Our Poets write, and Theologians preach ;

Our Arts and Induftry in times of need [feed—
Can proud and diftant empires clothe and
Parents and friends we find in ev'ry nation,
Where all fubfift alike by COMMUTATION.

VERSES written by the late JOHN THORN-
TON, Efq. a fhort time before his death,
on his receiving a MOURNING RING for
a RELATION of his NAME.

WELCOME, thou prefage of my certain
              doom !
I too muft fink into the darkfome tomb.
Yes, little Prophet, thus my name fhall ftand
A mournful record on fome friendly hand.
My name ! 'tis here, the characters agree,
And every faithful letter fpeaks to me ;
Bids me prepare to meet my Nature's foe
Serene to feel the Monfter's fatal blow ;
Without a figh to quit the joys of time,
Secure of glory in an happier clime ;
Then mount the fkies, forfake my old abode,
And gain the plaudit of a fmiling God.
Receive, Lord Jefus ! Body, Soul, and Spirit !
Behold my plea !--Thy fuff'rings and thy merit.

ELEGY,
By a YOUTH of Fifteen Years old.

AMID thefe much lov'd, well-known
        fcenes I'll ftray
  (Which once have witnefs'd many a joyful
              hour),   [ray
While Cynthia faintly fhoots her glimmering
  Athwart the abbey's ivy-mantled tow'r.

Sad Autumn's gloomy veil o'ercafts the day,
  Dims ev'ry flower, and ftains the vivid
              green ;
No more the warblers trill the melting lay,
  But mournful filence fills the faded fcene.

Far diff'rent 'twas when laft I view'd this
              place,
  Far diff'rent thoughts then warm'd my
      joyful heart ;   [trac'd,
With Lucy then thefe lovely fcenes I
  Alas ! we little thought fo foon to part.

" Ah, fhe was all my fondeft wifh could
      frame,"—   [partake ;
  'Twas fhe that did my woes and joys
'Twas fhe that lov'd me with the pureft flame,
  And left each fond connection for my fake.

Oft as I have return'd from evening walk,
  I've clafp'd my fmiling infant in my arms ;
Oft have I liften'd to its prattling talk,
  Or in its face have trac'd its mother's
              charms.

But when to diftant fhores I took my way,
  With her I bid farewel to each delight ;
Her abfence I deplor'd the live-long day,
  Her mem'ry ne'er was banifh'd from my
              fight.

                                      My

FIGURE 1.1. "Importation of Haydn," on a crowded page of the *European Magazine*, March 1791.

cultivation and organicist self-organization more striking even than Edward Young's 1759 account of the "vegetable nature" of original composition.[3]

> And now, to ease us of a useless toil,
> And fertilize our cold and barren soil,
> HAYDN celestial fire and *compost* brings,
> And seeds of Genius o'er each fallow flings;
> Plants fruits of sweetest savour through the land,
> Which (if allow'd to thrive and wide expand)
> May well enrich us for an age at least,
> And furnish out desserts for ev'ry feast.
> Thus in the *Commerce of the Arts* we find
> Resources for our wants of ev'ry kind.

This bioeconomic conception of the national musical body was earthier even than the celebrated vitalism of Adam Smith and his many acolytes.[4] The importation of Haydn—that divine fertilizer—was to guarantee the lasting fecundity of Britain's musical landscape.

The poem culminated with the colonial fantasy of a world connected by intimate family feeling—a globe newly spanned by the trade in sentiments and commodities:

> Our Arts and Industry in times of need
> Can proud and distant empires clothe and feed—
> Parents and friends we find in ev'ry nation,
> Where all subsist alike by COMMUTATION.

"Commutation," here meaning trade or barter, connoted the exchange of feelings and things—a self-regulating moral economy at once sociable and mercantile. (It had been an occasional motif of published debate and polemic since the passing of the Commutation Act in 1784, which dramatically reduced the tax on imported tea.) The last line may well have been an allusion to a much-anthologized passage from the sermon on ingratitude by the seventeenth-century churchman Robert South (cited by Samuel Johnson in his 1755 dictionary's entry on "commutation"): "the whole Universe is supported by giving and returning, by Commerce and Commutation." The register of popular moral instruction was thus blended with a more plainly materialist economics.[5]

Such a blend was common enough in the second half of the eighteenth century, when "commerce" encompassed all productive social intercourse, not exclusively the sort mediated by markets—the "commerce and society of men, which is so agreeable," as David Hume had put it.[6] Laurence Sterne's Parson Yorick, embarking on his digressive *Sentimental Journey*, had fretted over the "many impediments in communicating our sensations out of our own sphere,"

including "the want of languages, connections, and dependencies": "The balance of sentimental commerce is always against the expatriated adventurer," he
concluded, eliding the balance of trade with the desirable harmony of social intercourse.[7] Haydn prepared to leave Vienna with no such anxieties, it seems, in
part because of the nature of the goods that he exchanged: "My language is understood all over the world," he supposedly retorted when Mozart questioned
whether his older colleague knew enough languages to undertake a trip to
London.[8] This kind of enlightened cosmopolitanism typically accorded music
an honored place in its imagined geography of a connected world.[9] Music was
one of the master tropes of human connectedness—the vital, vibrational medium of connection itself, even. The poem *The Progress of Civil Society* by the
parliamentarian Richard Payne Knight (whose popular theories of landscape
Haydn surely encountered while in London) described the self-organizing
principle of civilization in overtly musical terms—as the growth of ideas that
"tune the heart" to gentler passions and so extend "chains of sympathy" across
the world.[10] Later in the poem, these sympathetic chains are overtly characterized as commercial, too—a characteristically eighteenth-century updating
of the great chain of being that, as Kevis Goodman has observed, was well
suited to the sweeping colonial "landscape view": the "golden chains" of "rich
commerce," writes Knight, connect "distant realms." As in the "Importation
of Haydn," commutation was at once musical, sentimental, and mercantile.[11]

Warehouse Aesthetics

Departing Vienna in the middle of December 1790, Haydn traversed Europe
in channels worn by years of this commutation. From Vienna to Munich,
from Munich to Wallerstein Castle in the Swabian countryside, from Wallerstein to Bonn, from Bonn to Calais, from Calais to Dover, from Dover to
London—Haydn entered the "world of moving objects" that J. G. A. Pocock
once proposed as the disruptive novelty of eighteenth-century life.[12] On the
road, Haydn became one more item amid the "porcelain and earthen wares,
looking glasses and glass wares, toys, apothecaries drugs, dye stuffs, tanned
leather, printer's black, manufactures and fabrics"—to reproduce only a few
examples from the lists of exports included in Thomas Clarke's *A Statistical
View of Germany*, published in the year that Haydn's journey began.[13]

But Haydn also conveyed valuable things within him. He would doubtless have agreed with Johann Mattheson's advice, relayed in the 1739 pedagogical monument *Der vollkommene Capellmeister* (a book that Haydn had
studied in his youth): the aspiring Kapellmeister should retain and replen-
ish a "stock" of musical formulas and gestures to be deployed whenever they

were needed.[14] Mattheson's word, *Vorrath*, connoted reserves, magazines, arsenals—collections of "necessary things that one may need in future," as the eighteenth-century dictionary compiled by Johann Christoph Adelung put it.[15] Mattheson was well versed in Lockean epistemology and shared its distinctively mercantile language: knowledge, maintained Locke, could be plausibly conceived as a "magazine of materials" inside one's head.[16] Knight's *Progress of Civil Society*, in explicit emulation of Adam Smith, would elaborate this Lockean principle into a vibrant somaeconomics—a conception of the human body as the microcosm of a successful trading nation, and of the nation itself as a vast circulatory system of transmission and storage: "every fibre to one centre tends, / And each impression to that centre sends; / Fix'd in the complex storehouse of the brain."[17] For his part, Mattheson, based in the northern commercial city of Hamburg, had spent most of his career in the service of the English diplomat Sir John Wich, translating pamphlets on economic policy and dealing on a daily basis with matters of trade and finance.[18] It is hardly surprising that he should have conceived of the Kapellmeister as nothing less than a packed musical warehouse, a person within whom an accumulated stock of musical techniques was stored.[19]

Toward the end of his life, Haydn was given to describing the years in which he worked in the rural estates of the Esterházy family as miserably secluded—a period during which he nonetheless laid up an ample stock of musical techniques, to be lucratively transported only later. "I was cut off from the world, there was nobody in my vicinity to make me unsure of myself or interfere with me in my course, and so I was forced to become original," Haydn told his biographer Georg August Griesinger, recasting his court career in the up-to-date terms of isolated genius.[20] To be sure, in the decade before he traveled to England, Haydn had begun to look to Vienna, with its material density and wide-ranging networks of association, as a respite from the closed court environments in which he had acquired his stock of musical technique. "My misfortune is that I live in the country," he complained to the Vienna-based art and music sellers Carlo and Francesco Artaria in 1781.[21] Nine years later, this frustration had turned into caricature melancholy: "Here I sit in my wilderness—forsaken—like a poor waif—almost without any human society," he wrote to his friend Marianne von Genzinger, Haydn having departed Vienna early in 1790, following the court's usual stay over Advent and Christmas. He contrasted his misery in the distant Hungarian palace of Eszterháza, at the southern end of the Neusiedlersee, with Vienna's "wonderful parties" and "musical evenings" at which "the whole circle is one heart, one soul." And he turned from this routine trope of sympathetic exchange instigated by music to all the other commutations that were contiguous and continuous with it:

> Here in Estoras [i.e., Eszterháza] no-one asks me: Would you like some choco-
> late, with milk or without? Will you take some coffee, black, or with cream? What
> may I offer you, my dear Haydn? Would you like a vanilla or a pineapple ice?[22]

Chocolate, coffee, vanilla: all products of colonial exploitation, the "proud and distant empires" imagined by the author of the "Importation of Haydn." Vienna, it seems, opened onto a world made by sentimental commerce. And from the perspective of this world, the magnetic courtly hub of Eszterháza suddenly seemed an outpost or periphery.

For most of Haydn's working life, Eszterháza would not have appeared this way at all—to Haydn or any of his admiring colleagues. The ancient pro-tocols and connections of the region's courts had crucially shaped how Haydn had stored up and transported the stock of his musical knowledge, and this had meant anything but isolation or stasis. Even before Haydn became Vice-Kapellmeister to the Esterházy family in 1761, his musical habitus had been formed by a potent transregional mix—a consequence, in large part, of the Italian musical diaspora that so decisively shaped eighteenth-century Euro-pean music.[23] As a boy in the choir of St. Stephen's, he found himself un-der the instruction of Georg Reutter, one of the most prominent students of the Venetian composer Antonio Caldara. And in the later 1750s, he endured a bruising period of apprenticeship with the celebrated Neapolitan master Nicola Porpora, with Haydn cautiously extemporizing keyboard accompani-ments during voice lessons. It was only then, so Haydn claimed in the 1770s, that he learned the "true fundamentals [*die ächte Fundamente*]" of compo-sition.[24] To enter the Esterházy court, whose architectural fabric included a palace on the Wallnerstrasse in the middle of Vienna and still grander resi-dences situated far from the Habsburg capital, was to enter a densely popu-lated musical contact zone.[25] From the beginning of his tenure, Haydn was in charge of an orchestra whose schedule was, so Charles Burney would report (via the Esterházy wind player Johann Christian Fischer), modeled on the working practices of the Neapolitan conservatories—which is to say, orga-nized around an intensive regimen of daily musical-technical drills.[26] And, especially as the focus of the court moved to Eszterháza, Haydn's main oc-cupation was to preside over a major opera house led almost exclusively by Italian singers. With the appointment of Nunzio Porta as theater director in 1781, Haydn spent his days trimming and adapting a distinctively Neapoli-tan operatic repertoire, by such musicians as Domenico Cimarosa, Giuseppe Sarti, and Niccolò Zingarelli.[27]

From the start of his career, Haydn made the kind of music whose very premise was to be portable and multipurpose. Looping around the tangled circuitry of the court, this music recalled the characters and registers of the operatic stage, quoted the stately or rustic dances of the ballroom, and appropriated the functional sounds of the hunt, chapel, and parade ground. And these gestures were bound together by the reproducible syntactical units that distinguished the Italianate music of the period, units entrained by such methods as partimento—the gatherings of haptic-mnemonic *movimenti* that Haydn had learned to command on the job with Porpora.[28]

Many of Haydn's Esterházy compositions exploited these sociotechnical principles of iteration to display collections of stock musical characters in rapid succession—a mode of musical organization that was made possible in part by the modular way in which this music was taught and learned. The opening presto of the Symphony no. 59, composed in the late 1760s, begins with an unusually large cast of contrasting characters—"annunciatory, misterioso, purposeful, agitated, urbane, rollicking, [and] valedictory," as Wye J. Allanbrook writes.[29] The emphasis on dramatic contrast—which continues in the austere-then-lyrical second movement, a minuet movement with a creeping *minore* trio, and a boisterous hunt conclusion—may well have been motivated by a theatrical function: as Elaine Sisman has discussed, several Haydn symphonies from this period were associated with dramatic performances in Eszterháza. Indeed, in 1774, the Symphony no. 59 was paired with Gustav Friedrich Wilhelm Großmann's play *Die Feuersbrunst* in a performance by Karl Wahr and his troupe.[30] In the opening section of the presto, every assertive or active character quickly yields to something more emollient or sentimental, sighing with two-note slurs. Within eight measures of the start, the exhortative staccato gestures, hammering away beneath an insistent pedal point in the violins, come to rest on the dominant with surprising gentleness. The subsequent passage of energetic transition, darkened by a swerve into the minor mode, emerges into a simple pastoral tune. And even this is swept away by a single flourish into a rustic, triplet-dominated dance—which, echoing the opening measures, soon dissolves into gentle valediction. This constant change of character is achieved in part by Haydn's treatment of pedal points: consonant triads frequently alternate over a continuous bass note, creating a pastoral ambience, while more mobile stock sequences cycle over the root. Indeed, the opening is woven together by an endlessly reiterated device from the period—a handy, tonally stable way to begin (or conclude) a keyboard improvisation, described most clearly in early nineteenth-century partimento collections by Zingarelli (fig. 1.2). Over a tonic pedal, the music moves from tonic to subdominant (in this, chromatic version, via a lowered seventh) and back to the tonic via the leading tone, producing the characteristic pattern of half steps heard in the second violins (fig. 1.3). Haydn

Il pedale si forma dall'accordo del basso fondamentale.

Si può dar parimenti la 7.ª minore come si andasse nella natura della 4.ª del tuono.

Derivati dal basso fondamentale.

Prima   Quarta   Quinta

FIGURE 1.2. Exemplars of a stock musical move in *Partimenti di Nicolò Zingarelli* (Milan: Ricordi, n.d. [early nineteenth century]).

FIGURE 1.3. Second violin part, from an early manuscript of Haydn's Symphony no. 59, Presto, beginning with the stock move. State Library of Mecklenburg-Vorpommern Günther Uecker, Mus 2556. Used by permission.

uses an identical maneuver twice at the end of the section—its circular quality now producing the sense of repose that prompted Robert Gjerdingen to
call the schema the "Quiescenza."[31] This was the most basic stock of Haydn's
musical knowledge.

Mobility and Credit

Scholars who have sought to theorize principles of expressive or syntactical iteration in eighteenth-century music have frequently turned to the concept of
stock, though without always pausing to consider its economic meanings: the
"repertory of stock musical phrases" that make up Gjerdingen's partimento-
derived compendium of musical schemata, the "stock musical figures and
patterns" discussed by Roger Grant, or the "gallery of stock characters" described by Danuta Mirka—the catalog of expressive types that present-day
music theory came to call topics.[32] "Stock," to these writers, denotes what is
repeatable, transportable, or citable: in order to mean, this music has to move.
Mirka has even proposed that musical topics are best understood as "*styles
and genres taken out of their proper context and used in another one*": as in the
Derridean conception of intelligible utterances, displacement paradoxically
appears to be their inaugurating principle.[33] Indeed, one could say that the
impression of "proper contexts"—that is, of originary functions and locations
now abandoned, as in the huntless hunt that concludes Haydn's Symphony
no. 59—is created and sustained in large part by the process of displacement
itself.[34] As in the increasingly unstable relation between music and the principle of mimesis that was widely noted by early critics of Italian comic opera,[35]
much late eighteenth-century music appears to heighten the poetic consequences of a newly audible semiotic and physical mobility—and the movements of this rootless musical stock made new worlds.[36]

    In the history of music, stylistic allusion and the circulation of recogniz-
able formulas are in themselves unremarkable, of course, and extend from
Tinctoris to Motown. Moreover, the historical basis upon which present-day
theorists of eighteenth-century music have gathered and cataloged musical
formulas, whether in the form of topics or schemata, remains contested, as we
will see.[37] But here I am concerned less with the mere presence of musical formulas or even the inherent mobility of any intelligible musical utterance, than
with the new vessels that increasingly mediated and constituted old formulas
in the late eighteenth century—an emerging set of technologies and social relations that enabled surplus value to be extracted from musical bits and pieces
that were in some cases centuries old. That is to say that I am concerned with
the economic mobilization of musical stock.

From a twenty-first-century perspective, the iterative principle of Haydn's inherited musical stock, shaped by many years of storage and transportation in the disciplined bodies of court musicians and their written pedagogical materials, seems oddly well adapted to a late eighteenth-century regime of print reproduction—even a kind of mechanical reproducibility avant la lettre. But during the 1760s, Haydn's musical stock had only intermittent encounters with the media structures that helped to produce the "world of moving objects"—the world that, by the time of Haydn's London visits, had abraded the borders of his court existence. This is not to say that Haydn's music had, until this moment, stayed put. Far from it: many of his compositions traveled from the Esterházy court during the 1760s, a substantial proportion of them in the form of clandestine duplications by unscrupulous music copyists.[38] Toward the end of the 1780s, Haydn still encountered this problem: "the rascals [Spitzbuben] put a piece of paper a parte under the music, and thus by degrees they secretly copy the part they have in front of them," he explained to Artaria.[39] Now and again, formally sanctioned routes propelled a composition over unprecedented distances: the 1767 "Stabat Mater" was one of the most widely disseminated works of Haydn's career, rapidly making its way from Vienna to the Parisian Concert Spirituel in the slipstream of Pergolesi's already famous version.[40] But at this time, Haydn remained a novice when it came to promoting such exports and commanded few mechanisms for extracting value from them. In 1768, he received the prestigious commission of an applausus (an allegorical cantata in Latin) from the abbey of Zwettl in Lower Austria, around eighty miles or so from Vienna. When Haydn delivered the manuscript, he included unusually extensive instructions for its rehearsal and performance and complained that he knew "neither the persons nor the place": "the fact that these were concealed from me made my work very difficult," he added.[41] How much credit Haydn was to receive, and how he in turn could trust a distant group of performers and listeners, was, it seems, unclear. At this stage in his career, the distance between music and place, addresser and addressee, caused him considerable anxiety.[42] For all that, over the subsequent twenty years, this division became a permanent reality, as Haydn embarked upon an immense project of reformatting: he increasingly employed the infrastructures of print commerce to generate value from his existing musical stock, in the process making his music more amenable to the logic of ownership and commercial exchange.[43]

To trace this development is not to describe changes in Haydn's musical style, then, as much as the interplay between his style and changing technologies, materials, and genres. Nowadays, a critical edition or a set of recordings creates relatively uniform media environments in which compositions or even single passages by Haydn from various points in his career can be treated as equivalent—comparable components of an entire oeuvre. In this context, the main questions one can pose about what appear to be stock musical devices inevitably concern how a composer appropriates and transforms conventions (the question of personal or regional style) or whether a composer was able to transform and supersede these inherited conventions with increasing maturity or artistic independence (replicating the old Romantic binary of original versus imitator). Haydn's music undoubtedly changed in the 1780s and 1790s—though it is by no means obvious that it became somehow less replete with standard musical gestures or deployed these gestures more creatively.[44] My intention in this chapter is not to enter into this debate but rather to rethink the stock devices in Haydn's compositions in these decades as inseparable from the changing media forms that his music occupied.

The long and uneven process of reformatting that Haydn began in earnest in the early 1780s might be understood as a complex historical encounter between contrasting, though in some respects highly compatible, principles of musical reproducibility—some originating in the old Italianate repertories and pedagogies that helped to form Haydn as a professional musician, others established by the commerce in printed music and the institutions of public performance that were growing within eighteenth-century urban centers.[45] From our standpoint, each of these principles of musical reproducibility can be seen only with and through the other.

For all its complexity, in Vienna and the wider sphere of the Esterházy court, the main agents of this historical encounter are not hard to discern. The year 1768 witnessed an important new associational practice and a simultaneous change in the law: the Kaiserlich-Königliche Vereinigte Akademie der Bildenden Künste (the Imperial-Royal United Academy of the Fine Arts) was created, combining and replacing the old Viennese guilds of copper engravers, while import taxes were substantially reduced on art engravings.[46] In this conducive environment, the brothers Carlo and Francesco Artaria sought and were granted permission by the crown to trade in maps and other engraved art items. By the end of the decade, their art shop, or Kunsthandlung, opposite the Michaelerkirche, counted many imported music engravings in its stock, sourced mostly from Paris. But, in 1778, the Artarias decided to branch out on their own and so became the earliest Viennese music publishers. (They would be joined by several competitors during the 1780s.)[47] Only months later, on New Year's Day 1779, a new set of legal protocols allowed Haydn to exploit this nearby infrastructure: he renegotiated his contract with Nikolaus I and was now allowed—by omission rather than permission—openly to provide music to paying customers beyond the court.

(The 1779 contract was probably one of several such documents, which served to acknowledge a number of informal arrangements that had been going on for some time.)[48] Straightaway, Haydn began to transfer his musical stock into genres well adapted to this new regime: before 1780 was a month old, he had produced three or four new solo keyboard sonatas; in 1781, six string quartets appeared (his first in a decade); from 1780 onward, more than two dozen simple solo songs with keyboard accompaniment.[49] This was musical matter that traveled well. These engravings were matched to the technical capacities of the growing ranks of amateur musicians, made ample use of the keyboard—the technological interface to which most consumers had access, whether in the form of the clavichord, harpsichord, or piano—and were replete with stock musical gestures that people already knew and could readily grasp.[50] Haydn's Sonata in C Major (Hob. XVI:35), which Artaria published in 1780, opens with a cheery, symmetrical folk tune, immediately repeated over a gamboling triplet accompaniment. And, having arrived squarely at its second full cadence, it is charmingly elongated with precisely the chromatic, tonally circular pedal-point gambit that once framed the opening section of the presto from the Symphony no. 59 (see fig. 1.4). Something long reiterated under Haydn's hands at the keyboard was now also reproducible as part of a saleable print object—the kind of object that launched Haydn into the relays of the early credit economy.[51]

By the end of the 1780s, Haydn had become skilled at using the emerging protocols of the Viennese print market to generate credit from musical

FIGURE 1.4. The stock move following the lively opening tune in the earliest London publication of Haydn's Sonata in C Major (Hob. XVI:35), Allegro con brio (London: Bland, 1780).

stock that, in some cases, remained stashed away in the Lockean "magazine of materials" inside his head. In August 1788, Haydn asked Artaria to send him "an *a conto* of 25 gold ducats next Wednesday by our outgoing hussars" on only the promise of either three quartets or three piano sonatas. (Haydn was asking simply for a signed letter, which he would have used to receive money from the court banker.)[52] By October, Haydn requested that Artaria loan him thirty-one gold ducats that he owed the Viennese piano builder Wenzl Schanz for an instrument he had bought "to compose your 3 piano sonatas particularly well": the music had still not appeared.[53] Toward the end of the following March, having met and negotiated with Artaria during a winter visit to Vienna, Haydn at last supplied his publisher with the third of his promised sonatas, throwing in what he called "a new *Capriccio*"—the C Major Fantasia—which, he added, "cannot fail to be received with approbation from professional and non-professional alike." He demanded the steep price of twenty-four ducats, which he asked to be subtracted from his debts.[54] In this way, music—and even merely the promise of music—was converted, via the newly available technologies of print commerce, into obligations, consumer items, hard cash, and credit.

Among the people who first sought to import Haydn himself to London was the banker Thomas Hammersley, who, in 1786, had cofounded Ransom, Morland, and Hammersley at 56 Pall Mall.[55] Early in 1787, the *Gazetteer* reported on his new musical endeavor and wryly equated the banker's and the musician's valuable paper currencies.

> Mr. Hammersley, the Banker, has now become the negociator, and as his *notes* are in as great estimation as those of Haydn, there is little doubt that he will prevail on him to visit England.[56]

As this report indicates, Haydn's potential visit caused such excitement because the importation of his music to London was already well underway. Early in the 1780s, the London-based music sellers Longman & Broderip had established a relationship with Artaria that led to an influx of new musical imports: already in 1781 Longman & Broderip issued a catalog titled *New Music Published in London, and imported from different Parts of Europe* (fig. 1.5).[57] Such was the volume of imports that Longman & Broderip updated these catalogs regularly: by 1786, *A Complete Register of all the New Musical Publications imported from Different Parts of Europe* indicates that Continental music was now pouring in to London via music sellers.[58] While Longman & Broderip occasionally used Artaria's publications as the basis for their own editions, they typically sold the Viennese prints with their own label attached to the title page, which boasted of extensive Continental connections:

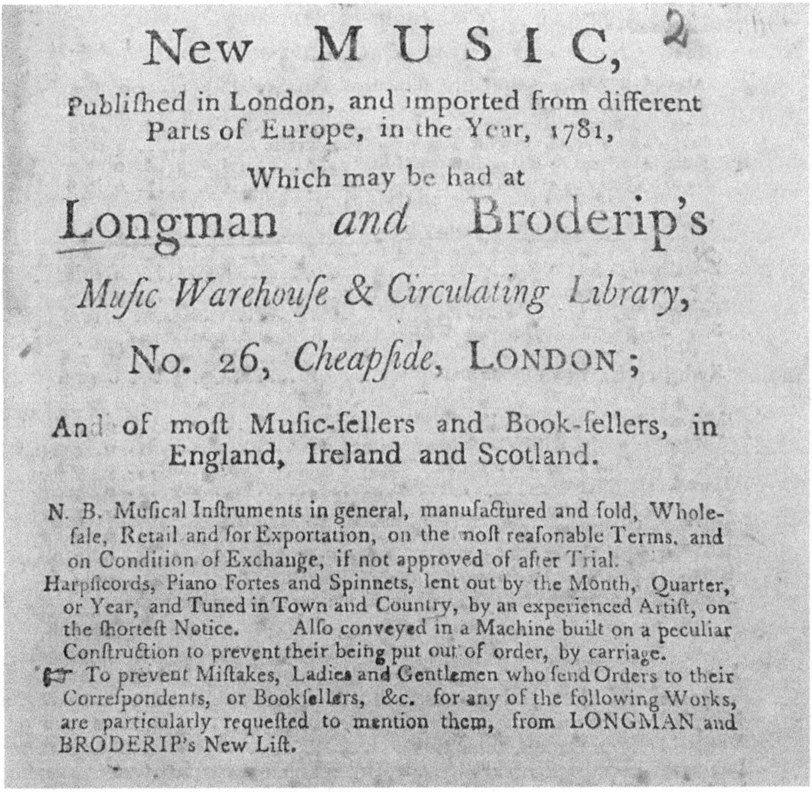

New MUSIC,

Publiſhed in London, and imported from different Parts of Europe, in the Year, 1781,

Which may be had at

Longman *and* Broderip's

Muſic Warehouſe & Circulating Library,

No. 26, *Cheapſide*, LONDON;

And of moſt Muſic-ſellers and Book-ſellers, in England, Ireland and Scotland.

N. B. Muſical Inſtruments in general, manufactured and ſold, Wholeſale, Retail and for Exportation, on the moſt reaſonable Terms, and on Condition of Exchange, if not approved of after Trial.

Harpſicords, Piano Fortes and Spinnets, lent out by the Month, Quarter, or Year, and Tuned in Town and Country, by an experienced Artiſt, on the ſhorteſt Notice. Alſo conveyed in a Machine built on a peculiar Conſtruction to prevent their being put out of order, by carriage.

☞ To prevent Miſtakes, Ladies and Gentlemen who ſend Orders to their Correſpondents, or Bookſellers, &c. for any of the following Works, are particularly requeſted to mention them, from LONGMAN and BRODERIP's New Liſt.

FIGURE 1.5. From Longman & Broderip's *New Music Published in London, and imported from different Parts of Europe* (1781). © British Library Board

> Imported and Sold by Longman & Broderip No. 26 Cheapside & No. 13 Hay Market London Who have a regular Correspondence with all the most eminent Professors and Publishers of Music in every part of Europe.[59]

Meanwhile, from 1781, Haydn himself sold new works (most of them also destined for Artaria) directly to the London music seller William Forster—which was to cause controversy and legal wrangling when more than one edition of new compositions by Haydn (to which several publishers believed they had exclusive rights) appeared in London simultaneously.[60]

Traffic also flowed from London back to Haydn. In 1789, the music seller John Bland, who had emerged as one of Longman & Broderip's fiercest competitors in London, undertook a journey between several European cities in search of publishers and composers who would agree to supply him with new works.[61] This was not the first of these speculative outings: Bland had traveled for a large portion of the previous year and, upon his return, had advertised in various published additions to his catalogs "Importations of the most eminent Composers," as a consequence of his "Connections, by a personal Application (of four months last Autumn) on the Continent, with the first Composers and Publishers."[62] This time, with the encouragement of the London-based violinist and impresario Johann Peter Salomon, Bland headed for the greatest prize: Haydn himself. Bland met Haydn in Eszterháza in November 1789. The result was musical traffic flowing in the opposite direction: Bland's London publication of the op. 64 string quartets, three piano trios, and the "cantata" (an Italian scena) *Arianna a Naxos*.

In the year that Bland visited, court records show that Haydn's prince graciously awarded him an extra pig—the very epitome of local stock—possibly as some kind of inducement to remain in the service of the court in the face of commercial temptations from elsewhere.[63] Bland, by contrast, brought Haydn the most up-to-date imported accoutrements—gentlemen's razors. Haydn's earliest biographers report that Bland rushed back to his lodgings to retrieve a razor, having heard Haydn complain about the bluntness of his own. The grateful Haydn supposedly gave Bland a string quartet in return—almost certainly not the op. 55 quartet currently known as *The Razor* but one of the op. 64 set, which had already traveled to Johann Tost in Paris.[64] The superior products of the Birmingham and Sheffield steel industries would have been known to Haydn—especially razors, which were among the earliest eighteenth-century consumer items to have been puffed by advertising campaigns.[65] A number of small metal things were on a wish list of desirable consumer items that Haydn jotted down at the very start of the notebooks that he carried with him around England: knitting needles, scissors, and a knife.[66] Whether or not there is any truth to the razor anecdote, Bland certainly sent English razors by post as soon as he was back in London. Haydn wrote back to him in April 1790, promising a second piano trio, vowing to retain his "valued friendship" and confirming that he had "received the razors in good condition," along with his fee.[67] This ensemble-cast it-narrative, driven by the energetic transcontinental commutations of friendship and trade, culminated in Bland's London edition of the six quartets op. 64, published in two volumes in June 1791.

By this time, Haydn himself was in London. Only a day after his arrival, the *Morning Chronicle*—presumably with the encouragement of Bland himself—reported, "Yesterday arrived at Mr. BLAND's, in Holborn, the celebrated Mr. HAYDN," and credited the publisher with being "the chief instrument of Mr. HAYDN's coming to England."[68] This was partly true, though the visit had been the subject of speculation in the London press for several years, and Haydn was only now easily transportable, owing to the death of Nikolaus I in September 1790 and the subsequent disbanding of the Esterházy orchestra. (Haydn remained in the service of the court but with minimal duties.) Upon hearing the news, Salomon, who had been staying in Cologne, rerouted his annual Continental tour to Vienna, where Haydn had relocated following the death of his prince. Still, Bland's earlier attentions had been critical. The music historian Thomas Busby later reported that Haydn had spent his first night in London, January 2, 1791, at Bland's lodgings.[69] Finally, it seems, Haydn had caught up with the mazy peregrinations of his own music. He was now the prize import amid the stock of books and instruments in Bland's Holborn warehouse.

The title pages of Bland's editions of the op. 64 quartets would proudly announce the hard-won copresence of the composer and his music: "composed by Giuseppe Haydn and PERFORM'D under his DIRECTION at Mr. Salomon's concerts, the Festino Rooms, Hanover Square" (see fig. 1.6). The earliest of these quartet performances had occurred, alongside grander orchestral fare, on the second of the Haydn-Salomon concerts on March 18. This would have been a new experience for Haydn, who had never previously encountered string quartets on ticketed concerts in front of a comparatively anonymous audience. Yet in London, the genre was absorbed into this relatively new media platform with considerable success: Salomon's press announcements show that the op. 64 quartet that premiered on May 6 was reprised "by particular desire" (as the standard formulation went) in concerts later that month.[70] Meanwhile, *Arianna a Naxos*—an operatic scena that was nonetheless intended to be easy enough for amateur singers (Haydn had studied the piece with Josepha, the sixteen-year-old daughter of the von Genzinger family)— was without doubt the hit of Haydn's earliest months in London.[71] This was in large part because *Arianna* was now coupled with the famous voice of the castrato Gasparo Pacchierotti: "Nothing is talked of—nothing sought after but Haydn's Cantata," gushed the *Morning Chronicle* following Pacchierotti and Haydn's appearance at the exclusive Ladies Concert on February 18, in the Marylebone home of the writer and society hostess Mary Blair. They reprised the performance only days later, on a concert organized by musicians of the New Musical Fund.[72] The last appearance of the cantata with Pacchierotti was on the Salomon series in Hanover Square on May 16—by which time hardly any of the audience would have been ignorant of the piece.[73] Bland showed impeccable timing and published *Arianna* the following June.

But even as Bland's early Haydn publications were anchored to these London events and spaces, they remained unavoidably vehicular, conveying musical stock that, though newly accessible to the bearers of tickets and the purchasers of engravings, had long been on the move. *Arianna a Naxos* begins

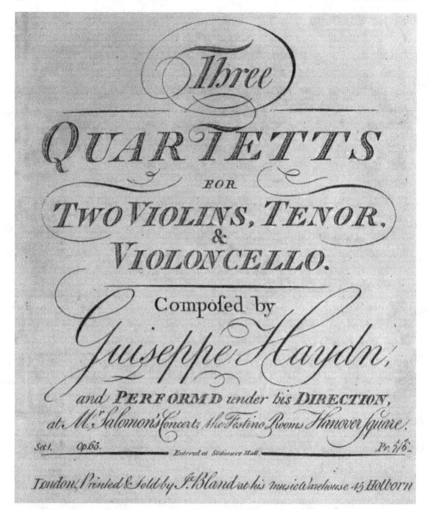

FIGURE 1.6. The title page of the String Quartets op. 64 (London: Bland, 1791).

with a diatonic version of the very pedal-point maneuver that had once opened the Symphony no. 59, the recitative unfolding with a typical keyboard improviser's gambit (fig. 1.7). And the op. 64 quartets reiterate the same move: it soothes the rustic dance at the end of op. 64, no. 4 (a purpose comparable to its calming role in the Sonata in C Major from 1780) and undergirds the spry contredanse that opens the last movement of op. 64, no. 6—Salomon's tune tripping exuberantly up through an octave before falling back to the root note (see fig. 1.8).

Thus did London's media landscape—its publications, its concerts—represent and reformat the well-used components of Haydn's musical style.

FIGURE 1.7. The same stock improviser's move, as the opening of *Arianna a Naxos* (London: Bland, 1791).

FIGURE 1.8. Salomon's tune, based on the stock move, beginning the last movement of op. 64, no. 6.

"My credit with the people [*mein Credit bei den Volck*] has been established," Haydn announced to von Genzinger following the successful season of 1791, using a word that denoted a favorable balance of both trust and cash.[74] His old musical stock had joined a new chain of exchanges: swapping places with razors, melting into money, transacting friendships, and earning credit.

A Resonant World

Like his letters to Bland, Haydn had headed along the route to London and ended up in 45 High Holborn. He had also carried all sorts of letters on his person to England: unassailably ancien régime letters of introduction—from the Austrian chancellor Prince Kaunitz to the ambassador Count Stadion and from King Ferdinand IV of Naples to Prince Castelcicala—and various bits of business on behalf of friends, such as letters from his admired colleague Paul Wranitzky to London music sellers.[75] The apparent spatial certainties of these terminating addresses—the locations between which music and musicians were transmitted—nonetheless enabled a new system of articulations and connections that created endless potential for onward journeys. "Addresses, literally, create channels," writes Friedrich Kittler.[76] Almost as soon as Haydn departed Vienna, a manuscript of the Symphony no. 91 had been interminably lodged in these channels: having neglected to bring it with him, Haydn requested that von Genzinger copy it onto appropriately "small postal-sized paper [*klein Post Papier*]" and send it to him by mail.[77] Months later, it had crawled only as far as Brussels.[78] (During his second London visit, Haydn noted the contrasting velocity of English mail coaches, which, he recorded, could manage 110 miles in twelve hours.[79])

Even when Haydn's music arrived, however, it rarely stopped at a single address. Sales of the music that had been imported to England represented only a small proportion of its onward journeys. Already by the early 1780s, Longman & Broderip began operating a circulating library from their Cheapside music shop, which promised "every publication, ancient and modern, that England, France, Holland, and Germany have produced, or may in future"—a claim that managed to imply a dramatic telescoping of space and time wrought by new commercial channels.[80] And they were joined by several more by the end of the century.[81] Richard Birchall, the music seller who was to take over many of Bland's publishing enterprises, started his own musical circulating library sometime in the 1780s on New Bond Street. A yearly subscription was eventually a steep £2.2.0—but this guaranteed access to a voluminous back catalog, including stacks of Haydn.

To circulate within London was also to slip into channels that led to the "distant empires" celebrated in the "Importation of Haydn." Longman & Broderip hired an agent in Calcutta in the mid-1780s and regularly shipped music publications, pianos, and other instruments to this large and established multiethnic city (this decade witnessed the earliest Indian performances of Haydn's orchestral music).[82] Busby would later claim that Longman & Broderip "created a commerce in [musical instruments] with every part of the world"—and, to be sure, their 1786 catalog of imported prints had advertised musical instruments that were "well seasoned, to stand all Climates," and "ready at the shortest notice for EXPORTATION." In what was doubtless a desirable piece of publicity, one of Longman's newest grands followed Haydn back to Vienna.[83] Pianos, along with some of Haydn's music, were among the commodities conveyed to China by the Macartney Mission in 1793—a trip that greatly interested Haydn upon his return to London the next year, doubtless in part because of Burney's close involvement with the musical elements of the mission.[84] It hardly needs saying that pianos were themselves intricate assemblages of widely dispersed materials: a late eighteenth-century English piano gathered together wool, silk, and leather, hardwood from the Americas (Haydn's own grand was in mahogany), as well as ivory from West and East Central Africa and, to a lesser extent, the Indian subcontinent.[85] Many of these materials thus journeyed back to the colonized realms from which they had been harvested, transformed in order to harbor the stock of European music.[86] Haydn's musical language, which he had claimed was understood "all over the world," was conveyed by materials harvested from all over the world.

Those attesting to the universal appeal of the piano's sound included what the *Times* described as six "Cherokee Chiefs"—three Cherokee and two Creek Indians, it seems, escorted by the adventurer and conman William Augustus Bowles—who made a much-publicized visit to Longman & Broderip's shop in 1790, where they witnessed a demonstration of the firm's "Grand Piano Fortes."[87] The Cherokee nation had sided with the British during the revolution, and Longman & Broderip had been one of several music sellers to publish songs that claimed to be of Cherokee origin. The most widely disseminated of these was the "Death song of the Cherokee Indians," an "Original Air Brought from America," published and republished by Longman & Broderip many times from 1780 onward.[88] The song paired a poem by Anne Hunter, who was later to collaborate with Haydn on most of his *Original Canzonettas* in the mid-1790s, with a tune provided by "a Gentleman long Conversant with the Indian Tribes" (see fig. 1.9).[89]

This song is a reminder that extracting and creating surplus value from ostensibly non-European sounds does not necessarily require those twentieth-century technologies that are typically denoted by the term *sound reproduction*.[90] These elaborately staged reverberations—Americans listening to European pianos, Europeans listening to American song—promoted the idea that London's music shops, and London's music, mediated the worldwide attachments of mutually enriching commerce. As Busby explained, the achievements of Longman & Broderip were not "confined merely to the purse"; they also kept "an open table at which professors and amateurs, from every part of the world, had the opportunity of meeting, and of eliciting from each other information of mutual and considerable advantage."[91] Standing in Bland's music warehouse or, later on, trying val-

FIGURE 1.9. From one of many later reprints of the "Death song of the Cherokee Indians" (London: G. Walker, 1810). Clara Thomas Archives and Special Collections, York University Libraries.

iantly to get work done in the shop of the piano builder John Broadwood on Great Pulteney Street, Haydn encountered not merely the brute spatial fact of London but the fantasy of a world mapped out by the concertina motion of things to and from London addresses. More than this, it was frequently a world made by music—by Haydn's music, even: "The musical world will rejoice to hear," began the *Gazetteer's* review of Salomon's concert of April 15, 1791, "that the celebrated *Haydn* has determined to fix the seat of his *empire* in this metropolis."[92]

Haydn had visited a mere fraction of his purported empire, of course. In 1791, his only sea crossing had been his trip over the English Channel on New Year's Day. He was nonetheless captivated by the idea of travel, and particularly by English ships. In his notebooks, he listed many details about masts and decks, captains and cockswains, merchant vessels and naval ships in the vast Portsmouth Dockyard. He was also fascinated by the technologies of British naval warfare: in 1794, he witnessed the wreck of the French ship of the line *Le just*, on display near Portsmouth, and even scrawled a tiny drawing of a fireship.[93]

It was around this time that Haydn started work on more than one composition celebrating Britain's naval prowess: the tub-thumping choral cantata *Invocation of Neptune*, which he took up at the behest of the Earl of Abingdon but put aside with only a chorus and a bass aria completed,[94] and the "Sailor's Song"—a canzonetta in the form of a sea shanty punctuated with bombastic passages of martial exhortation ("the roaring cannon loudly speaks, 'tis Britain's glory we maintain," proclaimed Hunter's poem).[95] As an honored guest aboard several of the opulent vessels that stopped in London, Haydn soon understood the "poetics of the ship's hold," to use Peter Sloterdijk's phrase—the principle of self-contained European interior spaces, designed to traverse globe-sized distances unbreeched.[96] Haydn even supplied a musical version of this poetics: one of his earliest, and most lucrative, English commissions came from an enigmatic sea captain, who requested some new marches before heading to America.[97] Thus did the plush sonic interiors of Europe embark.

Toward the end of summer 1791, Haydn was the guest of honor aboard an East India merchantman.[98] The conversation over the lavish lunch he was served would surely have turned to the long-running trial in Westminster Hall to impeach Warren Hastings, former governor-general of India, on twenty charges of high crimes and misdemeanors.[99] Indeed, almost for the duration of Haydn's time in England—the trial started in 1788, and Hastings was acquitted shortly before Haydn headed homeward in 1795—the Hastings trial provided a continuing public interrogation of British commerce and its potential to connect, improve, and exploit distant lands. Several of Haydn's closest acquaintances in London were vocal supporters of Hastings, especially the Burneys (Frances Burney had been present on the opening day of the trial in the "royal box," as if going to the opera).[100] Haydn's notebook indicates that he attended a public session of the trial on May 25, 1792. Consistent with his preoccupation with numbers, and especially money, he noted down Hastings's rumored three-million-pound personal fortune, as well as the ruinous expense of maintaining three advocates.[101]

The charges brought by Edmund Burke and the other so-called Managers responsible for the prosecution amounted to the claim that Hastings had harmed and exploited the Indian population during the confused period in which the East India Company became more or less the sovereign power in the region. For Burke, the trial was, perhaps above all else, a test of human sympathy when it was so thinly stretched across world-sized distances, as his voluminous speeches and publications on the subject continually repeated: "People that are wronged, people that are robbed, people that are despoiled have no other remedy but the sympathies of mankind."[102] His most famous, and, by the 1790s, venerable work, the *Philosophical Enquiry Concerning the Origin of Our Ideas of the Sublime and the Beautiful* (a book that Haydn made sure to purchase in an English edition while he was in London) had characterized sympathy in conventional eighteenth-century terms, as "a sort of substitution, by which we are put into the place of another man"—a form of imaginative exchange.[103] In his later publications on the Hastings trial, Burke repeatedly advanced the view, theorized in related ways by Hume and Adam Smith, that distance weakened sympathy—that India's subjects overburdened the colonizers' imagination, and the "sympathy which normally attaches you to men of feeling" was strained.[104] In many respects, Burke's rhetorically heated speeches and publications about Hastings, much like the early publicity campaigns of British abolitionists, were intended to redress what he perceived as an injurious imbalance in sentimental commerce.[105] As Mary Fairclough has argued, Burke and others, by the 1790s, had come to associate sympathy not only with the physiological operations of the imagination or the contagious properties of feeling but also with the "proliferative effects of the printing press"—an adaptation of the Humean conception of sympathy as the "communication of sentiments" to a changing media landscape.[106] "We transport ourselves in fancy to the scenes of those distant and forgotten adventures," explained Adam Smith, in his sympathetic account of the appeal of reading history books.[107] On this model, the travels of Burke's printed words about the fate of India under Hastings sought at once to arouse and perform the otherwise enfeebled reverberations of the sympathetic imagination.

One can trace something of this logic in Haydn's canzonetta entitled "Sympathy," published in the year of Hastings's acquittal—a strophic song on a Metastasian text, in which the singer describes a mutual love so absolute that "each affection of thy heart / By sympathy is mine." (In 1792, Rebecca Schroeter had used this formula in one of her passionate letters to Haydn: "I partake with the most perfect Sympathy in ALL YOUR SENSATIONS," she gushed.[108]) "The minds of men are as mirrors to one another," remarked Hume in a much-cited passage on sympathy from *A Treatise of Human Nature*, and Haydn's song performs just this specular structure in its constant recourse to internal repetitions and echoes, most clearly in the passages that require hand-crossing: a dactylic melodic fragment in the left hand (a pulsating heart or nervous frisson perhaps) passes from feminine treble to masculine bass over skittish thirty-second notes in the right hand (fig. 1.10).[109] This device is only the most blatant musical expression of a more pervasive pattern of self-conscious mirroring—between registers of the keyboard, between singer and keyboard player (who may frequently have been the same person), and perhaps even between the player and her instrument: one thinks of the many songs from the period, discussed by Annette Richards, that address the keyboard as a loving companion who resonates in sympathy with the feelings of an otherwise solitary performer.[110] "When thou art griev'd, I grieve no less. / My joys by thine are known," announces the singer, and these contrasting sentiments receive neatly successive treatment: groaning diminished sonorities and a turn to the minor mode with grief, then a string of pastoral skips in the major with joy. These are stock sentiments delivered in capsule form, subjunctive moods that belong to no one in particular yet: as Lynn Festa puts it, sympathy puts "emotions in motion," confusing the boundary between subject and object, self and other.[111] In other moments, the song aims to dissolve these stock sentiments into materials ostensibly more elemental:

FIGURE 1.10. Sympathetic mirroring in Haydn's "Sympathy" from *VI Original Canzonettas* (London: Corri, Dussek, 1795).

FIGURE 1.11. Vibrating nerves in "Sympathy."

the words "each affection of thy heart" are initially coupled with a closely voiced oscillation of thirty-second notes in the keyboard (fig. 1.11). This passage does not adopt a musical character as much as it mimics the vibrational substance of sound and feeling in themselves—though, of course, this is itself a stock musical gesture of nervous agitation, related to the theatrical tremolo: music that tells us what vibration should sound like.

These musical sentiments and sensations traveled from person to person not only because they were reproducible musical devices but also because they were captured in reproducible print objects. The communication of sentiments celebrated by Haydn's "Sympathy" was realized and sustained in large part by the motions of its printed form around the pianos and parlors of London—the motions of "musical characters" not only in the expressive sense but also the typographical one (in the eighteenth century, "musical characters" more frequently denoted forms of writing in any case).[112] "The circulation of print commodities allows for a sentiment to be broken off and sold separately," observes Festa.[113] Just as the song "Sympathy" hosted self and imagined other on a single keyboard—within a single performer, even—so the collection of circulating musical stock stored on its pages helped to promote its vibrant fantasy of sentimental commerce.

Among the assortment of engravings that Haydn carried back to Vienna from the unrivalled print shops of London was a picture that displayed the vast distances supposedly traversed by sympathetic fellow feeling even more pointedly than Haydn's canzonetta. It was a souvenir of Hastings's acquittal: *The Judgment of Britannia* by Henry Richter, engraved by the Florentine-born Francesco Bartolozzi, who had become a close acquaintance of Haydn's in London (see fig. 1.12).[114]

The picture triumphantly rebukes Burke and the Managers with a stark visual allegory. Hastings stands to the left of the picture, receiving a laurel crown from Britannia herself. He is presented to her by none other than Commerce, who wears a medallion of a ship and has an anchor at her feet,

FIGURE 1.12. *The Judgment of Britannia* (1795) by Henry Richter. Engraved by Francesco Bartolozzi. © The Trustees of the British Museum.

while Plenty stands beside her, cornucopia overflowing. Behind Hastings, a group of representatives from Bengal approach from the shadows, the foremost holding a scroll headed *Testimonial from Bengal.* Justice guards the whole scene from the conniving accusations of the Managers—including Burke and the distinctively big-nosed Charles James Fox—who cower behind a column to the right. Thus did the picture imagine a world connected by Commerce, a world crammed within Britannia's throne room, its distances shrunk by sympathy. This was a vision of commerce in its most capacious eighteenth-century sense—Hume's agreeable "commerce and society of men." *The Judgment of Britannia* portrays the grateful testimony of distant Indian people—never has the subaltern spoken so clearly—alongside the material plenty shared between colonized and colonizers, blurring any distinction between the reverberant exchanges of feeling and the material exchanges of goods. And, in a single image, it accomplishes the work that Festa ascribes to eighteenth-century colonial sentiment, imagining frictionless social intercourse even as it reinforces borders between the subjects and objects of colonial sympathy.[115] Hastings, the picture shows, had already secured the sympathetic attachments whose absence Burke had lamented—in the inclusive communications of commerce.

As it happens, the son of the picture's engraver, Gaetano Bartolozzi, had

met Haydn in Eszterháza several years earlier, where he had reportedly enjoined the composer to relocate to England. The only account of this visit, in
the *Gazetteer* in February 1787, caricatured Haydn's isolation, "unworthy of
his genius," the "pittance" he was paid, and his "miserable apartment in the
barracks," divided from the world across which his music now abundantly
moved.[116] In London, Haydn learned that many of his works had indeed covered distances as far as those portrayed in *The Judgment of Britannia*. To be
imported was not only to change address, but to acquire a global address
book—the impression of multiplying channels of communication and the
attendant fantasy of a world connected by sentimental commerce.

New Addresses

John Bland at High Holborn. Mary Blair and Alexander Blair at Portland
Place. John Broadwood at Great Pulteney Street. John Hunter and Anne
Hunter at Leicester Square. Addresses are precisely not the same thing as
people.[117] In the mega medium that is the modern city, the data of addresses
stand in for people: addresses are the points between which things can be
communicated. What is a music historian to make of the fact that, in the
1790s, hundreds of people placed upon their music desks compositions by
Haydn (and others) that they knew to have bounced from address to address
before pausing at their own? Or one could put the question in a more conventional way: To whom was Haydn's London music addressed?

For much of Haydn's long career, the question of musical address would
have been foundational. Before even starting work, he would have needed to
know the address—to know whom he was addressing. Festive court genres,
such as the 1768 *Applausus*, are full of apostrophic turns and nods to the most
eminent people in the room. "How blessed I am to be an inhabitant of this
building!" sings the character of Prudence in the *Applausus*—no wonder
that Haydn was anxious that he could not be there to oversee things. Music historians have frequently described Haydn's music from the perspective
of these changing addresses and addressees: the Eszterháza operas, the Paris
and London symphonies, the late Viennese oratorios, and so on. The impulse
to situate and localize Haydn's music—in the Festino Room, the Salle des cent
Suisses, or the Burgtheater—has produced generations of formidable and
imaginative scholarship. A recent ne plus ultra is Tom Beghin's *Virtual Haydn*
project, which pairs, in scholarship and performance, Haydn's keyboard music with particular instruments, spaces, and virtually engineered acoustics,
even particular historical hands and faces.[118] But the impulse to resituate this
music amid the plenitude of a historical place does not always sit comfortably

with the tendency of Haydn's compositions, especially those from the London period, to slip away—to move from address to address, to inhere as much in the mediating channels between addresses as in any point of historical termination. This is not to say that Haydn's music was unchanged by the people and places that he encountered in London or anywhere else, of course—although, to be sure, it has been notoriously hard to link Haydn's changing locations securely to any distinctive changes in his musical style or technique.[119] Rather, by the time he was in London, Haydn did not merely produce compositions with a changed address; his music had changed its relationship to address altogether.

On May 16, 1795, Haydn was witness to the marriage of the younger Bartolozzi, whom he had first met in Eszterháza around a decade earlier.[120] Bartolozzi's spouse was the British Scandinavian pianist Therese Jansen, for whom Haydn had composed a pair of piano sonatas the previous year. This most itinerant of genres seems to have found a home with Jansen in London: the Sonata in C (Hob. XVI:50) and the Sonata in E-flat, (Hob. XVI:52) have lent themselves to historical interpretations that acknowledge the impact, especially in texture and figuration, of Jansen's virtuosic version of London pianism, as well as the potential of heavier-actioned, more resonant English pianos.[121]

Yet the route by which the C Major Sonata turned up at Jansen's address was more circuitous than such linear conceptions of English pianism have typically implied. Haydn was notably economical with his materials in this sonata: he had already published its Adagio in Vienna with Artaria around 1793 or 1794, and he simply recycled the movement, with some adjustments, for its new London address. Meanwhile, the opening Allegro, which internally recycles a comically rudimentary thematic fragment almost unrelentingly—a descending triad plus a cadential mi-re-do pattern—seems to translate Haydn's material economy into an aesthetic principle: the extraction of maximum value from the barest minimum of musical materials. Griesinger reported that, late in Haydn's career, he criticized the tendency among younger composers to "string out one little idea after another" rather than exploiting the possibilities presented by a single one.[122]

From their ostensibly stable London addresses, the onward journeys of these sonatas began almost immediately. Jansen retained the C Major Sonata as exclusive to her performances around Britain and the Continent and did not consent to publish the piece until 1800.[123] The travels of the E-flat Piano Sonata were more complex still. Having given it to Jansen, Haydn returned home and published it independently with Artaria in 1798. The earliest edition is dedicated not to Jansen but to the Vienna-based pianist Magdalena

FIGURE 1.13. A pointed dedication on the frontispiece of the first English edition of the Piano Sonata Hob. XVI:52 (London: Longman, Clementi, 1799). © British Library Board.

von Kurzböck. Perhaps Haydn was not expecting to see the young Bartolozzi couple so soon. But it turns out that, having sold a huge stock of copperplates at Christies in 1797, they stopped en route to Venice in the very year that the Artaria edition appeared.[124] The couple were in need of cash, and the result was presumably a series of communications heading back along the route to England: in 1799, another edition, published in London by Longman & Broderip's successors, Longman, Clementi, & Co., appeared with the pointed dedication, "Composed Expressly for Mrs Bartolozzi" (see fig. 1.13). Beghin therefore locates the sonata in two distinct places: the 1798 Artaria edition frequently deviates from the English autograph—especially with respect to articulation markings—in order, he shows, to make the London sonata comfortable at its new Viennese abode.[125]

But was this piano sonata ever at home in either place? It accompanied Haydn on the road to Vienna and Jansen on the road to Venice (and one hardly need observe that it has been on the road ever since, which is how it continues to arrive at our door). Moreover, the musical materials of this last sonata, in particular the opening Allegro, are plainly a collocation of stock characters permanently "out of their proper contexts"—so much so that it served as a paradigm for Leonard Ratner's methods of topical analysis. Ratner's virtuosic rundown of the Allegro noted its opening French Overture, with its strong downbeats and dotted rhythms; the lyrical *stile legato* into which the majestic opening dissolves; the sudden irruptions of passagework in the brilliant style; the distinctive horn fifths, with their tripping right-hand embellishments; and the faintly exotic, Turkish-music recursions that interrupt them (see fig. 1.14).[126]

One should also note that the opening French Overture gesture is built

FIGURE 1.14. The Piano Sonata Hob. XVI:52, beginning with the stock move. Here, mediated by the inaugural 1799 volume of Breitkopf & Härtel's projected *Oeuvres Complettes*.

upon the old stock maneuver theorized by Zingarelli: a lowered seventh heading to the subdominant and a raised seventh heading back to the tonic—the one that Haydn had used to begin his Symphony no. 59 back in the 1760s. In its diatonic version, this device also begins the Piano Trio in E-flat (Hob. XV:30)—composed around the same time as the piano sonata and, like the sonata, dedicated to Jansen (fig. 1.15). Both of these compositions reproduce the pattern that opens Mozart's Second Piano Quartet—also in E-flat—which Artaria published in 1787 (fig. 1.16). In this key and at this time—and recall that Haydn had performed *Arianna a Naxos* many times in London, with its own opening deployment of the same gambit in E-flat—Haydn's hands were sliding into timeworn patterns.

The cluster of theoretical approaches that have aimed to acknowledge and categorize these stock patterns and characters—and even to valorize their stockness as a kind of mature worldliness—have by and large been united by a polemically localizing outlook, whose declared enemies are those

FIGURE 1.15. The stock move again, in the opening measures of Haydn's Piano Trio Hob. XV:30, piano part (Vienna: Artaria, 1797). Austrian National Library, Music Department. Used by permission.

FIGURE 1.16. The same stock move, and in the same key, beginning Mozart's Second Piano Quartet, K 493, piano part (Paris: Pleyel, c. 1803).

nineteenth- and twentieth-century modes of formal analysis, whose "principled neglect of [eighteenth-century music's] historically grounded features," as Allanbrook sardonically puts it, allegedly obscured the bodies and places that are inseparable from this music.[127] But topic theory has always grappled with its own somewhat attenuated historicity. It has never been clear where and how the clusters of meanings and feelings proposed by topic theorists are supposed to be "historically grounded," nor whether the problematically ecumenical modern-day concept of the topic is enough to turn our listening and performing practices into something historically informed.[128] The historical horizon is always receding: to enumerate stock characters or phrases is to describe not places of historical termination but principles of departure, of spatial and temporal motion—to describe not arrivals as much as journeys. And, crucially, by the 1790s, this principle of motion had been harnessed in new ways: Haydn's musical stock had been transformed by newly powerful technologies of storage, transmission, and reproduction—the technologies of print commerce.

It is no coincidence that the subjunctive mood of the characters, gestures, and symbols that are nowadays classed as musical topics also structured the sympathetic conception of beauty articulated by such eighteenth-century thinkers as Adam Smith: both are premised on the motion of the projective imagination. In *The Theory of Moral Sentiments*, Smith proposed that people derived greater pleasure from contemplating the means by which useful ends could be achieved than by any experience of those ends themselves, since, in the imagination, one could exchange places countless times with somebody who owns a luxurious mansion or consumes a sumptuous meal—and hence, through the faculty of sympathy, amass limitless pleasures. "The happy contrivance of any production of art," maintained Smith, is "more valued, than the very end for which it was intended"—an aesthetic principle that propelled economic expansion, as people were driven by the principle of sympathy to accumulate more than they could consume.[129] The structure of the musical topic similarly divides means from ends, making potential musical meanings from only notional functions: hunts without hunting, majesty without kings, characters without actors, sentiments without subjects.[130]

In the media landscapes of the late eighteenth century, the homelessness of these stock characters was newly discernible and newly powerful. The variety of gesture, character, and mood in a composition from the 1760s such as the Symphony no. 59—the variety that had propelled it into the theater at Eszterháza—took on a new potency in the format of the last piano sonata, which was designed to occupy commercial channels that cut across Europe. W. Dean Sutcliffe writes that this variety signals a "creative abdication of discursive authority": "A musical utterance marked by a variety of stance and gesture no longer seems to compel a particular response or enforce a single 'message.'"[131] The Haydn devotee Thomas Twining observed something similar in 1789, maintaining that the pleasure of the best instrumental music depended upon the "very indecision itself of the expression," "leaving the hearer to the free operation of his *emotion* upon his *fancy* and, as it were, to the free *choice* of such ideas as are, to *him*, the most adapted to react upon and heighten the emotion which occasioned them"—a description in which the Man of Feeling and the freely choosing consumer are barely distinguishable.[132] The "emotions in motion" in the opening movement of Haydn's last piano sonata might remind us that eighteenth-century sentiment is always about social circulation as much as private interiority—"passion that has been mediated by a sympathetic passage through a virtual point of view," as James Chandler puts it.[133] From this perspective, even Beghin's *Virtual Haydn* project is less the virtual making present of an absent past than an elaboration of the virtuality that this music has always implied.

Haydn's last solo piano sonata lived in the channels between addresses. Like the Longman & Broderip pianos where it would sometimes have rested, it was "ready at the shortest notice for EXPORTATION." And its huge potential to mean depended upon this very itinerance—upon innumerable, interminable journeys between a resonant collection of musical means and any particular meanings they may acquire. In the "anonymous freedom of the marketplace," writes Terry Eagleton, art addresses "anybody with the taste to appreciate it and the money to buy it"—which is to say that a deterritorialized market existence is more or less the same thing as vaunted aesthetic autonomy.[134]

Music before the Cliché

To Haydn, as to eighteenth-century thinkers such as Hume, "commerce" would have connoted the most agreeable forms of social intercourse, not the rapacious logic of economics. Haydn unabashedly cultivated and appreciated the "commerce of the arts": his years spent in London predate Romantic tropes of the artist's alienation from or resistance to the coercions of the market. The old aesthetic-economic concept of "stock" music was not yet pejorative nor yet interpretable as the technical trace of a constraining and standardizing system.[135]

Haydn would have understood his musical stock via the early modern principles of social circulation that allowed him to acquire it: the forms of musical training and dissemination honed by such institutions as the Neapolitan conservatories and such genres as Italian comic opera. These principles were never supplanted; but in the course of Haydn's career—and especially in London—they were absorbed into a mediascape and commercial infrastructure that mobilized and extracted value from musical stock in transformative ways. This was the moment of the "Importation of Haydn"—a moment of considerable promise, which made thinkable world-spanning communications of sentiment of the sort depicted in Haydn's engraving of the victorious Hastings. Only later would it be possible to denigrate the reproducible phrases and characters of eighteenth-century music as mechanistic "clichés" or "stereotypes"—words that, not coincidentally, derive from eighteenth-century print technologies.[136] The stereotype and the cliché were methods of cheap print reproduction that involved making a cast of a section of moveable type. English stereotype printing for music had not even started when Haydn left London. One of the earliest musical publications produced with stereotyped plates appeared in Strasbourg around 1803 and contained three quartets by Haydn's pupil Ignaz Pleyel (Pleyel had sold the quartets to the inventor of stereotype printing in 1795).[137] One might say, then, that—whether one means a technological innovation or an ethical-aesthetic value judgment—Haydn composed before the cliché.

The various musicologies of eighteenth-century musical stock—by which I mean studies of iterable conventions, characters, and technical common-places—are frequently driven by an ethical imperative: to recover in high-status eighteenth-century repertoires a worldliness and ordinariness that Romantic metaphysics has supposedly occluded.[138] On the model of Italian comic opera, argued Allanbrook, much late eighteenth-century instrumental music presents "an interminably varied, all-inclusive image of a peopled topographical space" in its dynamic mirror of the world.[139] But music makes as well as mirrors worlds.[140] The shape of Haydn's career, and the long process of reformatting his musical stock, might prompt us to consider his music's "varied, all-inclusive" ethos in a new light. The last solo piano sonata, with its whirl of musical topics, seems to celebrate and even overstate the dynamism of a world remade by the long-range commutations of commerce and, to that extent, could be compared to contemporary it-narratives, "novels of circulation," and treatises on political economy—genres that participated in and made the "world of moving objects," popularizing images of a perpetually mobile, interactive, truck-and-barter society.[141] There is more than an echo of this fantasy in more recent network-oriented and all-action conceptions of society—visions of a social world in which the only legitimate members are thrusting human and nonhuman actors, out there making things happen and forging new associations, "entering into commerce with what authorizes them and enables them to exist," to cite Bruno Latour's telling formulation.[142] In a certain strain of recent music research, observes Gavin Steingo, "relations and motion are valorized as being truer to music's inherent tendencies"—and perhaps even to the world as it really is.[143] But to portray mobility as an ontology is to ignore that it is a value. "To be doing something, to move, to change—this is what enjoys prestige," write Luc Boltanski and Eve Chiapello in *The New Spirit of Capitalism*.[144] This value can be traced to the urban commercial societies and colonial projects of the eighteenth century and the liberal philosophies that they nurtured. Patterns of global migration nowadays, no less than the changing circumstances of late eighteenth-century England—the upheavals described with such plangency by E. P. Thompson—is a reminder that movement is foisted on many people, while for others (as in Haydn's case) it remains a rare privilege.[145]

And so, to observe that Haydn was mostly enthusiastic about the commerce of the arts—or that he composed before the cliché—is not to say that his London years represent some moment of artisanal innocence, before musicians experienced the deleterious consequences of a more developed capitalism, or the Blakean forms of Romanticism that were, in part, responses to a changing economic reality. Rather, it is to acknowledge the shared provenance of versions of commerce that were to become mutually hostile in the nineteenth century: agreeable social intercourse and debased market relations. If the distant projection of the sympathetic imagination was Adam Smith's foundational principle of social harmony, it was also the Burkean solution to the crimes of British imperialists in India and, as we will see in chapter 3, the main abolitionist solution to the crime of slavery. But in many respects it was made thinkable by the distant projections of trade and imperial expansion themselves. It seems improbable that we could extract a more perfectible cosmopolitanism from such contradictory beginnings.[146]

These days, the Burkean remedy of imperialist sympathy, with its project of feeling for and with colonized others, is transparently inadequate— reinscribing as it does the boundaries between communities of sentimental sympathizers and their objects—while the theories of moral and economic equilibrium advanced by Smith have rarely looked less realistic. But the resonant ethic of mutual sympathy persists (though it is nowadays typically translated into the more usual postwar therapeutic terms of "empathy"), having again been given fresh impetus by new media environments, the forms of distance-shrinking social commerce they enable, and the virtuality of feeling that they promote.[147] What is more, as in Haydn's time, music has been mooted as the inevitable partner of this ethic: once again, music is vibrational but networked, physiological but mediated, something that confounds the feeling body and its virtual dispersion across space and time.[148] But Haydn's London music—the culmination of a period of ever-closer engagement with incipient urban capitalism—raises unsettling questions about this ethic and the dynamic social ontologies it proposes. It seems to me that it is no easy task to distill a more virtuous account of liberal human commerce from its economically compromised origins. And neither is it a simple matter to resume the old Romantic project of weeding out the reified materialist exchanges from the sympathetic ones that they made thinkable—the mere clichés from the sociable stock of musical communication.

Interest

Note down what you can see. Anything worthy of note going on. Do you know how to
see what's worthy of note? . . . Force yourself to write down what is of no interest.

GEORGES PEREC, *Espèces d'espaces* (1974)[1]

Taking Note(s)

Throughout his two stays in London, Haydn recorded many of his thoughts
and experiences in four small notebooks. These English-made books, roughly
six inches by four inches in size, were designed to slide into a gentleman's
pocket, and Haydn evidently carried them around the city with him at times,
writing things down in a haphazard way, in both ink and pencil. The resulting books are situated generically somewhere between the discontinuous
diary and the poorly organized commonplace book (a sort of scrapbook of
quotable extracts from other texts). They gather together personal encounters and concert programs, street scenes and public rituals, curious facts and
superlative measurements, classical epigrams, smutty stories, and earnest
theological tenets. The raw material they contain might seem well suited to
current disciplinary predilections: the materialist turn to objects and things,
and dispersed, network-oriented sociological paradigms, not to mention the
longer-established New Historicist claims on behalf of the radical potential of
the anecdote and the local detail.[2] Haydn's London notebooks are, from these
related perspectives, a treasure trove of marginalia, each entry a synecdoche
standing in for an ungraspable whole, pointing the scholar down new side
streets of microhistorical description, toward the elaborate reanimation of
past relationships. The second book begins with the recipe for Prince of Wales
punch (main ingredients: a bottle of champagne and a bottle of burgundy)
and within a few lines describes, with the anthropological fascination of a
Catholic, how a Quaker behaves at court (he "pays the door-keeper to take off
his hat for him," apparently) and, with the wide-eyed admiration of the Austrian landlubber, how to "preserve cream or milk for a long time" according
to the prescription of an English sea captain.[3] If, as Joel Fineman argued, the
value of the anecdote is that it disrupts formal historical narrative and "lets

history happen" with its lack of closure,[4] then Haydn frequently redoubles this force by leaving even his anecdotes incomplete: "Anecdote about the foot under her petticoat," he writes, leaving much to the imagination; "Mr. Fox's trousers. Story of a sedan-chair-bearer," runs another gnomic torso; and only a blank space follows the announcement of the "little story of an errand boy who ate cow dung."[5]

While the empty spaces that pockmark the London notebooks may be evidence of history happening in all its open-endedness, their ellipses and narrative blind alleys also remind the historian of the precariousness of this kind of data: Haydn jotted down what interested him; he noted only what he deemed noteworthy. The notebooks parade a medley of resonant historical things but provide, above all else, a record of Haydn's interests, how his interest was directed and commanded. One might even conceive of them as Haydn's "extended mind"—a claim that would be implausible were it not so widespread in eighteenth-century conceptions of the commonplace book: "A Book of this sort is in the Nature of a Supplemental Memory," wrote Jonathan Swift in his 1721 *Letter of Advice to a Young Poet*, "or a Record of what occurs remarkable in every Day's Reading or Conversation."[6] John Locke, who published the century's most widely cited essay on the technique of organizing commonplace books, had conceived of consciousness itself as the process by which experience was noted onto the blank page of the psyche—"white Paper, void of all Characters, without any *Ideas*."[7] The epigrammatic, the anecdotal, and the curious seem to have claimed the attention of eighteenth-century keepers of commonplace books,[8] yet such books themselves—like the published anthologies that proliferated during this time—created and reproduced what counted as remarkable in the very act of remarking upon things.[9] As Sianne Ngai has shown in her discussion of the "interesting" as an aesthetic category, the interesting thing is, in part, performatively generated—is brought into being in the moment in which it is observed and made available for discussion.[10] In the gesture with which Haydn's notes produced the noteworthy detail, then, he also produced materials for the historian—something that the present-day researcher understands all too well when faced with anecdotes that conspicuously lack punch lines. To record the spontaneous materials of a more formal history might have been part of Haydn's intention in keeping these notebooks, especially given that they were produced during his rapid rise to celebrity status: in the early nineteenth century, he showed them to his earliest biographers, Georg August Griesinger and Albert Christoph Dies. Nowadays, the original fourth London notebook no longer exists as a physical artifact but has been patchily reconstructed from citations that were preserved by these men, a notebook that is thus more about the noting than the book: a notional object made out of a historical succession of overlapping interests—Haydn's, his biographers', and ours.[11]

The London notebooks amply demonstrate that interest has always been bound up with economies of language: the interesting detail, as Ngai has shown, is not only produced by discourse but serves to generate more of it.[12] To judge something as interesting is to invite ramification, an explanation of why this should be so. To point out an interesting thing is thus to provide the premise for talk, to goad the discursive sense making of criticism, history, and aesthetics. The scholarly eye has roved variously over the notebooks since they were passed to Dies and Griesinger, attesting to changing interests and methodologies—from the secure dating of compositions and performances to the compilation and analysis of Haydn's numerous Latin aphorisms, staples of the eighteenth-century commonplace book.[13] These days, music historians might be equally attracted to the more blatantly quotidian, bodily, or appetitive moments and to the "reality effect" of entries that appear alluringly incomplete and inscrutable.[14] That every pattern of scholarly concern, however professedly "material" in focus, has depended on Haydn's inaugural act of noting down could seem ample demonstration of the once notorious Derridean dictum that there is nothing outside of the text.[15] And yet the related meanings of the word *noting*—that is, having to do with attentiveness on the one hand and writing on the other—serve less to undo the fallacies of logocentrism than to demonstrate that no materials are raw. To adopt Bruno Latour's terms, every "matter of fact" can be unraveled into a "matter of concern": a copiously mediated gathering of interests.[16]

Harold Innis, one of the progenitors of today's media studies, once described his intellectual program as an extended response to the question "Why do we attend to the things to which we attend?"—a challenge that he answered with recourse to the various techniques of human communication.[17] With Innis's question in mind, one might hazard the claim that noting down has been, for centuries, one of the core technologies of interest, which is in large part about discrimination, or what one chooses to note. One of the great eighteenth-century note takers, Johann Gottfried Herder, maintained that language was what allowed humans to make distinctions among the "mass of perceptions flooding" them—an operation that, in the psychological discourse inaugurated a century later by William James, became foundational to human experience itself: "Millions of items of the outward order are present to my senses which never properly enter into my experience. Why? Because they have no *interest* for me. *My experience is what I agree to attend to*."[18] Eighteenth-century readers had regularly testified to the ways in which the taking of notes, by sealing this experiential agreement, transformed and even produced attention itself. In his *Loose Hints upon Education*, first published in 1781, Lord Kames contrasted the reader who allowed ideas merely to "glide through the mind" with the more assiduous note takers: "But let a common-place book be in view: attention is on the stretch to find matter, and impressions are made that the memory retains."[19] Taking note thus became coextensive with taking notes.[20]

Though Haydn's London notebooks appear to promise a kind of material immersion—a compendium of cityscapes and soundscapes and all the other "scapes," alive with things and activities, that have preoccupied scholars of late[21]—the very business of noting could be construed as a way of keeping the sensuous abundance and disorder of the world in abeyance. This is no plainer than where Haydn notes, and notates, his encounters with music making—something of a disappointment if, with the sonically inclusive spaces of sound studies in mind, one is searching for continuities, rather than freshly inscribed boundaries, between musical objects and the less structured sonic environments that they inhabited. As it is, these notes only redouble the sense of separation between what one could call, in sound studies nomenclature, London "soundmarks" (sonic landmarks, in other words) and the sonic spaces from which they obtrude.[22] "No music ever moved me so deeply in my whole life," wrote Haydn of a chant by John Jones, which he had heard sung by several thousand orphans in St. Paul's. He was understandably moved to extract and preserve the tune with—and as—notation.[23] But Haydn also gave notational form to things that were closer to ambient noise: "A gang of rowdy fellows sang this song with all their might," he noted, presumably from within his apartments on Great Pulteney Street, providing an earnestly precise musical transcription, a jotting that may have represented the moment at which he acknowledged that resistance against so penetrating a distraction was futile: "They yelled so loudly that you could hear them 1000 paces away from the street" (see fig. 2.1).[24] Upon arriving in London, Haydn had observed in a letter to Marianne von Genzinger that he needed "more quiet in which to work, for the noise that the common people make as they sell their wares in the street is intolerable"—a situation that was apparently not improved by the offer of a work room in John Broadwood's music shop, just across the road.[25]

This confrontation of music and noise, musician and soundscape—dramatized most famously in this period by William Hogarth's 1741 etching *The Enraged Musician*, in which a violinist is surrounded by street hawkers in St. Martin's Lane—had long been an image through which Londoners commented on and made sense of their sometimes cacophonous environment.[26] In 1711 it was the subject of a widely circulated bagatelle in *The Spectator* by Joseph Addison, who noted that there is "nothing which more astonishes a

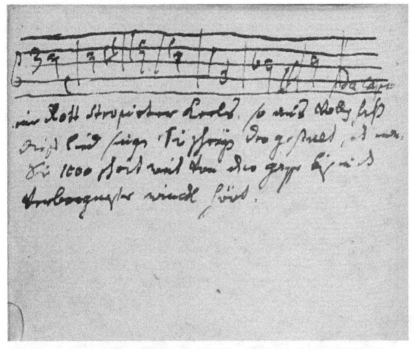

FIGURE 2.1. A street tune jotted down by Haydn in his notebook. Austrian National Library, Samm-
lung von Handschriften und alten Drucken, Vienna. Used by permission.

Foreigner, and frights a Country Squire, than the *Cries of London*." Addison
had accordingly dreamed up the correspondence of one "Ralph Crotchett,"
who nominated himself "Comptroller general of the *London Cries*," listing
among his qualifications "great Insight into all the Branches of our *British
Trades and Manufactures*" and "competent Skill in Musick." In this deadpan
comic vision, the sonic maelstrom of the city became more harmonious, the
cries of street vendors made musical by the attention of a man of taste: "Nor
can I forbear being inspired with a most agreeable Melancholy when I hear
that sad and solemn Air with which the Publick is very often asked, if they
have any Chairs to mend."[27]
    Distinguishing the various London criers and their cries within their
otherwise dense metropolitan habitats, and elevating them into something
altogether more picturesque, had a long history, especially in the visual arts.
John Thomas Smith's compendious *Vagabondiana* of 1817—a late contribution to the genre of cries of London portraits—traced its own encyclope-
dic project to Giuseppe Maria Mitelli's etchings of Bologna criers from the
previous century.[28] Yet engravings of the London criers and their cries had
been popular subjects since at least Paul Sandby's *Cries of London* from the

1760s.[29] Only two years before Haydn arrived in London, George Colman's theatrical version of *The Enraged Musician* had been presented to acclaim at the King's Theatre in the Haymarket.[30] And during all of Haydn's London years, Francis Wheatley was to exhibit his sentimental *Cries of London* at the Royal Academy—a series of mildly titillating pictures that circulated widely as a set of prints (and remain among the most frequently reproduced depictions of eighteenth-century street life; see fig. 2.2).[31] Songs that praised and incorporated the best-known London cries were also regularly served

FIGURE 2.2. *Two Bunches a Penny Primroses* (1793) by Francis Wheatley.

up to metropolitan audiences at this time. In 1792—the year that Haydn recorded his first visit to the pleasure gardens at Vauxhall—Anna Maria Leary
presented James Hook's "Two Bunches a Penny Primroses" (also the name
of Wheatley's contemporaneous picture): "How sweet to hear in London
streets / what's cry'd both up and down," ran the refrain (see fig. 2.3). And in
1795 the young chorister Thomas Welsh (who, incidentally, encountered and
made music with Haydn several times) performed Hook's "Ripe Cherries," a
song composed on much the same principle.[32] Both songs framed a moment
of direct quotation, emphasizing the naturalism of the street cries in question by changing the meter and tempo following whimsical fermatas. Thus
repackaging the sounds of the commercial streetscape for the more exclusive
commercial arenas of pleasure garden performance and the print market,
these songs represent one of the stylized ways in which Londoners aestheticized (and eroticized) urban experience—by discriminating, extracting, and
refining those sonic dimensions of London's street life that lent themselves to
tasteful citation.

Haydn's habit of noting and notating the city around him lay on a contin-
uum with such popular songs. No less than in the picturesque performances
at Vauxhall—or even in the absurdist comic vision of *The Spectator*—he recast the inextricable confusions of sound as the more precise discriminations
of music. Charlotte Papendiek recalled some decades after that the symphony
with which Haydn opened the 1791 season contained a movement that "was
to imitate the London cries," and even claimed that the cry in question was
"Live cod." This story is unreliable at best, and it remains unclear which
symphony Papendiek was dimly remembering, but it is telling that Haydn's
music should have been associated so directly with the urban commercial
streetscape.[33]

Though newly immersed in London's hyperstimulating environment,
then, Haydn also encountered, one could say, the techniques and technologies of abstraction—the social practices and material things that permitted
him to draw out and "attend to things" in particular ways. James Boswell, who
came south to London from Edinburgh in the early 1760s, had described his
arrival in terms of the bewildering proliferation of stimuli: "The noise, the
crowd, the glare of shops and signs agreeably confused me."[34] Haydn wrote to
von Genzinger in a similar vein, of the "endlessly huge city of London, whose
various beauties and marvels quite astonished me."[35] For all that, both dazzled
newcomers were equipped with a sense of place mediated in large part by
the written word, which circulated in unprecedented abundance within the
city. "I was full of rich imagination of London," remarked Boswell, recalling
his earliest stroll around town, "ideas suggested by the Spectator."[36] Haydn

6

FIGURE 2.3. James Hook's "Two Bunches a Penny Primroses," from *A Collection of Favorite Songs* (1793). © British Library Board.

boasts of fweets unknown to those in Town, how fweet to hear in London Streets, how

fweet to hear in London Streets, what's cry'd both up and down, what's cry'd both up and

down, what's cry'd both up and down. Two bunches a penny Prim ro ſes,

two bunches a penny.

2	3
Stern Winter may enrobe with Snow,	Thus, Winter must to Spring give way,
Each Valley Dale, and Hill;	As Seasons roll along;
Throughout the World bid Tempests blow,	The thorn-bud blofsom with the May,
And freeze the bubbling rill:	The Lark resume his Song:
Yet, Spring will come, with fmiling face;	And tho' the Country boasts of Sweets,
And fpread each joy around;	Unknown to thoſe in Town,
Give freedom to the wat'ry race,	How fweet to hear in London Streets,
And wake the pleasing Sound.	What's cried both up and down.
Two bunches &c.	Two bunches &c.

FOR THE GERMAN FLUTE

Allegretto

Slower

reported to von Genzinger that, amid the social calls and formal luncheons that marked his arrival, "I went the round of all the newspapers for 3 successive days."[37] To be in London was not only to live in its densely packed streets but to be written up, discriminated, and noted.

Psychic Investments

In the pages of the London notebooks, the impulse to abstraction also takes on a markedly quantitative character. "Every canal-lock costs £10,000," reported Haydn, in a characteristically terse entry.[38] With a distinctly mercantile eye, he continually noted these weights, measurements, and prices. Frequently they were the astonishing numbers—giant calculations that invisibly spanned city and nation—that were so often recorded in eighteenth-century commonplace books.[39] "The City of London consumes 8 times one hundred thousand cartloads of coal each year," wrote Haydn in the first notebook. "Each cart holds 13 sacks, each sack holds 2 dry measures: most of the coal comes from Newcastle. Often 200 loaded ships arrive at once. A cartload costs £2½." Beneath a draft of a canon that he regularly presented as a memento to friends and acquaintances, Haydn noted, "During the last 31 years, 38,000 houses were built in London." The second notebook continued in these superlative terms: "The City of London keeps 4,000 carts for cleaning the streets, and 2,000 of these work every day."[40] One of the earliest entries, about money, is perhaps the most fanciful: "The national debt of England is estimated to be over two hundred millions. Recently it was calculated that if they had to make up a convoy to pay this sum in silver, the waggons, end on end, would reach from London to Yorck, that is, 200 miles, presuming that each waggon could not carry more than £6000."[41] Haydn's fascination with man-made vastness surely registers what Anne Janowitz has called the "artifactual sublime"—a distinctively metropolitan slant on early Romantic aesthetics in which overwhelming immensity is "linked to the material excess of the production of goods."[42]

Yet Haydn's urban experience consisted of an assault of everyday material pleasures as much as these extravagantly supersensible notions. The earliest London notebook opens with a list of requests from friends back home, mostly for the superior metal products of the Birmingham and Sheffield steel industries. Below is a list of prices: shirts, a gold watch, a new watch chain, and so on. It seems that Haydn managed to acquire most of these items, since a table in the second notebook lists, with eccentric English spellings, "Stel Buttons," "a steel girdl," "a steel chain," "2 Secissars," and "7 Penn Knifes."[43] "A roasting chicken cost 7 shillings, a turkey 9 shillings, a dozen larks 1 crown," he scrupulously noted in 1792.[44] Sociologists of the city have long regarded the coexistence of an unending variety of appeals to the senses and the universalizing principles of equivalence—the principles that enable circulation and exchange—as one of the defining characteristics of modern urban life. Georg Simmel's 1903 account of the psychic impress of metropolitan existence was founded on the contrast between the "swift and continuous shift of external and internal stimuli" and "the reduction of qualitative values to quantitative terms"—a contrast that could equally describe Haydn's London notebooks.[45] The city, in other words, is the dwelling place—perhaps even the birthplace—of the commodity, that object insidiously divided, in the Marxian analysis, between the appeal of its sensuous surface and the calculable logic of its social life, a core existence characterized by the seriality of mechanical reproduction.

Haydn's compulsive pricing of the world reminds us that the concept of interest nowadays appears to shuttle between the separate and even mutually hostile discourses of aesthetics and economics, and so between the realms of the psychic and the monetary. That the concept had a mixed meaning in the eighteenth century is plain from the entries on "interest" in Samuel Johnson's dictionary, where the noun is said to denote "concern," "money paid for use," and "any surplus of advantage," while the verb encompasses "move" and even "touch with passion."[46] Haydn would surely have heard a lot of talk about interest in the economic sense from his banker acquaintances: since 1793, the war with France had driven up rates dramatically and had precipitated an equivalent decline in government bonds—consolidated annuities, or Consols—largely stable since their invention in the 1750s.[47] But the aesthetic and the economic are barely separable when Haydn, as in the occasionally blatant monetary obsessions of the century's most popular travel literature,[48] totted up the cost of even the most picturesque scenes he surveyed, perhaps echoing the boasts of some of his well-heeled hosts: "The castle chapel at Windsor is a very old but splendid building; the high altar cost 50,000 fl." Visiting the fashionable estate of the Duke of York at Oatlands in late 1791, he noted, "Among its many beauties is a most remarkable grotto which cost £25,000 Sterling."[49] In these oddly computational moments, Haydn appears to illustrate David Hume's explanation of "Our Esteem for the Rich and Powerful" in his *Treatise of Human Nature*, according to which the faculty of sympathy allowed the viewer of fine objects to experience a reflected version of an owner's less mediated pleasure.[50] "We enter into his interest by the force of imagination, and feel the same satisfaction, that the objects naturally occasion in him," wrote Hume: "the pleasure, which a rich man receives from his possessions" is thus "thrown upon the beholder."[51] Or, as Boswell was to put it, contemplating the glories of the London cityscape, "a person of imagination and feeling, such as the Spectator finely describes, can have the most lively enjoyment from the sight of external objects without regard to property at all." As in Hume's analysis, Boswell's interest sympathetically borrowed the enjoyment of owners, taking imaginative possession of their property.[52] The psychic and the monetary are inseparable in this conception of interest, and Hume's well-known inventory of riches suitable for sympathetic contemplation in the *Treatise* draws no distinction between practical tools and luxury items: "tables, chairs, scritoires, chimneys, coaches, sadles, ploughs, and indeed . . . every work of art"—everything passes by the reader in a typically urban muddle.[53]

The prices that Haydn recorded thus measured his interest in things. One might claim to witness in his relentless aesthetic-economic calculations—thinking along lines articulated by such critics as Jean-Joseph Goux and Marc Shell—the shared origin of the modern monetary form and modern conceptions of the psychic economy.[54] In this way of thinking, interest becomes a kind of speculation with the coinage of one's mind and describes the return or profit that one's attention might yield. Attention is something that we *pay*. "If we think of attention as a resource, or even a kind of currency," writes Tim Wu, describing the attentional models of advertisers from early nineteenth-century newspapermen to the designers of Facebook, "we must allow that it is always, necessarily, being 'spent.'"[55] By noting the price of picturesque grottoes, canal locks, or high altars, Haydn was conceiving of his psychic investments in part via monetary ones.

Beyond the obvious fact of their predominantly urban-oriented content, then, Haydn's London notebooks seem to bear the traces of his new metropolitan experience. The capricious organization of his notes, in which one runic entry follows another without connection, is reminiscent of Michel de Certeau's oft-cited account of walking in the city—the "rhetoric" of urban pedestrianism, which, Certeau claims, is characterized by the tropes of synecdoche (part standing for whole) and asyndeton (the omission of usual syntactical links).[56] The extended mind that Haydn bequeathed to his biographers might accordingly be regarded as a quintessentially psychogeographical text, confounding mind and world, parsing the cityscape via dislocated points of interest. Each act of noting stands in for and produces an urban whole that cannot be synoptically grasped, much as the anecdote might be conceived as a synecdoche for distant historical circumstance. Moreover, though Haydn captured his metropolitan experience in the profusion of things that he noted, he discriminated these things at once in sensuous isolation and according to abstract principles of equivalence, primarily market price. In the expanding spaces of urban commerce, art objects and market objects, as well as the psychic and monetary forms of investment in them, were mixed together, just as they were in liberal empiricist theories of interest, before the discourses of aesthetics and political economy went their separate ways.

Disinterest and Boredom

In the eighteenth century, the concept of interest acquired what might seem to be a pair of antonyms, whose relationships to interest nonetheless turn out to be more complex than straightforward antitheses. First is the term that became notorious as a motif of Kantian aesthetics: *disinterest* (the "interesselos," as in "interesseloses Wohlgefallen," or disinterested pleasure).[57] This concept came to mark the very distinction between art and craft, purposiveness and purpose, aesthetic value and market value,[58] that appears to have had barely any presence in Haydn's London (the publication of Kant's third *Critique* in 1790 notwithstanding).[59] During the eighteenth century, disinterest came to denote not lack of attention but rather a lack of investment, an absence or virtuous subtraction of personal drives or monetary stakes—"no possession, no enjoyment or reward," as Shaftesbury had put it in his *Characteristics*.[60] The resulting problem would trouble theories of art and moral philosophy for generations: while theoretically desirable as an ethical stance, perhaps, one cannot *arouse* disinterest. To be sure, being interested might appear to be a low-intensity feeling.[61] Albert Otto Hirschman's *The Passions and the Interests* once claimed that the concept of interest gained currency in the seventeenth and eighteenth centuries precisely as a staid corrective to older conceptions of the volatile passions—a foundational transformation that shored up the "political arguments for capitalism before its triumph," as Hirschman's subtitle ran.[62] Still, however attenuated, interest, unlike disinterest, was about arousal. As the entry "Interessant" in Johann Georg Sulzer's *Allgemeine Theorie der schönen Künste* explained, the interesting is "whatever is a concern for us and to a degree compels us to exert our capacity to desire": to be interesting is to inspire a basic dynamic of attraction.[63] No wonder that the word should have cropped up, in block capitals, in the series of ardent letters written to Haydn by the widow Rebecca Schroeter in 1792: "EVERY circumstance concerning you MY BELOVED H^dn is INTERESTING to me."[64] The sentiment interested Haydn enough that he transcribed all of Schroeter's letters into the back of the second London notebook. "She was . . . a beautiful and amiable woman whom I might very easily have married if I had been free then," he confessed to Dies.[65]

Interest's second apparent opposite, boredom, has a less elevated intellectual history. Boredom is about disinvestment through inattention.[66] The cast of mind that tended to become bored was central in Simmel's analysis of urban experience, the corollary of constant and varied stimulation: "There is perhaps no psychic phenomenon which is so unconditionally reserved to the city as the blasé outlook," he argued.[67] Over the eighteenth century, as Patricia Spacks has shown, published discussions of boredom in England gradually turned from long-standing theological concerns over the corrosive spiritual consequences of ennui to address a condition now considered endemic among overstimulated urban consumers.[68] The invention and commercialization of "leisure time" during this period in turn produced the idea of "diversion," whose purpose was to forestall the ever-present risk of boredom.[69] "So few of the hours of life are filled up with objects adequate to the mind of man," moaned Samuel Johnson in *The Rambler*, "and so frequently are we in want of present pleasure or employment."[70]

At the beginning of his *Philosophical Enquiry*, Burke argued that "restlessness and anxiety" inevitably attended the basic state of "curiosity."[71] The notion of curiosity had its own distinctive history, which, even more plainly than interest, reveals the oscillation between subject and object set in motion by such theories of mental arousal, as in the "curiosities" (which aroused curiosity) displayed by eighteenth-century antiquarians, or shared by members of the Royal Society.[72] To Burke, curiosity was simply "whatever desire we have for, or whatever pleasure we take in novelty"—an impulse that nonetheless "soon exhausts the variety which is commonly to be met with in nature."[73] As Simon McVeigh has shown, novelty was one of the recurring claims among London's concert organizers in this period.[74] "Something New," a song performed at Vauxhall Gardens by Elizabeth Addison in 1791—self-consciously new, as well as wholly generic in form and style—satirized and celebrated the caprice of London's beau monde and addressed the matter straightforwardly: "each Change of the Fashion you fondly pursue / You'll own that it pleases because it is New" (meaningful fermatas accompanied the word "new").[75] In this novelty-driven landscape, packed with curiosities, boredom was not only a constant threat but could even become a sign of distinction and discrimination, as the many mild diversions of the interesting threatened to dwindle into precisely the opposite.[76] "Among the higher classes, whether in the wealthy, or the fashionable world, who is unacquainted with *ennui*?" asked the noble protagonist of Maria Edgeworth's story "Ennui"; "unless roused by external stimulus, I sunk into [a] kind of apathy, and vacancy of ideas."[77]

While it had been a commonplace of early eighteenth-century thought to censure the "vacancy of ideas" promoted by instrumental music, later in the century Adam Smith was only one of many prominent thinkers to marvel that music, even when it was not obviously imitative, should be "so agreeable, so great, so various, and so interesting" that it could occupy the mind completely.[78] Still, in the years before Haydn appeared in London as the latest diversion, Johann Peter Salomon had experienced some excruciating failures as a result of unexpected audience disinvestment. In early May 1789, he directed an evening of music in which the opening act contained the usual mix of genres: a Haydn symphony, a quartet by Ignaz Pleyel, a concerto, and several songs and choruses. The second act, however, was taken up entirely by a cantata by Vincenzo Federici, an associate of the Italian Opera in London. This turned out to be a poor programming decision. Susan Burney, who attended with several acquaintances and, inevitably, ran into her father there, reported on the musical part of the evening in her diary: "The Second Act consisted of a Cantata the Music very good by Federici, tho' rather monotonous & lugubre, wch being sung only by Mr Harrison & Mrs Ambrose, was tedious & heavy beyond most things I have heard." The result was a major embarrassment for Salomon: "before it was concluded, almost every body had been driven from the Room—I was sorry for poor Salomon—He spoke a few words to me at the end of the Concert, in evident vexation & low spirits."[79]

Music historians have frequently considered the attention-seeking devices scattered across the twelve London symphonies—the stark contrasts, imagistic passages, and unexpected narrative twists—to be audible traces of Haydn's exposure to London's competitive concert-giving business.[80] Not that these were by any means unprecedented in his music, which had long been noted for such curiosities. Rather, one might say that London's musical life appears to have encouraged Haydn to pursue this tendency with a new consistency, and even a new blatancy. Aside from the six symphonies that he produced as a lucrative commission from the concert society of the masonic Loge Olympique in Paris, the London symphonies were the only works in this genre that Haydn expressly directed at audiences beyond his court bases in Eszterháza and Eisenstadt and their wider Viennese networks. While he never traveled to the French capital to witness the reception of his Paris symphonies, in London he was in the thick of things.

In advance of the 1792 season, Haydn's former pupil Pleyel showed up to bolster the fortunes of the Professional Concert—the older Hanover Square series led by Wilhelm Cramer that directly rivaled Salomon's—and bearing works not yet heard in London. It precipitated what Haydn rather histrionically called a "bloody harmonious war," waged in the press as much as in the concert room. "Haydn and Pleyel are to be *pitted* against each other this season; and the supporters of each are violent partizans," announced the *Public*

Advertiser, with undisguised glee.[81] "The newspapers are all full of it," Haydn reported to von Genzinger, proud to be at the center of such a widely noted imbroglio.[82]

The consequence was a series of compositions by Haydn that aimed to be—to quote the correspondent of the *Morning Herald* who reported on the premiere of Symphony no. 93 in February 1792—"distinguished above all common competition," symphonies that were, as the *Herald* noted of the D Major, "original, various, and interesting."[83] It is surely no accident that, almost as soon as they had been performed, two of the London symphonies came to be known by their most interesting features (the *Military* and the *Surprise*), while two more (the *Drumroll* and the *Clock*) acquired nicknames early in the nineteenth century.[84] These were the distinguishing marks, even trademarks, of the symphonies—explicit bids to generate and sustain audience investment. As such, they share something of the "synecdochal esthetic" that Leah Price sees in many eighteenth-century literary works—the formal principle that seems to anticipate a reception consisting of intermittent attention, critical citation, and excerpting.[85] The interesting features of Haydn's London symphonies were designed to be talked about, to be written up in newspaper reports and commentaries. The nicknames accordingly turned each point of interest into a synecdoche for the symphony as a whole, conveying a noteworthy musical feature through a metropolitan landscape clamorous with attention-seeking things.

Making Musical Interest

Amid this clamor, the celebrated "surprise" chord (the unexpected drum stroke and orchestral tutti) in the theme of the Andante variation movement of the *Surprise* Symphony is something of a synecdoche of these synecdoches: a symbol of Haydn's impulse to command the attention through a notable musical device—a reductio ad absurdum, even, inasmuch as it consists of parameters as elementary as contrast, loudness, suddenness, and textural repleteness, all compressed into a split second. From one perspective, Haydn's surprise is barely more than an abstract template for what makes something interesting at all, since its identity is almost entirely dependent on the background of seriality from which it stands out—the successive iterations of what would rapidly become one of his most reiterated tunes. When the opening variation begins with an orchestral tutti of similar suddenness, it is as though the bang of the surprise chord has been relocated to a new corner of this recursive musical landscape, and one might imagine the attention roving around, kept busy by noting a moving musical target.[86]

The repetitions that make up this piece were in some ways continuous with the many repetitions of the tune that reverberated beyond the formal limits of the Andante: in the print market, on concert programs, and in the fashionable parlors of London and other European capitals (several piano reductions, solo and duet, were published soon after the symphony was performed by Salomon; see fig. 2.4).[87] According to Dies, the Andante followed Haydn to an inn in Wiesbaden on his return journey to London in 1794, echoing through the wall as it was pounded out on the piano by an unsuspecting group of Prussian soldiers.[88] And Haydn even repeated the tune himself, in a joke precisely about its ubiquity, when the orchestra quotes the Andante in his 1801 oratorio *The Seasons*, imitating the merry whistle of a ploughman. In 1790 Ernst Ludwig Gerber concluded that Haydn had a knack for writing music that appeared *bekannt*, or already known.[89] In the case of the Andante, it surely helped that the tune was itself constructed from precirculated musical materials, the basis of its curiously fungible character. Foursquare trips up and down tonic and dominant triads conclude with calculatedly formulaic cadential approaches, while the dominant pedal following the double bar consists of a standard disposition of parts that the eighteenth-century theorist Joseph Riepel might have called a Ponte (see fig. 2.5; the passage would work, in the most elementary form of this schema, with dominant sevenths and 6-4 chords alternating).[90]

Aside from its one calculated gestural imperfection, the tune seems to aspire to a proportionality bordering on blankness—the kind of typicality that Deidre Lynch associates with the worthy gentleman protagonist of the early novel, which "authorized him to oversee the social world's diversity": a pure standard, around and through whom the distinctive and distorted "characters" of the lower orders or exotic outsiders became legible.[91] This was the comparative neutrality of the eighteenth-century beautiful, the blankly universal background against which locally interesting characters became distinctive: the ultimate specimen of beauty, argued Adam Smith, was at once "the rarest of all things" and "the most common," because "all the deviations from it resemble it more than they resemble one another."[92] (Not coincidentally, this is an adequate description of the formal principle of many eighteenth-century variation sets.) Character consists of "a small deviation from general Proportions," explained a 1775 advertisement for a print of Hogarth's *Characters and Caricaturas*.[93] And, to be sure, the repetitions in Haydn's Andante unfold as a parade of interesting "characterizations," each refocusing the attention: an opening Grazioso with delicately curtseying embellishments; a turbulent and stormy contrast, beginning in the minor mode; a pastoral variation presided over by the flute; and an expanded closing variation that swings back

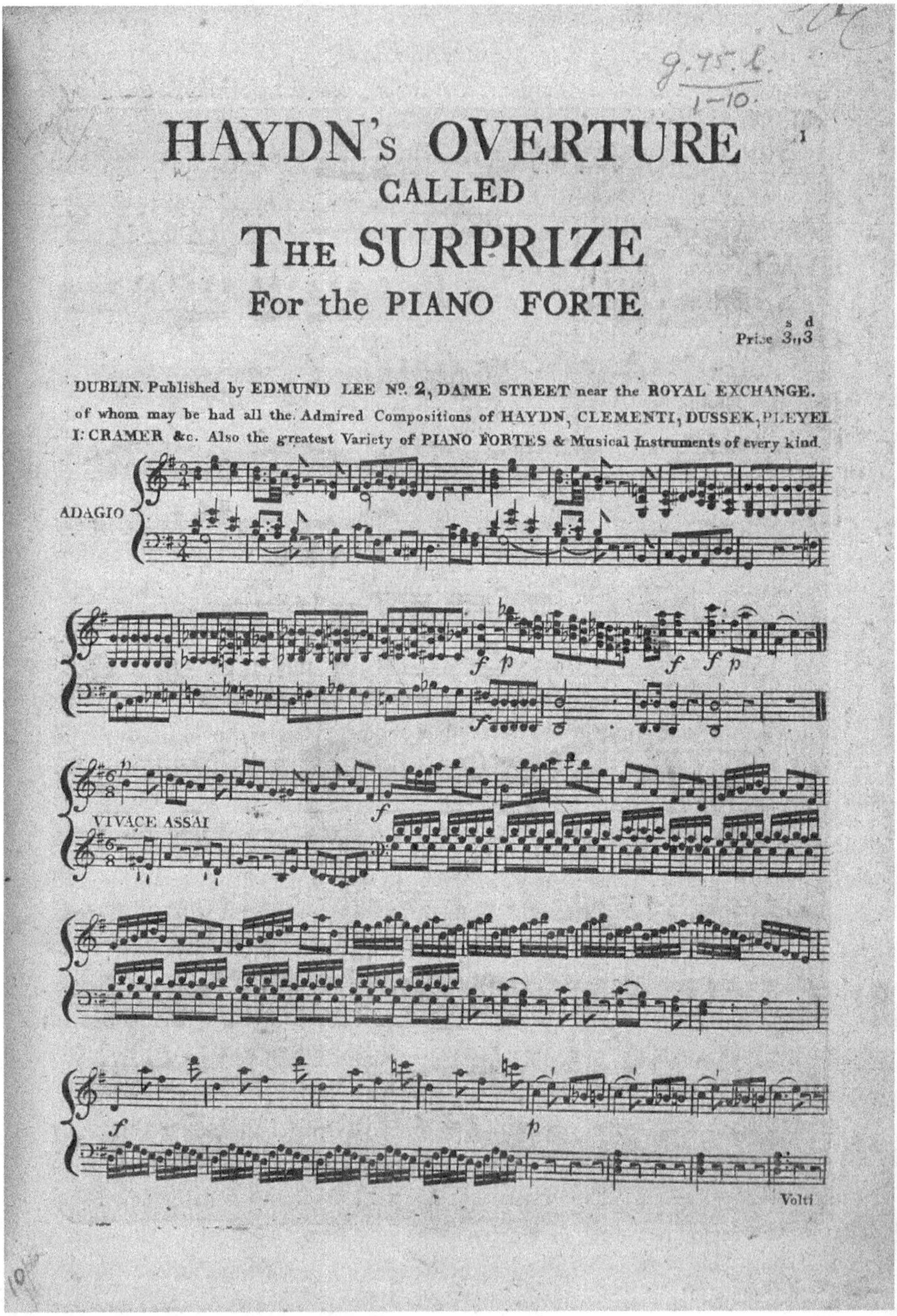

FIGURE 2.4. Piano reduction of the opening of Haydn's *Surprise* Symphony, from *Haydn's Overture Called the Surprize* (c. 1800). © British Library Board.

FIGURE 2.5. Piano reduction of the theme of the Andante of Haydn's *Surprise* Symphony, from *Haydn's Overture Called the Surprize* (c. 1800). © British Library Board.

and forth between a public martial register and an interior sentimental style. This is *characteristic* music, perhaps less in the recent musicological sense— that is, a historically sensitive way of describing music that refers to things or tells stories through a heightened iconicity[94]—than in the sense of popular eighteenth-century "characteristic" engravings and writings: picaresque depictions of human diversity, typically in urban locales, that scholars nowadays tend to regard as part of the early history of the novel.[95]

The interplay of seriality and unpredictability, of blankness and characterfulness, in this Andante doubtless contributes to the impression of "expressive ambivalence" that Sutcliffe derives from several of Haydn's earlier symphonic slow movements. The "unusual gestures or oddly timed events" in these pieces generally do not disturb "an equanimity of tone and a polished style of delivery," writes Sutcliffe; rather, they call attention to the techniques by which the attention is called.[96] "The focus is less on expression and more on discourse, on the mechanisms that underpin what we believe to be natural or touching or melancholy in expression. Haydn seems above all interested in perception—in what it means to sit and listen."[97] In other words, he is interested in interest.

Perhaps one cannot even give an adequate description of the surprise of the *Surprise*—or even of the drumroll of the *Drumroll*—exclusively in terms of musical materials, so obviously are these gestures implicated in an audience's interest in them. Ciphers, conduits for attention, they exist only to be noted, much as the curiosity embodies our curiosity. "I christened it the *Surprise* when I announced it for my Benefit Concert at the opera Room, the year it was composed for Salomon's concerts at Hanover Square & my valued friend Haydn thank'd me for giving it such an appropriate Name":

thus jotted the flutist Andrew Ashe on an 1803 concert program, on which the *Surprise* was the opener (by this time routinely called by its synecdochal nickname).[98] The stories that circulated early on about the surprise chord—that it was Haydn's bid to startle sleeping concertgoers or to scare inattentive ladies—may have been fictitious, but they show that it was understood to be fundamentally "about" attention.[99] Haydn's tamer but nonetheless revealing version of the story was reported by Griesinger:

> I was interested in surprising the public with something new, and in making a brilliant debut, so that my student Pleyel, who was at that time engaged by an orchestra in London (in 1792) and whose concerts had opened a week before mine, should not outdo me. The first Allegro of my symphony had already met with countless Bravos, but the enthusiasm reached its highest peak at the Andante with the Drum Stroke. Encore! Encore! sounded in every throat, and Pleyel himself complimented me on my idea.[100]

For all that, a vivid report of the premiere of the *Surprise*, in *The Oracle* on March 24, 1792, barely mentioned the audience reaction at all, instead describing Haydn's Andante as a depiction of surprise itself, a portrayal rather than cause of shock: "The surprise might not be unaptly likened to the situation of a beautiful Shepherdess who, lulled to slumber by the murmur of a distant Waterfall, starts alarmed by the unexpected firing of a fowling-piece."[101] As Raymond Williams once observed of late eighteenth-century urban poetics, the new pushes and pulls of city life are here representable as a kind of rhetoric that distorts the inherited vocabularies of the pastoral—and one could say the same of the Andante's self-consciously "pure" musical register, upon which the surprise encroaches (a register easily adapted to the ploughman in *The Seasons*).[102] The nervous, abrasive musical stimuli typical of the metropolitan landscape here seem to intrude upon and disrupt a clichéd pastoral scene. The image of the alarmed shepherdess teaches us what attention is and turns Haydn's surprise from a real-time shock into a musical reification of attention itself.

The opening drumroll of the Symphony no. 103 works in a similar way: it is an attention-grabbing audiovisual device emanating from the back of the orchestra that alerts the listening public to its own attentiveness, or distraction—though the *Morning Chronicle* reported that "the Introduction excited the deepest attention."[103] Rhetorically coming "before" the beginning—and arguably before any introduction too—the opening drumroll is a timbral moment unconducive to Haydn's usual kinds of musical elaboration: like the surprise chord, it seems to reify the focusing of attention itself and, in this case, sets up the ominous unfolding of the Adagio introduction. Its return near the end of the Allegro seems to function as an uncanny "refocusing" moment before the last measures of the coda—a glimpse of the fundamental state of interest-edness that lies behind one's experience of the diverse elements of the piece, perhaps. A clever, attention-seeking trademark accordingly sets in train the rhetorical move, proceeding "gradually from dark confusion to clarity and reason," which Marshall Brown once exalted as the analog of the "infolded, temporal self-consciousness" posited by Kantian critical philosophy.[104] Thus does marketing become metaphysics.

Reporting on the ninth concert of the 1794 season in Hanover Square, the *Morning Chronicle*, by way of defending the music of Giovanni Battista Viotti (another of the season's attractions), complained of the "quirks and quackery, in which modern music is so apt to indulge"—an ambiguous comment, to say the least, when the newest music by Haydn (which the reporter made sure to praise) was the greatest draw of the evening.[105] On this occasion, the main attraction was a repeat performance of the Symphony no. 100, whose second-movement Allegretto, with its military-themed quirks, had been a sensation: "The middle movement was again received with absolute shouts of applause: Encore! encore! encore! resounded from every seat."[106] When Haydn decided to repeat the symphony once more in his own benefit concert on May 2, 1794, it was trailed in the press as "the Grand Overture . . . with the Militaire Movement," the Allegretto already moving to center stage.[107] And by the time the symphony was reprised yet again during his last season in London—in the third of the Opera Concerts at the King's Theatre on February 23, 1795—the piece had become the "*Military* Overture." The Allegretto, now a synecdoche for the whole piece, was encored, as it had been on its previous outings. "Of all the instrumental pieces HAYDN's *Military Overture* was the most conspicuous," concluded the short newspaper report.[108]

The Allegretto of the *Military* was certainly designed to be conspicuous. Like the Andante of the *Surprise*, it presents its interesting features against a background of seriality: repetitions within repetitions of an entirely four-square tune, not as blatantly featureless as the earlier Andante, perhaps, but simple and singable nonetheless and constructed from similarly common-place musical materials (including a four-measure Ponte before the conclud-ing eight-measure phrase of the main tune). Haydn produced the bulk of the Allegretto from a measure-for-measure reorchestration of the naive second-movement romance from his concerto for two *lire organizzate* (composed in 1786–87 at the behest of King Ferdinand IV of Naples). As Emily Dolan has shown, within a fundamentally repetitive formal scheme, the Allegretto creates interest primarily through timbral variation.[109] In the opening section of the movement, the tune is divided into repeating chunks, each one presented by strings and flute and then echoed by a wind ensemble: the opening eight measures, then the subsequent eight-measure answer, the connecting Ponte, and the concluding eight-measure phrase. Even the ensuing dramatic minor-mode episode—which, partly because it barely deviates from the even phrase structure of the main theme, seems as much like a minore variation as a contrasting middle section—derives a large part of its interest from the incursion of janissary percussion instruments: cymbals, bass drum, and triangle. In Dolan's account of the piece, the repeat of the main theme—just pizzicato strings and wind to begin with—eventually "absorbs" these sonic intruders, creating the opportunity for still more timbral variety. The added percussion results not only in a strident, martial character but also the delicate, music-box timbres into which the tune dissolves.[110] While there is every reason to consider the Allegretto a ternary form, the principle by which it unfolds is nonetheless comparable to the variations of the Andante of the *Surprise*: a simple tune is subjected to a series of interesting timbral "characterizations," although in this case the movement ultimately describes a more decisive process of change, whereby the unadorned romance fully takes on the military character by which the symphony became known. Even so, the Allegretto ultimately compresses this overarching principle into a synecdochal moment almost as sudden as the chord in the *Surprise*. At the end, Haydn deviated from the scheme of his earlier romance and added something especially for London: the most overtly characteristic gesture in the piece, a bugle call for solo trumpet, as much an uncanny incursion into the surrounding musical discourse as the reprised drumroll in Symphony no. 103 (see fig. 2.6).[111] And, here too, a drumroll follows the bugle call: a steep crescendo to an orchestral tutti on an abrasive, unexpected chord—a "climax of horrid sublimity" according to the *Morning Chronicle*.[112] (The chord soon turns into a harmless augmented sixth and so introduces a series of cadences and the closing fanfare, reminiscent of the C major tattoos that punctuate the opening movement of the Symphony no. 97.) More than the synecdochal moments of the *Surprise* or the *Drumroll*, the bugle call of the *Military* operates according to an existing conception of attention and what it means to capture it. It is a reminder that "attention" was (and remains) a key concept in the parade-ground drill as well as in the consumption of music. One could even say that the bugle call hailed and interpellated its audience, wittily adapting long-standing musical technologies of military discipline to the purposes of capturing the interest of London consumers.[113]

Well might Haydn's former pupil Pleyel have congratulated his teacher on

FIGURE 2.6. The surprise at the end of the Allegretto of Haydn's *Military* Symphony, as mediated in a piano trio reduction printed by Johann Salomon, *Haydn's Celebrated Symphonies* (1797). © British Library Board.

such winning ruses. For there are similar attention-seeking strategies in the three Pleyel symphonies that it seems were composed newly for the London season.[114] On February 14, 1792, the day after the opening Professional Concert of the season, the *Morning Herald* pronounced that a new "overture" by Pleyel "was elegant, interesting, and scientific"—though it is not known which symphony this referred to.[115] In the second movement of Pleyel's London Symphony in B-flat, an Andante Grazioso in 6/8, the progress of a delicate siciliano-like melody is upset by several fortissimo surprises, which are given added force by a trombone (see fig. 2.7). Particularly disconcerting for those invested in questions of priority and precedent, Pleyel also produced a grand Symphony in E-flat in which the imposing horn chords that begin the slow introduction to the opening movement make a surprise return before the coda; this was more than two years before Haydn dramatically brought back the drumroll and slow introduction in the opening movement of his own E-flat Symphony.[116] These were the weapons in the "bloody harmonious war" of the 1792 season, waged for possession of the audience's interest.

Granted, especially with *The Oracle*'s picture of the alarmed shepherdess in mind, one might justly wonder whether Haydn's symphonic surprises are truly examples of the typically low-intensity arousal of the interesting. Is a surprise not more instantaneous and startling than that? Annette Richards has argued that the Andante of the *Surprise* is best understood as an instance of the musical picturesque—that aesthetic of artful detour and carefully modulated imbalance—and that the surprise chord is too physically comic and imagistic to be the kind of thunderbolt associated with the eighteenth-century sublime.[117] As a blemish or detour from the serene beauty of the Andante theme, the surprise chord is perhaps an example of what Uvedale Price's 1794 essay on the picturesque called "deformity"—a feature that, by contrast with the beautiful, "makes a quicker and most distant impression, and strongly rouses the attention" (music was Price's main example).[118] Yet one can also easily overlook the fact that a surprise can be literally surprising only once. "Time poisons perception," writes Michael Clune, in a slightly disheartening neurological reading of Romantic poetry (among other things). "The more we see something, the duller and feebler our experience of it becomes." Or, as Burke wrote, sounding for all the world like one of Simmel's blasé metropolitan consumers, "The same things make frequent returns, and they return with less and less of an agreeable effect."[119] Be that as it may, Haydn's surprises compensate by becoming rhetorically "surprising," as much formal functions as phenomenal experiences.[120] The name with which Ashe claimed to have christened the *Surprise* Symphony required no accompanying spoiler alert: we remain surprised by Haydn's chord in much the way that we are still

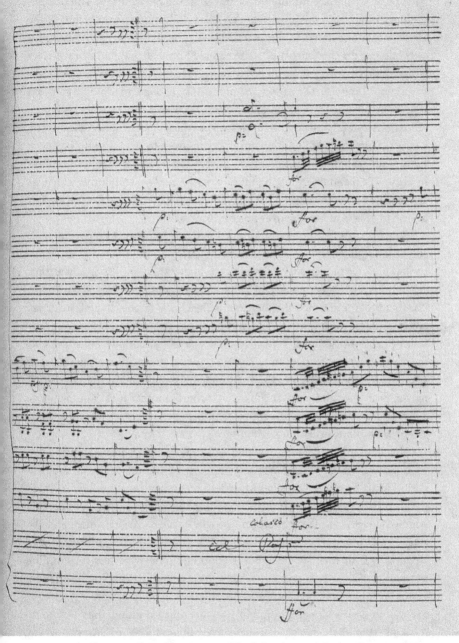

FIGURE 2.7. Surprises in the Andante Grazioso of Pleyel's Symphony in B-flat (1792?). Autograph, British Library [RPS MS 155]. © British Library Board.

"surprised" by the last-minute rescue in Beethoven's *Fidelio* or by Janet Leigh's premature exit from the movie *Psycho*. The many piano transcriptions of the *Surprise* that circulated in the years following the symphony's premiere not only allowed for the "surprise" to be revisited time after time but invariably announced the surprise on the frontispiece (see fig. 2.8): What could be less surprising? Likewise, the early years of the *Military* were marked by constant repetition—in the immediate encores, in successive concerts, in published reductions and critical commentaries, all of which capitalized on the already harvested attention of London consumers in order to sell more newspapers, more piano transcriptions, and more concert tickets. Salomon wasted no time in printing a piano trio version of the "*Grand-Military* Symphony," which, as announced on the title page, was "printed for Mr. Salomon the Proprietor and to be had of him at the Hanover Square-Rooms."[121]

Pace Karl Heinz Bohrer, for whom "suddenness" is the foundation of all aesthetic experience,[122] it seems, then, that iterability—the ways in which something can be revisited, reproduced, and rethought, especially within critical discourse—is the very principle of art's continuing social existence. The image of the alarmed shepherdess in *The Oracle* implies that all surprises creep up upon us unawares. Yet this image was in itself a whimsical invention of critical discourse—was, that is, a way of pleasurably revisiting and more precisely discriminating a favorite musical moment in print. Haydn's surprises thus come closer to the open-endedness of the interesting than they may appear: though instantaneous, they compel another look, another consideration. First they produce alarm, then they produce talk; what starts out as surprising ends up as interesting.

This temporal trajectory becomes especially clear when listening to the 2010 live recording of the *Surprise* Symphony by Marc Minkowski and the period instrument orchestra Les Musiciens du Louvre, which boldly replaces the surprise chord, first with an unexpected silence, then, in the course of an additional repeat, a piercing scream from the entire orchestra, which audibly alarms the Viennese audience, who subsequently dissolve into self-conscious laughter at their own surprise.[123] It is tempting to describe this substitution in terms of Peter Kivy's rather crudely subject-object-congealing distinction between "sonic" and "sensible" authenticity: that is, as an attempt to recreate the way in which something might have been heard rather than the noise it might have made.[124] But, of course, even this refurbished surprise wears off after an initial listen and, by the time you read about it here, has long since transformed from something that instigates astonished laughter into something that prompts musicological theorizing. Replacing the chord with a scream may even look like a vain attempt to forestall this transformation,

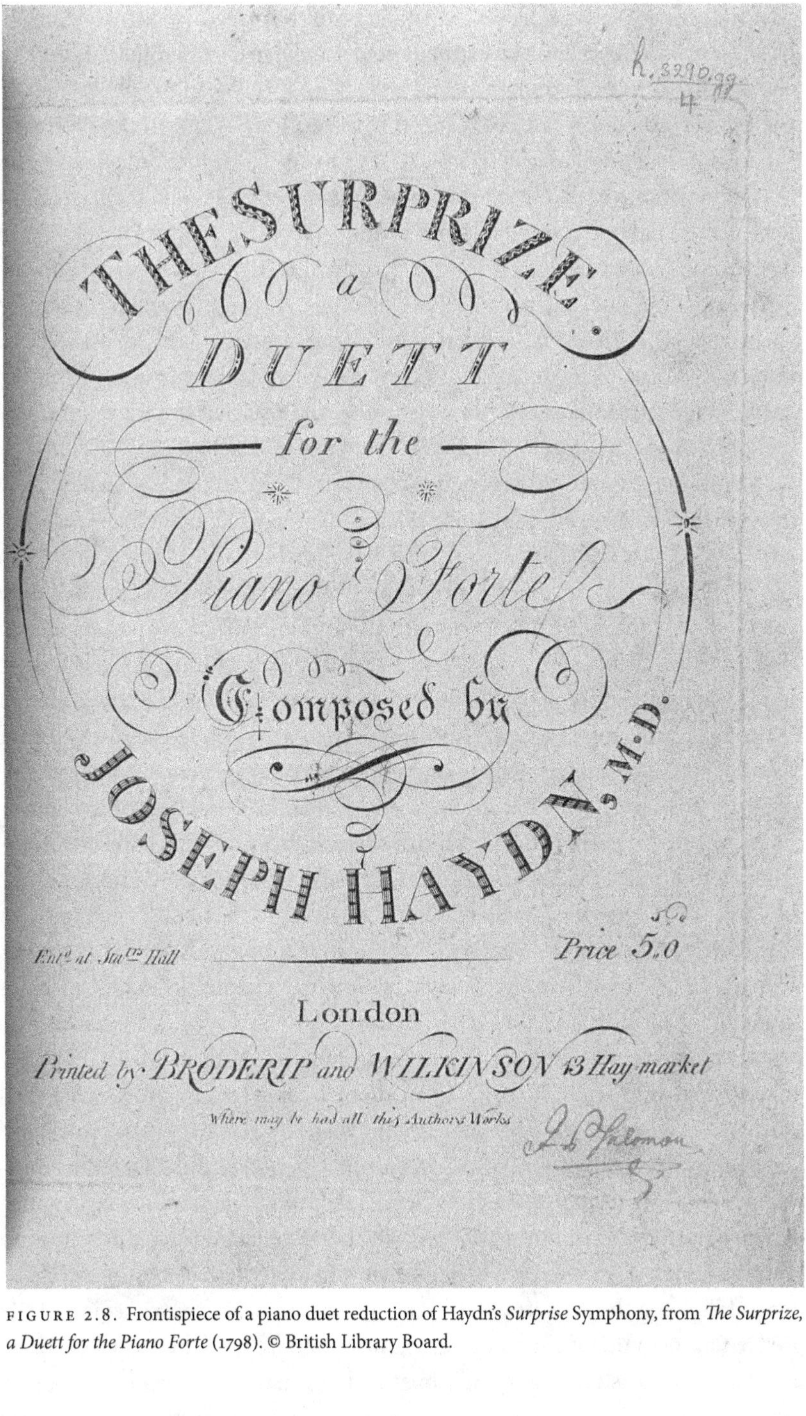

FIGURE 2.8. Frontispiece of a piano duet reduction of Haydn's *Surprise* Symphony, from *The Surprize, a Duett for the Piano Forte* (1798). © British Library Board.

which in the process endorses the impression that Haydn's surprise consists of a dynamic of audience investment before any particular materials and, as such, is liable to become hackneyed before long. One can hardly imagine a period instrument orchestra substituting the errant C-sharp of the *Eroica* for the frisson of a more dissonant pitch. As Dolan has argued, musicians and musicologists have tended to understate the importance of the surprise chord within the movement—as "an aural promise of the orchestra's potential," in her reading—because it is primarily a timbral device, less amenable to the pitch orientation of most formal analyses, where it tends to emerge as "a mere special effect."[125] The Musiciens du Louvre's substitution of the surprise chord implies a degree of anxiety, over not only the inevitable transition from the surprising to the interesting but, even more, the risk that the interesting will turn into the boring.

Certainly, generations of analysts have lined up to profess their lack of interest in the surprise chord—a musical device widely considered so banal and populist that Donald C. Johns was moved to call his 1963 article on the *Surprise* Symphony, which dwells on every part of the piece other than the one by which it is known, "In Defence of Haydn."[126] Long before, Tovey had set the tone by calling the surprise chord "the most unimportant feature in all Haydn's mature works," thus ritualistically abjuring the attractions of those musical features that try most openly to arouse our interest in order to achieve the disinterestedness required of the more serious contemplator of art.[127] The chord has "no special relevance to the unfolding of the movement," writes A. Peter Brown, in much the same spirit.[128] It is surely no coincidence that Johns's disinterested perspective on Haydn's Andante consisted of a map of the piece as opposed to any more capricious pedestrian journey through it—a synoptic vision of formal proportions rather than Certeau's street-level metropolitan immersion, with its synecdochal relation to passing items of musical interest. Accordingly, the seriality of variation procedure itself—more recently theorized with more nuance in terms of the rhetoric of parataxis by Elaine Sisman—is a cause of concern for Johns, who aims to demonstrate that the *Surprise* variations are not "merely" strophic.[129] He thus reinscribes the interesting detail at the level of musical form, promoting an acute sensitivity to Haydn's deviations from proportional correspondence between theme and variations (in the second, minor-mode variation and the coda). It hardly needs saying that Johns's analysis is best understood when following the progress of the Andante closely with a score, a view of the music that no audience member in Hanover Square would have adopted. By and large, Haydn's London symphonies address an audience of pedestrians.[130] And yet it would be wrongheaded merely to privilege a notional street-level perspective over the supposedly up-in-the-air abstractions of analytical close reading—or, for that matter, to valorize the "free" play of a musical "surface" over some questionable metaphysics of depth.[131] For, even equipped with synoptic maps, analysts will produce interesting details just as they have always been produced: by noting them into existence. In the end, a map supplements the many technologies of discrimination, and such technologies, as we have seen, have always lived in the street. Though some analysts might wish a diagram to be a distancing tool of scholarly disinterest, interest always resurfaces, attesting to the dynamic of attraction that necessarily secures any form of attention at all.

Besides, the kind of close reading that Johns pursued had its origin in the very forums of critical discussion that were starting to appear during Haydn's lifetime, and with which his later music was closely linked. Like the emerging notion of "round character" in eighteenth-century literature, which Lynch traces in part to the new Shakespeare criticism of the 1780s, some musically interesting features are only fully apprehended via critical rumination, which elaborates upon and magnifies the smallest textual clues and mildest sensuous experiences: "The beauties of Shakespeare . . . are not forward nor obtrusive," wrote William Richardson in 1783. "They do not demand although they claim attention."[132] Not long before this, Carl Ludwig Junker had praised Haydn's adagios for their "serious, interesting whimsy," which he compared to "the tragic sentiments of a Shakespeare."[133] Junker thus deployed a relatively new critical vocabulary that would eventually be elevated into art theory by Friedrich Schlegel in his 1797 essay *On the Study of Greek Poetry*, which associated the modern age with what he called "interesting poetry" ("interessante Poesie"). In Schlegel's view, interesting art, with its cultivated open-endedness and perpetual invitations to be read, became more or less continuous with the explanatory discourse that it eagerly solicited; it was partly directed, that is, at the unceasing debates of a rapidly expanding critical sphere.[134] Schlegel's "interessante Poesie," as Ngai notes, "seems to mark a convergence of art with conceptual discourse about art," and with this in mind, one could say that Haydn provides ample musical evidence that his were among the earliest instrumental compositions to be so widely written up.[135] Focusing "less on expression and more on discourse" (to quote Sutcliffe again), Haydn's music, as critics have noted for some time, frequently takes on the character of discourse itself. The Andante from the *Surprise*, the opening movement of the *Drumroll*, and the Allegretto of the *Military* might even be said to blur the distinction between musical discourses and the critical discourses that impinge upon them, so overtly do they thematize their own interesting features.

The Fate of Interest

This chapter has concerned itself, at least in part, with late eighteenth-century urban soundscapes and material culture—those wide, discipline-traversing spaces that have recently allowed musicologists to assemble networks of people, practices, and things in new and illuminating configurations.[136] But the idea of interest has complicated matters. For, absent such an idea, these capacious conceptual spaces can sometimes appear too passive or inert to sustain the acts of discrimination that produce our objects of attention to begin with—acts that, as we have seen, Haydn's London music frequently thematized and even modeled. However thickly textured our historical accounts, all description works through synecdoche; however brutely material our focus, all networks are held together by the selectivity of our interests and the interests that we inherit.[137] In the inevitably partial historical data that we invoke, in the necessarily curtailed musical excerpts that we repeatedly discuss in our classrooms, synecdoche goes all the way down.[138] It may even be that synecdoche is the ubiquitous figure of interestedness, the material-linguistic trace of changing techniques and technologies of discrimination, whether these take the form of a popular nickname, a critical practice, a composer's notebook, or a music analyst's diagram.[139] These tools create hierarchies, establish salience, generate and pluck out discrete objects of knowledge to be shared, construct and condition how and why "we attend to the things to which we attend," to recall Innis's formulation. Synecdoche reveals the speciously level landscape of mere facts as an arena of variegated concerns.

And yet, heeding Latour's energizing call to rethink "matters of fact" as "matters of concern" is surely only possible if scholars are equipped with a clearly formulated idea of what "concern" is—and, especially, of the places and historical periods in which it became newly viable to conceive of one's relationship to the world in terms of this special kind of interestedness. As Isabelle Stengers has noted, in Latin-derived languages "interesse" is, etymologically, "situated between"—is apparently nothing but the empty dynamic of subjects binding themselves to their subjects.[140] How have people conceived of and naturalized this in-between stuff, this force that supposedly glues people and things together? Thinking about Haydn's London compositions and the market in which they were produced helps us to formulate a distinctively musical answer to this question. It has frequently been observed that, in the London of the 1790s, Haydn was introduced to a new "patron," with whom he had never worked so closely—the largely anonymous general public.[141] One of the few ways in which he, or any of his colleagues, could conceive of the wishes of this radically distributed patron, whose desires were revealed in many atomized acts of purchasing and exchanging the steep half-guinea tickets, was via the concept of interest, a concept that, as we have seen, appears curiously divided nowadays between distinct aesthetic and economic meanings but that, in the eighteenth century, denoted a form of individual investment that was necessarily both psychic and monetary. Now that, in several areas of music studies at least, the relational network of people and things is one of the main methodological paradigms, and even, to some, one of the privileged social ontologies, it is easy to forget that this idea has a historical point of origin.[142] Indeed, the notion that the social body is a "vast, heterogeneous, intricate Mass of Interests," as Burke once conceived of the distant inhabitants of Bengal,[143] originates precisely in Haydn's metropolitan world: in early liberal philosophies of taste and civil society; in the eighteenth-century imaginative prose that explicated and celebrated the vibrancy of social circulation; and, of course, in the incipiently capitalist systems that these writings sought at once to theorize and produce.[144] Haydn's London music, as I have argued, encourages us to conceive of our attention in terms of the psychic economy of interest and, in the process, teaches us to be interested in music in particular ways, which is perhaps why it has rarely sat comfortably with later aspirations to disinterested contemplation.

In 1795 Haydn returned home, to a city that was never to match London's commercial intensity. It would be some time before Vienna hosted a concert series on the scale of the Opera Concerts or those in Hanover Square, although the number of music publishers and piano workshops, as well as the circulation of advertisements and music criticism, expanded rapidly in the years around 1800.[145] Yet the most momentous changes that Haydn witnessed in the city were brought about by the wars with France, which prompted the Austrian state to promote a bellicose public ambience, through increased sponsorship of newspapers and other publications, and a new emphasis on civic ceremony and collective celebration.[146] As Thomas Tolley has argued, the kinds of audience engagement and musical attention seeking that Haydn had cultivated in London thus proved useful in his late Vienna years, now that music was regularly called upon to address and shape collective sentiment.[147] In wartime Vienna, cultivating interest became a fraught political matter.

Given that these years witnessed the convergence of Haydn's interesting music, market interests, and the ideological interests of wartime administrators, it may seem paradoxical that intellectual historians should so frequently associate the years around 1800 with the ascendancy of the philosophical ideal of disinterested contemplation.[148] To be sure, the critical reception of the canonical symphonies of Beethoven, produced during Haydn's last decade, might sometimes imply that these works are better suited to this ideal than the London symphonies.[149] Yet, as music critics have long observed, Beethoven's music, especially in its exhortative Napoleonic vein, trades in many of the same strategies of interest arousal as Haydn's. One hardly need list all the formal swerves and uncanny incursions in a composition such as the Fifth Symphony, quirks that have been consistently interesting across generations of reviews and critical exegeses: the horn calls and pleading oboe solo of the opening Allegro, the dark-to-light transition into the finale, the added "surprise" of the scherzo's ghostly return before the concluding recapitulation.[150] With these interesting details in mind, it is hard to avoid the idea that the forms of contemplation promoted by some Beethovenians were (and still are) made possible only by repressing and sublimating the many forms of arousal that inevitably underpin them, much as Tovey disdained the interest in Haydn's surprise. And, as we will see, the apparent opposition between interestedness and disinterestedness is the psychic analog of the Romantic distinction between "market value" and that new nineteenth-century thing called "aesthetic value"—codependent notions that share an intellectual origin, even as they now appear antithetical.[151] Haydn's London symphonies were composed before—*just* before, one might say—Romantic thought divided up our values in this way.[152] As such, Haydn's music reveals not only the market origins of many of the vaunted musical strategies and high-minded aesthetic values that came to prominence in the nineteenth century but also the institutional changes, technological developments, and conceptual contortions that made the now familiar Beethovenian position viable.

It is not my intention to conclude this chapter (or this book) with a predictable material turn, however, yet again unmasking the unworldly fantasies of bad old Romantic idealism as thoroughly and inescapably "worldly." Indeed, now that many music scholars are turning to materialist approaches of various kinds, the very implicatedness of Haydn's London music with listeners' growing conceptions of their own interest should steer us away from the ontological extremes of some of the newer materialisms: those inspired by Martin Heidegger, for whom the artwork is a special instance of the inscrutable "thing," oblivious to human intentions and purposes,[153] or those who would disperse musical subjects and objects into the supposedly liberating, supposedly more fundamental, materials of sound or vibration—"unencumbered by humans," as Nina Eidsheim puts it.[154] All description is "a directed, *interested* simulacrum," as Roland Barthes once said of structuralist analytical methods.[155] To imagine that one can simply assign to music (or sound or vibration) a position amid an array of implacable things "out there" is, under the guise of a virtuous rejection of anthropocentrism, to indulge the fantasy that one can intimate a view from nowhere, a view accomplished with no hard-won techniques, no particular interests.[156] This is a distinctly (neo) liberal vision: a self-organizing network of material relationships, mysteriously divested of—indeed, wondrously liberated from—our own concerns.[157] It amounts to a posthuman version of the tendency that Gayatri Chakravorty Spivak once cautioned against in postcolonial studies—that of the intellectual "masquerading as the absent nonrepresenter who lets the oppressed speak for themselves."[158] Haydn's London music forecloses this politically dubious fantasy, I would argue, because, produced before the ascendancy of the Beethovenian notion that art and the market are irreconcilable, it revels in the fact that art—no less than Haydn's London notebooks—makes, and is made by, our interests. Just as coinage reifies and teaches a particular understanding of desire by giving our as yet undirected drives a material form, so one could say that Haydn's music gave sonic shape to the psychic reorientations of interested attention. In the eighteenth-century urban environments in which the concept of interest acquired its modern meanings, Haydn made interest itself audible.

3

Objects

I came into the world imbued with the will to find a meaning in things, my spirit filled
with a desire to attain to the source of the world. And then I found that I was an object
in the midst of other objects.

FRANTZ FANON, *Black Skin, White Masks* (1952)[1]

Woman is opaque in her very being; she stands before man not as a subject but as an
object paradoxically endued with subjectivity.

SIMONE DE BEAUVOIR, *The Second Sex* (1949)[2]

Little Boxes

In the last years of his life, Haydn received a stream of respectful visitors, and
he would routinely request that a servant produce for them the precious objects and mementos that he had collected over a long career—the curiosities
by which one could command a view, in material terms, of the public suc-
cesses and private connections of his biography. One item in his collection
was a ribbon bearing the name "Haydn," which had been presented to him
(so Haydn recorded in his notebook) by the wife of a "Mr. Shaw" following a
party at the Shaws' house on December 14, 1791. Mr. Shaw was, it seems likely,
the musician Thomas Shaw, who led the orchestra at the Drury Lane theater.[3]
The opportunity to receive Haydn would have been thrilling for any of London's fashionable set at this time, especially following the success of Salomon's
1791 seasons in Hanover Square. If the Mr. Shaw in question was indeed a fellow musician, one can only imagine how much more excited he would have
been to host his period's towering musical celebrity. But, as Haydn's account
of the party makes clear, the elegant ribbon was not a record of any theatrical
success or public honor but rather of the more intimate exchanges through
which the paraphernalia of his celebrity were now dispersed.

> He [Mr. Shaw] received me downstairs at the door, and then led me to his wife,
> who was surrounded by her 2 daughters and other ladies. As I was bowing
> around the circle, all at once I became aware of the fact that not only the lady
> of the house but also her daughters and the other women each wore on their
> headdress *a parte* over the front a most charming curved pearl-colored band
> of 3 fingers' breadth, with the name Haydn embroidered therein in gold; and
> Mr. Shaw wore this name on his coat, worked into the very ends of both his

collars in the finest steel beads. The coat was made of the finest cloth, and with elegant steel buttons. The mistress is the most beautiful woman I ever saw.

With a characteristically gendered sense of social space, Haydn cast the scene as an overwhelmingly female one, in which women and luxurious objects were displayed side by side. Mr. Shaw, in his lurid Haydn-studded coat, also requested an everyday object from Haydn as a souvenir of the evening:

> Her husband wanted a keepsake [*Denkmahl*] from me, and I gave him a to-bacco box which I had just bought brand new for a guinea; he gave me his in-stead. Several days later I visited him, and saw that he had had a silver case put over my box, on the cover of which was very elegantly engraved Apollo's harp and the following words: *Ex dono celeberrimi Josephi Haydn* [a gift of the re-nowned Joseph Haydn]. N. B. The mistress gave me a stick-pin as a memento.[4]

It was only during the 1790s that the word *keepsake* entered the English language, as people sought to forge new kinds of intimacy with materials ex-tracted from an increasingly cluttered marketplace.[5] Judging from Haydn's note, practices of this sort, depicted and popularized in the works of Laurence Sterne and others, were relatively new to him, and he was amused to learn that his generic, if expensive, tobacco box had acquired another box of its own.[6] One could position this curious instance of boxes enclosed within boxes within the sentimental prehistory of a nineteenth-century bourgeois pre-occupation, once noted by Walter Benjamin: cases. "Pocket watches, slippers, egg cups, thermometers, [and] playing cards," which took their place along-side lustrous envelopes for the person, such as "jackets, carpets, wrappers, and covers"—the epidermal extensions of self that, so Benjamin intimated, pro-duced and reinforced a new conception of human interiority.[7] Like Mr. Shaw's steel-buttoned coat, the box enclosed not only an object but a relationship—the feelings that were his true and permanent possession.[8] "*Ex dono celeber-rimi Josephi Haydn*": the box now recounted its own sentimental story.

This chapter follows Haydn's music, and the music of his contemporaries, across this new world of intimate consumer objects. Away from the presti-gious venues of Hanover Square or the largest London theaters, whose newest products were preannounced and scrutinized in journals and newspapers, music was not so readily extricated from an array of fashionable distrac-tions and desirable things. While in London, Haydn contributed to a range of small and commutable musical genres—especially popular song and sim-ple chamber music—that traveled between private houses and commercial printers, music libraries and pleasure gardens, grand outdoor performances and the pages of ladies' magazines. To follow these journeys is to map out an eighteenth-century musical public decisively shaped by changing economic behaviors—a "counter-public" of the sort described by Deidre Lynch, encompassing a new regime of consumer practices associated predominantly with women.[9]

Eighteenth-century writers had long dramatized the Sternean allure of consumer objects by conferring voices upon them, most conspicuously in the genre of the it-narrative, in which small consumer items—hats, pens, handkerchiefs, and so forth—personally recounted their picaresque adventures.[10] Haydn's songs, and even his chamber works, were well suited to a commercial landscape populated with such voluble things. Popular songs were (and in many respects remain) the quintessential modern consumer items, in part because they literalized the ubiquitous eighteenth-century trope of the seductively vocal object. This chapter approaches the consumerist aesthetic of popular song as a tuneful ancestor of Marx's uncannily envoiced commodity, which unexpectedly speaks up toward the end of the first chapter of *Capital* to confess that it has no intrinsic or fixed value.[11] But, whereas the voice of the Marxian commodity stood for the mendacious intimacy of the soulless object, animating and concealing a system of economic exchange, the eighteenth-century habit of attaching voices to inanimate objects—and uncoupling them from persons—was, as we will see, ethically more ambiguous. London's commercial music scenes were dominated by women's captivating voices, often performing popular songs in the sentimental vein. But the value of the sentimental voice was inseparable from a newly consumerist conception of desire—as unending pursuit, aroused by the sympathetic imagination—and an attendant aesthetic of enticing objects. These principles of exchange and desire permeated even the century's best-known theories of art. The Hogarthian account of beauty, whose visual frame of reference was repeatedly adapted by later eighteenth-century writers to describe music and sound, accorded special status to undulating lines, opaque rhetorical boundaries, and quavering voices: like the gleaming second skin of Haydn's tobacco box, an aesthetic of seductively iridescent surfaces dramatized the boundaries between desiring subjects and desirable objects.

The politics of the sentimental voice, and its relationship to an economic system in which people and objects constantly swapped places, comes into sharpest focus in one further instance of late eighteenth-century popular song that features in this chapter—ballads in service of the antislavery cause, which, especially from the late 1780s, were sung in the theater and in private homes. The most widely circulated abolitionist songs shared a basic rhetorical device: they envoiced enslaved Africans, with the ostensible aim of restoring a lost interiority to people who had been violently reduced to what the Jamaican planter Edward Long called "objects of purchase and sale."[12] Simon

Gikandi argues that European thinkers of the eighteenth century sought to "quarantine one aspect of social life—the tasteful, the beautiful, and the civil—from a public domain saturated by diverse forms of commerce, including the sale of black bodies"; yet we will see how the sentimental voice allowed these tenuously separate spheres to mingle.[13]

To recognize that voices do not always index personhood, and may even work to produce and enclose objects, is to imperil the ongoing liberal project of recovering and listening to subaltern voices.[14] Indeed, the aesthetic-economic past of the vocal object may ultimately hold some discomforting methodological lessons. Not only does it remind scholars, once again, that new histories of marginal or quotidian things cannot be created merely by prompting their materials to speak more clearly, but it also hints at foundational problems with the ethic of envoicing that typically guides more politically fraught histories, especially those of colonialism and slavery.[15] For, as we will see, many of the most clearly audible—and the most touching—voices that resounded across the public spaces of the late eighteenth century were produced by distinctively modern economic arrangements, which promoted the newly intimate commingling of people and things.

Pursuit of Objects

It was not only domestic music making that, as in the Shaw's home, occasioned this commingling. In Vauxhall pleasure gardens, where Thomas Shaw was a regular in the band,[16] Haydn's music had been performed since the early 1780s, rubbing shoulders on set lists with songs, operatic excerpts, and comic turns—all within a space laid out to display people and consumables.[17] These, too, were organized into boxes. Like many appreciative foreign visitors, Haydn, who attended Vauxhall on at least one occasion (on June 4, 1792), remarked on the rows of "supper boxes," enclosed on three sides and painted with Hogarthian scenes of everyday pleasures (fig. 3.1).[18] "There are 155 little supper boxes [*Butticken zum Speisen*] situated very cutely [*gar niedlich*] in various locations, each of which can comfortably hold six people," noted Haydn, with his characteristic attention to numbers.[19] Haydn's use of the word "niedlich" is notable, given its associations, especially in anglophile German art criticism, with the gendered values that Annette Richards parses as the "popular, the lively, the charmingly naïve, and the comic."[20] The boxes were a site of manifold consumer pleasures. In the 1790s, the memoirist Henry Angelo recalled the Duchess of Devonshire and her entourage seated in boxes at Vauxhall "supping in the rooms facing the orchestra—French horns playing to them all the time," indulging in a mélange of sonic

FIGURE 3.1. Technologies of viewing and being viewed: the famous rows of supper boxes at Vauxhall Gardens (from *Gentleman's Magazine* 35 (August 1765), between pp. 356 and 357).

and culinary enjoyments.[21] Partly because of the variety of coexisting pleasures that Vauxhall displayed, the *Monthly Mirror* asserted in 1801 that great
singers were "never listened to in Vauxhall Gardens," by contrast with the
elite London theaters.[22] And, to be sure, even Haydn's musician's view of the
gardens only mentioned the "pretty good [*so ziemlich gut*]" music as part of
a varied survey that included tea, coffee, almond milk, and the extravagant
illuminations.[23] But, as Angelo's description makes plain, the supper boxes
were arranged to promote mutual inspection as well as a degree of separation and privacy, offering up their occupants as a spectacle in themselves.
On his visit to Vauxhall, the "Chinese" narrator of Oliver Goldsmith's *The
Citizen of the World*—a satirical epistolary novel produced throughout the
1760s—remarked that the genteel Mr. and Mrs. Tibbs required "a box where
they might see and be seen—one, as they expressed it, in the very focus of
public view."[24]

On chilly evenings such as the one Haydn described, the music and musicians, too, were frequently presented in their own luxurious architectural re-
ceptacle: the Vauxhall Rotunda—a circular neoclassical structure, portrayed
as a stylized box-within-boxes on the cover of several Vauxhall song com-
pendiums (fig. 3.2), which functioned not only as an enclosed acoustic space

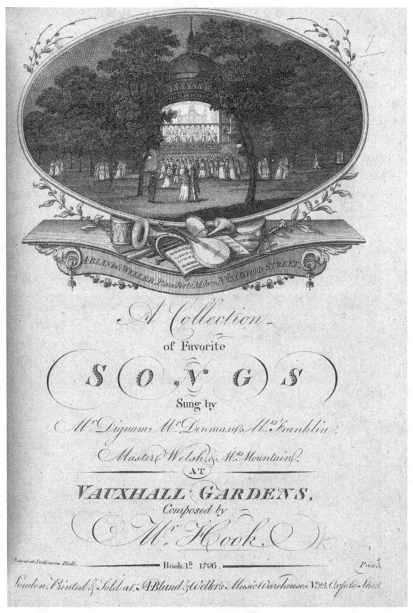

A Collection
of Favorite
S (O , N G) S
Sung by
Mr. Dignum, Mr. Denman, Mrs. Franklin,
Master Welsh, & Mrs. Mountain,
AT
VAUXHALL GARDENS,
Composed by
Mr. Hook.

Entered at Stationers Hall. ———— Book 1st 1796. ———— Price 5

London, Printed & Sold at A. Bland & Weller's Music Warehouse. No. 23. Oxford Street

FIGURE 3.2. The Vauxhall Rotunda, depicted on the frontispiece of *A Collection of Favorite Songs sung by Mr. Dignum, Mr. Denman, Mrs. Franklin, Master Welsh, & Mrs. Mountain at Vauxhall Gardens . . . Book 1st* (1796). © British Library Board.

but as the grandest of all the pleasure gardens' many technologies of viewing and consuming.[25]

It is in Vauxhall that Haydn may have heard some of the most explicit musical appeals to consumer desire. One of the hit songs to emerge from the pleasure gardens in the mid-1790s was a saucy number entitled "The Female Auctioneer," by the veteran composer James Hook. Published in 1797 in one of the regularly issued Vauxhall compilations, the song continued to circulate in individual broadsides with Hook's music (and other tunes, too) on both sides of the Atlantic for the duration of the nineteenth century (fig. 3.3).[26] In London, "The Female Auctioneer" was popularized by Anna Maria Leary—inheritor of the title of "Vauxhall Siren"—who had lately married and become

FIGURE 3.3. "I'm going, going, going": from James Hook's "The Female Auctioneer," in *Second Collection of Favorite Songs sung by Mr. Dignum, Mr. Denman, Mrs. Franklin, & Mrs. Mountain, at Vauxhall Gardens* (1797). © British Library Board.

Mrs. Franklin.[27] "I am come to sell if you will buy," announces the auctioneer. But what is being auctioned? Following some musical delaying tactics, which mildly disrupt the symmetry of a downbeat-heavy country-dance tune, the opening stanza supplies the answer in the form of a punning punch line (as though London's beau monde would have been unable to guess, having paid to see the performer in front of them): "Ah, no, the lot I have in hand is now to sell myself." The subsequent refrain is a direct address, through which Leary would surely have encouraged various kinds of audience interaction when she appeared at the Rotunda, adorned with her signature ostrich feathers: "And I'm going, going, going . . . Who bids for me? Who bids for me?"

The overt combination of the erotic and the pecuniary in "The Female Auctioneer" would have been charged, to say the least. In 1790, the Russian poet and historian Nikolai Karamzin observed upon his visit to Vauxhall that "the actors and actresses of the London theaters sing, and the listeners show their appreciation by throwing them money."[28] Earlier in the century, Vauxhall's proprietors had been hesitant to employ singers as permanent attractions because London sex workers so frequently advertised themselves via song.[29] Prostitution was common in the more secluded and unlit areas of the gardens—the so-called Dark Walks, where Frances Burney's eponymous heroine Evelina had an unpleasant encounter with "a large party of gentlemen, apparently very riotous," having just enjoyed a genteel performance of an oboe concerto.[30] Hook's song professes to be about the more decorous negotiations of the marriage market, asking, "Pray where's the Girl, I wish to know / Would not become a Wife?" But it answers this question with a sly celebration of the unending pursuit of love, as opposed to its respectable conjugal legitimation: "At least I own I really would, / In spite of all alarms, / Dear Bachelors, now be so good, / Do take me in your arms."

Like Leary herself, the country-dance tune, with its fermatas and cheeky hook, presented itself neatly packaged, boxed within generic instrumental episodes that redoubled the syntactical function of cadential closure and enclosure. Especially in the bounded material form of an exchangeable print object, this was fungible, repeatable music.[31] Reprised night after night at the Rotunda, relayed between friends in fashionable houses, reproduced in the seasonal Vauxhall anthologies, Hook's little song crowded together and switched places with a hundred others, a great many also by Hook.[32] And, with its open invitation to be pursued, "The Female Auctioneer" laid bare the transactional logic of its genre, which not only turned women performers into consumer objects but also portrayed consumer desire itself as an eternal pursuit—its objects forever going but never wholly gone.

Pursuit was the subject of another comic Vauxhall song by Hook from around this time, though in a radically contrasting register—a "favourite hunting song" entitled "In Pursuit of the Fashion," replete with horns and a galloping 6/8 meter. In this self-conscious and even self-celebrating satire, the evocation of country sports perversely described the metropolitan pleasures of Vauxhall's arena of pastoral fantasy (fig. 3.4): "After Fancy and Folly

FIGURE 3.4. "All join in the Chace": the beginning of James Hook's "In Pursuit of the Fashion," in *A Third Collection of Songs Sung by Miss Milne et al. at Vauxhall* (1791). © British Library Board.

we eagerly fly; / In pursuit of the Fashion, Hark forward's the Cry." As in the "Female Auctioneer," the chase—not the capture—was the point.

At Vauxhall, to witness the pleasurable spectacle of consumption was at least as important as acquiring the objects of consumption themselves, especially given the much-ridiculed meagerness of the overpriced consumables on offer (so translucently thin were the notorious ham slices that they were widely known as "sliced cobwebs").[33] With a pointed pecuniary metaphor, the narrator of *The Citizen of the World* found "every sense overpaid with more than expected pleasure" upon his visit to the gardens, because the sight of others' pleasure fueled his imagination to "an ecstasy of admiration" ("the company gaily dressed, looking satisfaction, and the tables spread with various delicacies").[34] This imaginative principle was the main attraction of that new eighteenth-century leisure activity for which Burney's *Evelina* deployed the neologism "shopping": not the acquisition of objects as much as the pleasurable pursuit of them.[35] Shopping was the most visible symptom of the "contagion of desire" among the London beau monde that Samuel Johnson diagnosed in *The Idler*. "We see all about us busied in persuit of imaginary good, and begin to bustle in the same chase," he observed. "Whom shall we find among these . . . that is not tormenting himself with a wish for something, of which all the pleasure and all the benefit will cease at the moment of attainment?"[36] Johnson's derision was directed at the emerging forms of social behavior that the sociologist Colin Campbell once called "modern hedonism": the deferrals of appetitive satisfaction allowed by the exercise of the sympathetic imagination—the aesthetic principle essential, so Campbell argued, to a new Romantic ethic of consumerism.[37]

Hook's "The Female Auctioneer" rehearsed a widespread trope of eighteenth-century popular art: a seller became the wares. It was the very premise of picturesque depictions of street hawkers, such as Wheatley's *Cries of London*, which elaborated an erotics of the lower-class female vendor, framed by the gaze of well-heeled purchasers. Wheatley's portrayal of a female ballad seller, "A New Love Song, Ha'pence a Piece," was arranged around the charged look that the crier shares with her customer—palm open to receive his payment, naked wrist turned toward the viewer—and so echoed in formal terms the relation of the purchasing public to Wheatley's print object itself. Around the central pair stood representatives of motherhood and infancy, while an eager dog that worried away beneath the transaction (and perhaps also the gentleman's prominent whip) emphasized the erotic nature of the exchange (fig. 3.5). Each picture in Wheatley's series had a distinctive surface character—primrose seller, milkmaid, strawberry seller, and so on—yet several of his vendors were identical in appearance, in

FIGURE 3.5. *A New Love Song, Ha'pence a Piece* (1793) by Francis Wheatley.

large part because they had all been modeled by his wife: the object of desire turned out to be as fungible as the prints themselves.[38] The street cries that these prints rendered in visual terms were cited at the foot of each picture: "Turnips and Carrots, Ho!"; "Round and Sound, Fivepence a Pound, Duke Cherries"; "Milk Below." Extracted from London's streets, and reframed within the elegant borders of Wheatley's prints, these voices, like the voice of Hook's "Female Auctioneer," now circularly advertised themselves.

Isabella Kelly's 1797 novel *Joscelina* displayed a more tumultuous version of this trope in a key moment of recognition—indeed, the pivotal episode of anagnorisis—when a voice, in the guise of a street vendor, alerts the noble Errington to the plight of his serially unfortunate beloved. By this stage, Joscelina is living in penury alongside the prostitute Jessy on the streets of London. Reduced to singing for coins outside a coffeehouse, Joscelina's feeble rendition of the song "My name is poor Mary, Primroses I sell" secures her transformation into a vulnerable, and available, object.[39] "God of my soul! that voice," cries Errington, aghast. In the spectacle that greets him as he rushes from the coffeehouse, the "affecting, soft, plaintive, tremulous" voice is translated into the formal terms of a tableau. Kelly, with the signal self-consciousness of the sentimental mode, announces that this moment is designed for and created by the aroused observer: "What a scene for the melting heart of sensibility! . . . To give her air, Jessy had a little uncovered her snowy bosom, and her cap falling off as she sunk, her hair hung in beautiful luxuriance about her neck and shoulders." Here, the gentle, tremulous voice becomes the indistinct outlines and shimmering surfaces of Joscelina's body, the desire-made threshold between object and subject.[40]

Ideas of beauty in eighteenth-century Britain were relentlessly epidermal, preoccupied not with objects or bodies as such but with their seductive skins: lines, borders, and contours. Burke's account of the beautiful directly connected this preoccupation to an aesthetics of pursuit: the *Philosophical Enquiry* distinguished the mere lust "that hurries us on the possession of certain objects" from the kind of imaginative attachments that allow us to contemplate their form.[41] The sympathetic contemplation of objects, to Burke, constituted a higher order of mastery than mere ownership and was expressed in formal features associated with weakness and pliancy: smallness, delicacy, and smoothness.[42] His exposition of these features emphasized appealing outlines above all else and so drew substantially on the popular theories of Hogarth: the concept of the "serpentine" line appears as soon as Burke seeks to explain the appeal of "gradual variation"—of "parts not angular, but melted as it were into each other."[43]

While the Hogarthian conception of line foremost concerned the sense of vision, Burke was one of many eighteenth-century thinkers to translate it into aural terms. The *Philosophical Enquiry* did so via the Miltonic image of the singing voice in the *Allegro*: "the *melting* voice through *mazes* running." This voice, maintained Burke, was the musical version of beauty's "winding surface"—its alluring aural-sonic epidermis.[44] By the end of the century, the association of beautiful surfaces with the "melting" voice was commonplace: "To produce the Beautiful in music, all must be soft, smooth, and flowing; the melody must be vocal," explained William Crotch in his lectures on the taxonomy of musical styles.[45]

Crucially, in Hogarth's theory of beauty, the line—and especially the "waving" line that aims to replicate the animacy of moving objects—is more than a straightforward imitation of anything in the world: it materializes a primal principle of human desire.[46] A material inscription that the artist makes in the service of representation, a line, proposed Hogarth, nonetheless corresponds to no stable or self-evident contour in reality. It is best considered a composite of bodies and the searching gaze that delineates them: the waving line "leads the eye in a pleasing manner along the continuity of its variety," wrote Hogarth. But because it implies so much more variety than anyone could perceive, it appears as a representation of a worldly body only with the "assistance of the imagination"—a mental capacity that Hogarth regarded as a form of endless pursuit.[47] "Pursuing is the business of our lives," he announced, and intricate lines "*lead the eye a wanton kind of chace*": a line is not the self-evident boundary of an object, so much as a technical approximation of the animating human principle of pursuit.[48]

It was this philosophical principle of eternal pursuit—not the acquisition of objects in themselves, however luxurious—that Johnson had condemned in his abstemious dismissal of London's fashionable world. For, as Johnson's own dictionary explained, an object is primarily "that about which any power or faculty is employed," even "something presented to the senses to raise an affection or emotion in the mind"—meanings that survive in the use of the word *object* to denote a goal or purpose.[49] Objects, that is, do not inertly establish the limits of the self, like the stone against which Johnson reportedly struck his foot to refute George Berkeley's extreme brand of idealism.[50] For this reason, some scholarship across the humanities, particularly in literary criticism, has endorsed Martin Heidegger's distinction between "objects," inextricable from our needs and desires, and "things," supposedly oblivious to human purposes.[51] But in light of the talkative, songful, and seductive eighteenth-century landscape of objects, I remain unconvinced that the supposedly implacable "thing" can accomplish much for historians of the arts, except perhaps to provide a modernist frisson of alienating materiality in the midst of methodologies that sometimes tend toward abstraction or tidy explication. It seems to me that, were we on the lookout for "things," beguiling literary texts or musical compositions would not be the most promising places to uncover them. These are, after all, Johnson's "objects" par excellence, raising an "emotion in the mind," whose melting voices and hazy contours constitute the uncertain threshold where desire meets and is materialized as form.[52]

Objects, Animals, People

Even though eighteenth-century thinkers routinely claimed that the social improvements fostered by commerce would be secured by the increasing prominence and proximity of women,[53] contemporary feminists were quick to observe that particular classes of women were at once the subjects and objects of the century's growing consumerist outlook. "Strength of body and mind are sacrificed to libertine notions of beauty," argued Mary Wollstone-craft in her 1792 *A Vindication of the Rights of Woman*, and these notions reduced women to "mere animals," ornamental nonpersons.[54] Beauty as it was theorized by Burke certainly seemed to ply between people, animals, and objects, indiscriminately gathered beneath a gaze perpetually oriented toward glossy surfaces. In his disquisition on "smoothness," Burke adduced the "smooth skins" of women alongside the "coats of birds and beasts" and the "polished surfaces" of "ornamental furniture": these were all items of property that a gentleman of taste might expect to have around the house.[55] Thus were women classed among the beautiful objects of the eighteenth century. The tremulously singing Joscelina, the beckoning ballad seller, the seductive female auctioneer—these were persons-turned-objects, turned back into persons via the sentimental conferral of voice. And, more even than the envoiced banknotes and hairpins of contemporary it-narratives, these feminized person-objects undermine any stable equation of voice and personhood, voice and agency.

To summon voices from objects, animals, or people was also to assert a degree of mastery over them. This power dynamic is on display in one of the prints that Haydn acquired while he was in London: a 1791 illustration by Henry Bunbury, engraved by Haydn's friend Francesco Bartolozzi, to accompany the opening four stanzas of Anna Letitia Barbauld's 1773 poem "The Mouse's Petition" (fig. 3.6). The poem, a favorite of the time, took the form of an address to the natural scientist Joseph Priestley from a mouse. (Priestley had conducted a series of famous experiments wherein he trapped mice in sealed containers with and without potted herbs, in order to demonstrate—when some mice suffocated—that the animals relied on the oxygen that the plants supplied.)[56] Adopting the up-to-date language of individual liberty, the mouse makes a self-conscious appeal to sentiment aroused by its newfound voice:

FIGURE 3.6. *The Mouse's Petition* (1791) by Henry Bunbury. Engraved by Francesco Bartolozzi. © The Trustees of the British Museum.

> O hear a pensive prisoner's prayer
> For liberty that sighs;
> And never let thine heart be shut
> Against the wretch's cries!

The third stanza even contained the kind of language that led contemporaries to suspect that Barbauld's whimsical poem implied a more radical political message (a suspicion that she denied).

> If e'er thy breast with freedom glowed,
> And spurned a tyrant's chain,
> Let not thy strong oppressive force
> A free-born mouse detain.[57]

As Bunbury's picture makes clear, however, "The Mouse's Petition" is intended to be amusing even in its poignancy, predicated as it is on an exaggerated mismatch between the gravity of the rhetoric and the tiny scale of the creature who adopts it: all eyes are directed toward the tiny mouse at the center of the engraving, while successive boundaries both box it in and guarantee that it is the focus—a cage, a tabletop, the limbs of the onlookers, and then their bodies and the trees that frame them. The open-palmed gesture of one of the standing ladies, interposed between the mouse and the face of the seated Priestley figure, seems to intercede on the mouse's behalf, implying that the voice in the poem may be a sentimental (female) projection (perhaps even concocted to entertain the observing child). Even as the poem aggrandizes the fate of the mouse, then, it also miniaturizes and minimizes the principles at stake. If the mouse's embodiment of smallness is hardly beautiful in the Burkean sense—though the composition in which the mouse is encased may meet the description—it nonetheless partakes of the related, more overtly consumerist, aesthetic that a handful of writers have since elaborated under the rubric of the "cute," which intensifies the impression of vulnerability that Burke regarded as essential to the beautiful.[58] "Pity is the primary emotion of this seductive and manipulative aesthetic," writes Daniel Harris. "A class of outcasts and mutations"—"stationary objects and tempting exteriors"—inspire a perverse kind of love tinged with sadism.[59] Not coincidentally, one of the opening chapters in Wollstonecraft's *Vindication* indicted earlier generations of revered male thinkers who had turned women into mere "objects of pity."[60]

By the 1790s, Barbauld had joined Wollstonecraft in observing the moral limitations of pity, and sentiment tout court. By this time, however, her target was Britain's failure to end the epochal crime of slavery. Her "Epistle to William Wilberforce," published in the aftermath of the 1791 parliamentary defeat of Wilberforce's bill to abolish the slave trade, noted that this political disaster had happened in spite of wave after wave of sentimental abolitionist publicity, not least in poetry similar to her own. "The Muse, too soon awakened, with ready tongue, / At Mercy's shrine applausive paeans rung." But, concluded Barbauld, artists' overeager efforts to "rouse, to melt, or to inform the breast" ultimately did nothing to challenge the mechanisms of greed: "Where seasoned tools of Avarice prevail, / A Nation's eloquence, combined, must fail."[61] As a poet who had herself contributed to a corpus of eighteenth-century sentimental literature that sought to arouse pity by urging enslaved Africans to speak, Barbauld knew all about this. The eighth of her 1781 *Hymns in Prose for Children* addressed, in its vision of a globe encircled by God's mercy, a "Negro woman, who sittest pining in captivity." "Raise thy voice, forlorn and abandoned one," wrote Barbauld: God alone—though, crucially, the readers of her poetry, too—will hear and take pity.[62]

Suspicion of the political efficacy of feeling—especially as a tool of resistance to the economic logic of slavery—has a long history.[63] Indeed, as Brycchan Carey points out, the condemnation of misplaced or false senti-

ment was itself a commonplace of eighteenth-century sentimental writing—an ethic that required the constant policing of authenticity.[64] James
Gillray's lacerating antisentimental satire from 1798, *The New Morality*, portrayed a generation of professed radicals, including Samuel Taylor Coleridge
and Robert Southey, in various states of destructive feeling, urged on by a
stack of pamphlets and polemics, spewing forth from a bottomless Cornucopia of Ignorance. Behind a preaching Priestley, the haggard and murderous
personification of Justice wields a dagger, Philanthropy clutches the globe in a
suffocating embrace, and Sensibility weeps over the fate of a dead bird, a book
by Rousseau in hand, even as her foot crushes a severed human head (fig. 3.7).
Yet as these grim masterpieces of Tory propaganda reveal all too clearly, the
antisentimental attitude was also one of gleeful misogyny. As E. J. Clery argues, when eighteenth-century writers associated women with "economic innovation," this was also an ideological bind, linking "new and extreme forms
of social injustice" with female consumers.[65]

Hence the equivocation in such texts as Wollstonecraft's *Vindication*,
which portrayed women as enslaved people, even as it accused many of complicity with the exploitative transformation of themselves and others into ornaments.[66] Driven by base desire, maintained Wollstonecraft, men will always
"endeavour to enslave women"; yet she also decried "English women whose
time is spent in making caps, bonnets, and the whole mischief of trimmings,
not to mention shopping"—zealous consumers who energetically reduced
themselves and others to mere surfaces.[67] By contrast, Barbauld's contemporaneous poem "The Rights of Woman" celebrated these attractive surfaces
as a source of power, and in overtly sonic terms: "soft melting tones" were,
wrote Barbauld, in Miltonic vein, the feminine equivalent of the "thundering
cannon's roar" that accompanied the "boasted rule" of men.[68] But, to Wollstonecraft, such dubious agency—barely any distance from the manipulative
vulnerability of Barbauld's cute mouse—was more adequately understood as
yet another way in which people were turned into objects.

It is hard to ignore that the abolitionist accoutrements that were ranged
against slavery, armed with all the weapons of sentiment, at times appeared
to reiterate, in miniaturizing terms, the very transformation of people into
objects that antislavery campaigners condemned. The most famous of these
items was the cameo produced by Josiah Wedgwood, based on the seal of the
London Committee of the Society for the Abolition of the Slave Trade, which
depicted a kneeling African man in chains. These cameos rapidly became
fashion accessories. As Thomas Clarkson recalled in his 1808 chronicle of the
abolitionist movement,

FIGURE 3.7. Detail from *The New Morality* (1798) by James Gillray.

Some had them inlaid in gold on the lid of their snuff-boxes. Of the ladies, several wore them in bracelets, and others had them fitted up in an ornamental manner as pins for their hair. At length the taste for wearing them became general.[69]

Aware of the unpleasant paradox implicit in selling representations of Black bodies in order to argue against the violent appropriation and sale of Black bodies, Wedgwood and the committee distributed his cameos but never sold them.[70] Even so, this impulse to distance lofty expressions of fellow feeling from the less noble consumer sentiments aroused by manufactured luxury items was arguably undermined by the aesthetic principle of the cameo itself. Around the picture of the enslaved African, as on the seal of the committee, ran the epithet "Am I not a man and a brother?"—a question emanating from yet another voice conferred on yet another eighteenth-century object. As Festa has argued, this positioned Wedgwood's cameo in a politically hazardous series of substitutions all too familiar in the gendered landscape of eighteenth-century object-persons, uniquely freighted in this instance by the scale of the violence to which it referred: objectified persons now became personified objects, circulated ostensibly to reclaim a stolen personhood.[71] With this in mind, one can hardly fail to note the proximity of the Wedgwood cameo to other luxury items depicting people of African origin, especially Black child servants, who featured in the margins of enduringly popular paintings (including the Vauxhall supper-box painting *The Game of Quadrille and the Tea-Equipage*, from the studio of Francis Hayman) and on such household goods as Worcester china tea sets.[72] Here, the surface of the Black body merged with the desirable surfaces of luxury objects under the gaze of the white sympathizer, as Clarkson made plain in his description of Wedgwood's "beautiful cameo": "The ground was a most delicate white, but the Negro, who was seen imploring compassion in the middle of it, was in his own native colour."[73]

The Wedgwood cameo generated still greater surplus sentimental value by reproducing the scene of the Black body in pain. Saidiya Hartman and others have since dwelt at length on this iteration of the Aristotelean moral problem of deriving aesthetic pleasure from the spectacle of cruelty—on the "spectacular nature of black suffering" and the "repression of black testimony" that can ensue.[74] This spectacle—and, through it, the sentimental conferral of voice on the suffering object—was, without doubt, central to eighteenth-century abolitionist publicity. During the earliest coordinated wave of campaigning in the late 1780s, the best-known antislavery verse was William Cowper's ballad "The Negro's Complaint"—one of several poems, published in 1788, ordered by the ardent abolitionist (and repentant former slave trader) John Newton.[75] As in John Bicknell and Thomas Day's widely read "The Dying Negro" of 1773,[76] Cowper's "The Negro's Complaint" gave a voice to an African in order to inspire pity ("Forced from home and all its pleasures / Afric's coast I left forlorn"). And the climax of the poem rehearsed the sentimental trope in which false sentiment is condemned: "Prove that you have human feelings, / Ere you proudly question ours!"[77] Over the next decade, Cowper's African would be granted several musical voices—many of them, in scenarios reimagined by Julia Hamilton, composed by, and intended to be sung by, women.[78] The earliest publication of Cowper's ballad, as

FIGURE 3.8. William Cowper's "The Negro's Complaint" as a song in the *Lady's Magazine*, December 1793.

Clarkson observed, had already signaled its intended audience—genteel and possibly female—with the subtitle *A Subject for Discussion at the Tea Table*.[79] Late in 1793, *The Lady's Magazine* published a musical setting credited to a "Female Correspondent—an Amateur."[80] The sigh-laden tune unfolds as a succession of touching musical formulas, the most daring being a winding chromatic ascent on "to increase a stranger's treasure" (see fig. 3.8). Musical publications of this kind attest to the presence of abolitionist singing in fashionable English parlors, where women in particular could try on the voices of enslaved African men as a kind of sentimental role play.[81]

This role play also had its more public face, one that leads back to the exuberantly commercial space of Vauxhall Gardens. The earliest published song called "The Negro's Complaint," which appeared around the same time as Cowper's poem, was by the English actor and musician Charles Dibdin (see fig. 3.9), though his song was based on "The African" by the Liverpool abolitionist William Roscoe (another poem released amid the wave of abolitionist campaigning in 1788), and borrowed only Cowper's more emotive title. Like Cowper, Roscoe also envoiced an enslaved African man, torn from the prelapsarian "groves of Angola" and "severed from all I held dear," whose copious tears and sighs provide evidence of his humanity.[82] The introductory and closing borders of Dibdin's song display its one distinctive surface hook: a series of ornamental heart palpitations on a standard cadential descent by thirds.

While celebratory accounts of the abolitionist cause, from Clarkson's history onward, have tended to describe such songs as distinct in kind from

FIGURE 3.9. The opening of Charles Dibdin / William Roscoe, "The Negro's Complaint" (London: Preston, c. 1788). © British Library Board.

the forms of blackface that were increasingly standard fare on the London stage, one only need follow the musicians and actors involved in their performance to see the continuities between them. Dibdin's "The Negro's Complaint" entered a theatrical scene in which racial mimicry was ubiquitous.[83] The song was first performed in Vauxhall Gardens by Charles (née Benjamin)

Incledon, a former sailor with a particular line in naval musical camp, who had shared a platform with Haydn's music at Vauxhall countless times.[84] Dibdin, meanwhile, was at this time much celebrated for his portrayal of the Black servant Mungo in his and Isaac Bickerstaffe's Drury Lane farce *The Padlock*, dating back to the 1760s.[85] And, by the late 1780s, Dibdin's so-called negro impersonations were a fixture in his informal *Table* entertainments, which remained popular well into the nineteenth century.[86] *The Gentleman's Magazine* even published a denunciation of slavery by the Rev. Samuel Disney (of Corpus Christi College, Cambridge) in the voice of Dibdin's Mungo, presented as an "Epilogue to *The Padlock*," beginning with the kind of racist patois that Cowper's poem eschewed but gradually adopting the ostensibly universal register of contemporary moral philosophy as it continued ("I am a slave, where all things else are free").[87] Around the same time, George Colman and Samuel Arnold's long-running hit *Inkle and Yarico* premiered in the Haymarket—a vaguely abolitionist version of a story, frequently retold since the seventeenth century, of love between a European trader and a native American (who, in Colman and Arnold's version, is ultimately rescued from a life of slavery when Inkle's heart, "long callous to the feelings of sensibility," can bear it no longer).[88] The 1792 Covent Garden version of the opera promised a "negro dance" following the second act.[89] The aesthetics of sentimental abolitionist art thus oscillated between a collection of apparent opposites: racist mimicry and sympathetic representation, consumer items and cherished objects, the grotesquely vulnerable and the beautifully melting, inert objects and animate persons.

The touching voice, the sentimental register, the appeal to feeling—these were also the few viable forms of self-presentation available to African people seeking political redress. The desperate petition from a group of enslaved people to the Massachusetts legislature in 1777 cited, alongside the principles of individual liberty and rights that were bound up with their newly founded state, "the tender feelings of humanity" that their plight ought to arouse.[90] Abolitionists frequently reported on the passionate singing of enslaved Africans in the Middle Passage in order to assert their status as people: "Their songs are songs of lamentation upon their departure which, while they sing, are always in tears," professed Wilberforce in a widely disseminated passage from his parliamentary speech of May 12, 1789.[91] The sentimental logic of personhood extended even to those of African origin who had achieved a degree of liberty and status in the European metropolis. Describing the epistolary style of the formerly enslaved writer and musician Ignatius Sancho, Gikandi observes that "performing the culture of taste" in ways consistent with "the pleasurable habits of the London metropolitan culture" was one of the ways in which prominent Africans in England could lay claim to their full human-ity.[92] This is especially clear in Sancho's *Collection of New Songs* from the late 1760s—settings of fashionable verse by Shakespeare, Garrick, Anacreon, and others (including simply "a lady"): as in the genre of the slave narrative, the emotional propriety of these songs supposedly humanized the author, named on the title page only as "an African." Likewise, concert reviewers habitually treated the moving performances of the mixed-race violin virtuoso George Bridgetower, who appeared in several concerts alongside Haydn in the 1790s, as proof that those with dark skin had the full complement of sensibility.[93]

To provide this proof was surely one reason why the enslaved African-born poet Phyllis Wheatley was received in the Jermyn Street home of Haydn's future collaborator Anne Hunter in 1773.[94] Anne Hunter was already well-known in British letters and hosted salons in the same spaces that her husband, the distinguished Scottish surgeon John Hunter, performed medi-cal demonstrations and dissections. Before a select gathering, Wheatley read aloud from her new volume of verse amid John Hunter's copious anatomi-cal specimens. These included human remains that, according to the trader George Cartwright, had deeply upset the group of Indigenous people from Labrador who had visited earlier that year. Hunter's collection would eventu-ally include a cast of Ignatius Sancho's arm.[95] Wheatley's poem, "On Being Brought from Africa to America," which represented the story of her own enslavement as an act of divine mercy, concluded with a couplet that adduced the poet's own voice as evidence of Black personhood: "Remember, Chris-tians, Negroes black as Cain, / May be refined, and join the angelic train."[96]

But what did the Hunters hear? During the reading, John Hunter, an early proponent of racial science, took notes on what he considered the perceptible imperfections in Wheatley's vocal apparatus. The notes were later published under the heading *Of the Voices of Animals*.[97] John Hunter was without doubt attentive to the voice and the secrets it might disclose. Yet it is hard to avoid the conclusion that even, or perhaps especially, in the instant of aesthesis, a voice—that Hogarthian sonic line, sustained in part by the pursuit of an ac-quisitive ear—did nothing to prevent Phyllis Wheatley from joining his col-lection of specimens.[98]

In excavating the aesthetics of eighteenth-century popular song via the political strategies of abolitionist publicity, I do not intend to invest a small-scale vocal genre with graver ethical import than it can reasonably sustain. Still, as Gikandi has argued, the repression of slavery structured eighteenth-century discourses of taste and beauty in pervasive ways—perhaps especially in the strategies by which European thinkers displaced, elided, and explained away slavery's very existence. From this perspective, sentimental abolitionist publicity could be conceived less as a discrete context in which to locate a particular musical genre than as a bundle of historical practices in which an economic, calculable logic of human desire, beautiful objects, and touching voices was unusually salient.[99] This logic is clearer still given that so much abolitionist art was produced by and for women: as Wollstonecraft and others insisted, the sentimental blurring of personhood and objecthood engendered by eighteenth-century market society profoundly shaped women's lives, and in ways that were periodically in tension with the violently extractive kinds of human objectification that abolitionists decried. And, as we will see, in the popular song's beautiful confusion of subject and object, we may detect glimmers of a more recent antagonism—between artwork and commodity.

Haydn's Musical Objects

Haydn began to produce simple songs in bulk only once he had access to a viable local print market: his first twelve lieder, from around 1780, were part of a creative response to the expansion of the Vienna-based Artaria brothers into music publishing. These lieder soon reappeared in Britain and Ireland furnished with new texts, recast as English "ballads." Moreover, throughout the 1780s, English music sellers reprocessed much of Haydn's existing music into this most readily consumable form. Gretchen Wheelock has shown how several song collections bearing Haydn's name appeared in England in the 1780s.[100] Describing their contents as "ballads" or one of the variants of the term *canzonets* (canzonetts, canzonettas),[101] these new Haydn songs were created by pairing a varied selection of light English poetry with tunes extracted from music already in circulation: parts of string quartets, piano sonatas, and even large-scale orchestral compositions.[102] Creating these songs involved locating the smaller musical morsels contained within longer works—those beautifully bounded episodes of implicit vocality—and conferring actual voices upon them: the singable portions of instrumental Adagios and Andantes, the evenly phrased melodies of variation movements, and the recurring dance tunes of rondo finales. The prolific Samuel Arnold, who came to know Haydn personally in the 1790s, published a set of these arrangements with Longman & Broderip in the year that his *Inkle and Yarico* was premiered; in the preface to the volume, he pronounced that Haydn's "beautiful melodies" were "so truly vocal" that they would not suffer from the addition of English poetry.[103] Arnold was one of several arrangers to create snug generic borders around the elegant A major melody from the Andante double variations of the Symphony no. 53—a composition that had been performed regularly in England since the earliest generation of Hanover Square concerts.[104] His version coupled the tune with "Morning," the first of the three verses (along with "Noon" and "Evening") that made up *Day: A Pastoral* by the Anglo-Irish poet John Cunningham. Poems that described themselves as pastorals were one of the verse types that dominated song collections—especially those designated canzonets—alongside an assortment of love songs, elegies, and sea songs.[105]

This was precisely the poetic mixture that Anne Hunter supplied for the first volume of Haydn's *Original Canzonettas* published by Corri, Dussek & Co. in 1794—"original," presumably, because they had not been quarried from existing works and were instead planned from the outset as small, vocal consumer items. Though the printed forms of these canzonettas were oriented toward domestic spaces organized around the piano, they nonetheless found their way quickly into the public arenas where many of Haydn's earlier "canzonetts" had originated. On February 1, 1795, at the residence of the Duke of York, Haydn reportedly performed at least one of these new songs himself at the behest of the king and queen, following an orchestral concert consisting mostly of his own music, though the description of the event in William Parke's *Memoirs* made sure to characterize the episode as one of female domestic intimacy even amid the court spectacle: "Haydn, by desire of the Queen, sat down to the pianoforte, and, surrounded by Her Majesty and her royal and accomplished daughters, sung, and accompanied himself admirably in several of his *Canzonets*."[106] Three days earlier, on an otherwise antiquarian program of the Concert of Antient Music—directed, incidentally, by the ever-present Samuel Arnold—the teenage singer Caroline Poole (who had made her name at Vauxhall) unusually chose to sing what *The Sun* called "a beautiful new *canzonet* by HAYDN"—doubtless one of those most recently published.[107] Performances such as these, which mediated the identity of a celebrity through a popular musical object, were the basis of the later public face of Haydn's canzonettas: the "Pastoral Song"—the third canzonetta in the first volume, whose text paints an innocent picture of youthful pining after an absent love, too cute to be grief—was a favorite with mid-nineteenth-century operatic celebrities, such as Jenny Lind. Early on, critics began to describe this song in particular as the quintessence of daintiness in music. The Leicester industrialist and exuberant musical amateur William Gardiner, in his notes to the 1817 English edition of Stendhal's *Vie de Haydn*, called the "Pastoral Song" a "perfect exhibition of the line of beauty in music" and turned upon its lilting A major tune the full range of Hogarthian adjectives: "The intervals through which the melody passes are so minute, so soft, and delicate, that all the ideas of grace and loveliness are awakened in the mind."[108] As if materializing its status as the very ideal of a luxury musical object, in 1804 Gardiner—who was the heir to a substantial hosiery manufacturing business—chose the opening of the "Pastoral Song" as one of a handful of tunes by Haydn to stitch into several pairs of stockings.[109]

More even than the "Pastoral Song," however, it was the opening canzonetta of the 1794 collection that was most overt in transforming the female performer into an appealing object. Less explicit than such Vauxhall hits as Hook's "Female Auctioneer," "The Mermaid's Song" was nonetheless a barely veiled song of seduction: "come and I will lead the way / Where the pearly treasures be," sings the mermaid in the opening stanza, promising in the second yet more treasures that lie "far below the rolling waves / Riches hid from human eye." These coquettish enticements bring to mind the Austenesque role of female singing and keyboard playing in the theater of eighteenth-century marital negotiation—the kind of ornamental social performances that Wollstonecraft so deplored.[110]

Partly because of its subject, "The Mermaid's Song" radically heightens the impression of attractive surfaces and sonic boundaries that characterized so many eighteenth-century popular songs. It is, above all else, a lavish display of Hogarthian waving lines: the introduction presents a succession of undulating shapes made by sixteenth-note triplets and the burbling ebb and flow of broken chords (fig. 3.10). The initial poetic pretext is clear: these are Hunter's "rolling waves," translated into sound. Yet these waving sonic lines seem also to represent, at other moments, the ululating call of the mermaid herself, perhaps mingling with the sound of the ocean—the keyboard's supernatural supplement to the mermaid's existing vocal line. A warbling sequence of descending triplets in thirds, already introduced from the second measure of the keyboard introduction, later returns as a prelude, and then as an accompaniment, to the vocal refrain, "Come with me and we will go / Where the rocks of corral grow" (fig. 3.11). The triplet motion brings a hazy sparkle to an otherwise straightforward stepwise descent—almost a rhetorical translation of the ambiguous status of Hogarthian waving lines themselves, positioned uncertainly between object and desiring perceiver.

The text repeatedly invokes gleaming or opaque surfaces—the "dancing sunbeams" that "play on the green and glassy sea" and the treasures that "dimly shine in Ocean's caves"—as the waves and voices sonically intermingle. Here is the waving line as alluring voice as soft contour as listener desire—all leading the ear "*a wanton kind of chace*," to recall Hogarth's formulation. And in the refrain that closes each verse, even the passage that establishes the most precise syntactical border serves at the same time to convey the mermaid's most sweetly dangerous appeal, "follow, follow me": a simple ascent from 5 to 1, with an interrupted cadence landing on vi, answered by a plain descent from 4 to 1. At the charming boundaries of this musical object, the

2

THE MERMAIDS SONG.

Canzonetta I.

FIGURE 3.10. The undulating beginning of Haydn's "The Mermaid's Song" from *VI Original Canzonettas* (London: Corri, Dussek, 1794).

text articulates an aesthetics of pursuit: the wanton chase, the sentimental fantasy, produces greater pleasure than any more finite satisfactions.

Haydn's prominent dedication of the 1794 volume of canzonettas to Anne Hunter not only acknowledged his poetic collaborator, who was not credited as coauthor anywhere else in the publication, but also located his songs in a

FIGURE 3.11. Voices, waves, and gleaming surfaces in "The Mermaid's Song."

primarily female economy of interpersonal exchange. This was not without considerable prestige, given the well-known salons at the Hunters' palatial Leicester Square residence, where they had relocated in the 1780s (complete with a purpose-built theater in which John Hunter had performed dissections before paying audiences before his death in 1793).[111] As Emily Green argues, intimate dedications tended to reinforce rather than subvert the principle of market exchange, partaking of the impulse to personalize consumer items, as well as the newer forms of public intimacy that were increasingly part of celebrity self-presentation.[112] Haydn's songs were at the center of exchanges between several prominent women with whom he was friendly during this period in London—not only Anne Hunter but also Rebecca Schroeter, who, it appears, borrowed and copied out Hunter's verses and would surely have played or heard Haydn play his new songs as he produced them.[113] The pianist and composer Cecilia Barthélemon—the daughter of Haydn's friend and colleague, the violinist François-Hippolyte Barthélemon and former student of Johann Samuel Schroeter, the late husband of Rebecca—recalled Haydn performing the canzonettas with his London friends. He presented copies of them to Barthélemon,[114] and her surviving inscriptions on both volumes not only personalize these print objects still further but also describe the sentimental practices that they inspired. "I had the great pleasure to hear the famous Dr. Haydn play & sing his beautiful Canzonetts (in my youth) in my Dear Father's House at Vauxhall," wrote Barthélemon on the second set of canzonettas.[115] Above the second song of the first book, "Recollection," a tender F major Adagio, darkened by passages of chromaticism and throbbing heartbeat figures in the keyboard, Barthélemon wrote, "I heard dear Dr. Haydn, sing this, with peculiar expression—with grateful recollection of his English friends" (fig. 3.12).

She described the same scene in more rhapsodic terms on a surviving manuscript of an Italian aria: "Often have I sat with him when he play'd his Sweet Canzonetts & he used to shed tears *when he sang* 'The Season comes when *first we met* but you return no more' [the canzonetta 'Recollection'] & I said to him, 'Papa Haydn, Why do you cry?' & he said, 'Oh! *my dear Child*. I do not like to leave my English Friends, they are so kind to me!'"[116] This stylized recollection of the weeping Haydn—anticipating his own future recollections via a song about recollection—exemplifies the specular self-awareness of the sentimental mode: pleasure is generated by the fantasy of absent or unattainable things, activated by an object that speaks of them.[117] This is another version of the aesthetics of pursuit, here refracted through an elegiac register. "Why cannot I the days forget / Which time can ne'er restore?" asks the poet. And Haydn's canzonetta transforms the "days too fair, too bright to last" into the melancholy of a permanently desirous present.

Cecilia Barthélemon reciprocated Haydn's musical gift. In 1794, she joined the ranks of eighteenth-century musicians who had dedicated works to Haydn when John Bland published her Keyboard Sonata in G, op. 3.[118] Barthélemon was surely deliberate in her choice of tune in the sonata's rondo finale (the sort of clear-bordered, repeatable musical object that was easily detachable from its formal context): a "hornpipe"—a dance that appeared frequently on the London stage, which had acquired increasingly maritime and national associations in the course of the century.[119] Undeniably neat, the winding line of Barthélemon's hornpipe, with its distinctively short-winded melodic repetitions and heavy downbeats, hardly counts as beautiful (fig. 3.13). It is closer, perhaps, to the comic, neither-beautiful-nor-sublime register that Crotch called "ornamental," at least in its "playfulness of melody" (one of his stylistic criteria).[120]

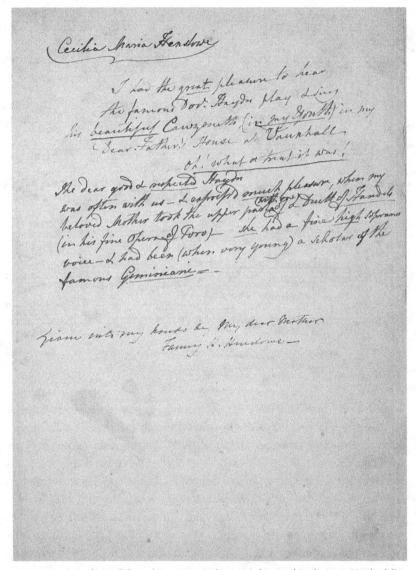

FIGURE 3.12. Cecilia Barthélemon's inscription (in her married name of Cecilia Maria Henslow[e]) on the second volume of Haydn's *Original Canzonettas*. Memorial Library of Music, MLM 493. Courtesy of the Department of Special Collections, Stanford Libraries, Stanford, California.

Notably, in the English-inspired music criticism of Friedrich Rochlitz, Crotch's third aesthetic category was rendered as the *Niedlich*, or cute.[121]

To close a sonata dedicated to Haydn with a hornpipe was to endow a musical object with a cutely ornamental English surface—a memento of the English friends that Haydn professed he would miss, perhaps. Matthew Head

FIGURE 3.13. The opening tune of Cecilia Barthélemon's "Rondo alla hornpipe," from the Piano Sonata op. 3, dedicated to Haydn (London: J. Bland, 1794).

suggests that Haydn may have done something similar in the rondo finale of his Piano Trio in G (Hob. XV:25)—the "Rondo, in the Gypsies stile," one of three published by Longman & Broderip in 1795 and dedicated to Rebecca Schroeter (fig. 3.14).[122] Haydn's vigorous, chattering contredanse tune, and especially the wilder stomping and flourishing in the episodes that frame it, drew on various "national" *verbunkos* idioms associated with the itinerant musicians of Hungary and the Burgenland—idioms that, as Catherine Mayes has shown, were domesticated alongside a range of saleable musical exoticisms in the expanding sphere of printed music.[123] "Haydn may have been representing—or constructing—himself as exotic," proposes Head.[124] In this presentation to his English lover, then, Haydn had perhaps sought to distinguish himself as an audible exotic type—to convert himself into a distinctive ornamental surface.

Surface Fantasies

In a much-discussed passage in *Capital* on commodity fetishism, Marx mused on what the commodity might say if it could speak.[125] As many commentators

FIGURE 3.14. The start of Haydn's "Rondo, in the Gypsies Stile," from the Piano Trio Hob. XV:25, piano part (London: Longman & Broderip, 1795).

have since observed, even though Marx proposed that the commodity would confess that its value consists in nothing but the endless equivalencies of exchange, the unexpected piping up of its voice in the midst of a knotty critique of capitalism uncannily reinforced the very intimacy that its message was supposed to contradict.[126] Even in the very instant of its theoretical disenchantment, the commodity possessed an enchanting voice.

A certain Marxist tradition, especially in the twentieth century, has treated the commodity's seductive voice as mere phantasmagoric mystification—the vocal facet of its gleaming surface, which occludes the reality of exploitative social relations. Thus Adorno, borrowing from Schopenhauer, characterized phantasmagoria—one of the keywords of his Wagnerian critique—as "the outside of the worthless commodity": the enchantingly nebulous exterior of late Romantic orchestration, concealing an essentially mechanistic, reproducible interior.[127] Yet the performative contradiction of Marx's speaking commodity—the voice that persists, in spite of itself—expresses a more complex conception of the relation between people and objects than could feasibly emerge from an analysis predicated on the mere bifurcation of violent economic reality and consoling ideological illusion. As Terry Eagleton has pointed out, *Capital* ultimately indicates that the beautiful surfaces of commodities, and the human intimacies that they foster, are not mere masks, covering deeper realities of economic domination; rather, they are integral to the self-presentation of capitalism—not its mendacious appearance as much as its native sensuous form.[128] Arguably, it is for this reason that Marx begins the exhaustive critique of *Capital* not with one of the usual zero points of classical political economy—labor or nature, say—but with aesthetics: the phenomenal relation of people and the powerful objects among which they must live.

None of this should be surprising from the perspective of the incipient consumer societies of the late eighteenth century. There, as we have seen, consumer objects that acquired voices, as well as voices that were turned into alluring consumer objects, were commonplace. Music historians have long noted that eighteenth-century conceptions of musical beauty were largely coterminous with music's newly marketable object status.[129] Even widespread eighteenth-century notions of sympathetic feeling, as Jean-Christophe Agnew has argued, might be considered the prototype of the commodity, "a universal equivalent into which all other goods could be converted" (a claim that seems far from outlandish nowadays, in the era of calculable sentimental exchanges transacted via social media).[130] Generations of Romantics have sought to distinguish art from commodity, the voices of others from self-centered projections, true feeling from false sentiment, and the deep interior of subjects from the shining exterior of objects—but, from the eighteenth- and twenty-first-century perspectives, these distinctions look like anxious (and almost always doomed) attempts to prize apart concepts that are inseparably conjoined.

Consider the *Specimens of Various Styles of Music*, compiled by that theorist of ornamental musical surfaces William Crotch—a multivolume publication that synthesized materials from the courses of lectures he had delivered at Oxford University and the Royal Institution in London in the early years of the nineteenth century. In this curiosity cabinet of musical excerpts, mostly culled from existing printed sources, the Allegretto from Haydn's Symphony no. 82 sat alongside the songs of ancient Greece, Israel, and China; sections of oratorios by Handel, overtures by Gluck, and a Sanctus by Gibbons; not to mention all sorts of "national music," from Canada and Scotland to Madras and South Africa, from an English "Cobbler's Hornpipe" (one thinks of Barthélemon) to Hungarian dance melodies (one thinks of Haydn) (fig. 3.15).[131]

Crotch described his sample of global musical types as *specimens*—exemplars of various species or kinds, as in the natural sciences.[132] If, as Sarah Day-O'Connell has proposed, Haydn and Anne Hunter's musical collabora-tions bear the traces of John Hunter's proximate anatomical preoccupations, then here we see Haydn's music positioned among myriad sonic specimens of humanity.[133] Each one is distinguishable by its musical surface, its own musi-cal voice—appreciable even though (or perhaps because) Crotch had made every specimen knowable and comparable via the medium of the keyboard.

This appealing storefront of voice-specimens, neatly boxed and ready to be examined upon the family piano, should, I think, give music schol-ars pause. For it recognizably exhibits, and trains listeners to identify, the distinctive "surfaces" that many theorists of eighteenth-century music, es-pecially practitioners of topic theory, have since valorized, often with po-lemical urgency—the "images of our own humanity [that] define the surface of late eighteenth-century instrumental music and constitute its power," to quote Allanbrook.[134] As we have seen, the eighteenth-century aesthetic of small musical consumer objects, to which Haydn responded most directly in his London songs and chamber music, was predicated on the very idea of such musical surfaces, and arguably even made the counterintuitive idea of a Hogarthian musical surface plausible: the gleaming boundaries, alluring contours, and intimate voice of the musical commodity. Haydn's "Rondo, in the Gypsies stile," Barthélemon's English "Rondo alla hornpipe"—each in-scribed its author and the author's "nation" in the ornamental surface of a sentimental consumer item. James Currie advocates suspicion of these varied yet legible surfaces, and particularly the virtuous, "democratic" pluralism that a critical attention to them is sometimes taken to imply: a "musical surface,"

FIGURE 3.15. The world's voices become audible: from the index to William Crotch's *Specimens of Various Styles of Music*, vol. 1 (London: Robert Birchall, 1807).

he observes, is neither historically given nor phenomenally self-evident.[135] Indeed, as Crotch's collection of diverse musical specimens clearly shows, these multifarious surfaces were taxonomized and made available in large part by the economically acquisitive and omniaudient colonial ear.[136] Moreover, even though the disciplinary regimes of modern racial science did not yet determine how most eighteenth-century Europeans conceptualized race,[137] the surface-oriented gaze of eighteenth-century beauty, enshrined musically in such publications as Crotch's *Specimens of Various Styles of Music*, was surely among the preconditions for Europe's emerging "racial epidermal schema," to use Frantz Fanon's phrase.[138] Not yet the scientifically racialized hierarchies of late nineteenth-century style criticism, Crotch's collection of distinct musical specimens nonetheless represented their epistemological premise.[139]

The eighteenth-century prehistory of the musical commodity is another reminder, then, of the limits of the liberal politics of voice—the assumption, recently unsettled in music studies by James Davies, that "speech equates with freedom" and that "political and moral emancipation" can only be secured by the possession of voice.[140] Wendy Brown's critique of "compulsory discursivity" and the attendant "fetish of breaking silence," from which Davies draws his inspiration, describes a dynamic whereby "those historically excluded from liberal personhood" are forever enjoined or obliged to emerge from the discursive shadows, to attain a new articulacy in the form of "slave ballads, the flaunting of forbidden love, the labor theory of value, or the quantification of housework"—confessional and reparative genres that are inevitably subject to their own regulatory norms and disciplinary strictures.[141] Everything must have its own voice—its own recognizable surface, its "own native colour," as Clarkson put it—in order to register as a political agent. More than that, even: every voice must come in its own box. Ellen Lockhart elegantly demonstrates how near-metaphorical voices and boxes became conceptually intertwined in the early nineteenth century—not least in the invented "voice box" of contemporary medical discourse: to be a vocalizing subject was to be contained within clear proprietorial boundaries.[142] It seems to me that the gendered and racialized history of garrulous or songful objects in the eighteenth-century marketplace should make us more cautious still. The blatant political shortcomings of an anthology such as Crotch's *Specimens of Various Styles of Music* are not curable with the usual liberal remedies: including more specimens, or taking greater care to listen out for misrepresentation or mere ventriloquism (an echo of an old sentimental anxiety). Having one's own voice is not inconsistent with being a mere specimen; it is a prerequisite.

It is partly for this reason that several theorists of race, and especially of Blackness, have turned away from the most articulate instances of apparent subaltern testimony and toward moments of meaningful inarticulacy, untranslatable bodilyness, or historical uncertainty as the basis of an emancipatory politics. Stephen Best has even queried the ethics of the "recovery imperative" so central to the historiography of slavery, with its foundational metaphor of "giving voice" to the voiceless.[143] Are voices always so legible? Some time ago, Lindon Barrett insisted that the answer should be no: the aesthetics of the Black voice, he argued, refuses the subordination of "singing voice" to "signing voice" that supposedly inaugurated the European enlightenment subject.[144] And Fred Moten went further still, reinterpreting Marx's speaking commodity not beside its chatty eighteenth-century forebears but against the scream that Frederick Douglass recalled hearing from his aunt Hester as she was beaten—an extreme vocal disruption issuing from the person-made-object that, argued Moten, resists the violent logic of exchange value.[145] This commodity has a voice but neither signs nor sings. Even so, the resistance of this human object became, in Moten's interpretation, the basis of a coherent—if fissured and paradoxical—"aesthetics" and so retained something of the old avant-garde promise that even the most radical rupture or disjunction might, however transiently, congeal as an involuted formal process, quicksilver performance, or knotty artwork, with the potential to elude or subvert capitalist principles of value.

Whether or not we still believe in the critical potential of a "radical aesthetics"—especially in the avant-garde spirit—it is plain, I hope, that Haydn's commodity aesthetic entertained no such resistance. Within a predominantly female sentimental economy, Haydn contributed to a musical corpus in which people became beautiful objects and objects acquired beautiful voices, in a never-ending exchange. To that extent, the small-scale music of London's early commercial society might be positioned in the deep history of what, in theorizing the modern construction of Asian femininity, Anne Cheng calls "ornamentalism": the aesthetic principle according to which commodified identities are wrought through "fabrics, ornaments, and 'skins' that never enjoyed the fantasy of organicity," the epidermal thresholds of the self upon which meanings and emotions are impressed.[146] Haydn's musical commodities were not produced or consumed on the assumption that art is a humanizing corrective to the alienating reifications of capitalism; rather, they celebrated a new human economy in which objects and people increasingly constituted one another.

4

Work

Human productivity was by definition bound to result in a Promethean revolt because it could erect a man-made world only after destroying part of God-created nature.
HANNAH ARENDT, *The Human Condition* (1958)[1]

Chapel Master, Chapel Servant

For most of his life, Haydn was constantly busy. Besides the daily business of rehearsing and directing the orchestra maintained by the Esterházy family, and supplying music for the court's chapels and ballrooms, Haydn oversaw the practical side of the family's major theater for over a decade. And yet, until late in his career, it is not obvious that Haydn had been busy with *work*—that value-producing discharge of human energies that was to underwrite the nineteenth-century regime of wage labor. Duties he had in abundance. His terse 1761 contract, drawn up when he accepted the post of Vice-Kapellmeister with the Esterházy court, had listed several of them, decidedly routine sounding by the standards of the modern culture hero:

> Joseph Heyden shall appear daily (whether here in Vienna or on his estates) in the *antichambre* before and after midday, and inquire whether a high princely *ordre* for a musical performance has been given; to wait for this order and upon its receipt to communicate its contents to the other *Musici*; and not only himself to appear punctually at the required time but to take serious care that others do so as well, specifically noting those who either arrive later or absent themselves entirely.[2]

This was less *work* than *service*—a principle of zealously performed loyalty that would continue as long as the hierarchical social relations that it helped to sustain. Even in 1802—which is to say, by the time that Haydn was a wealthy musical celebrity—his latest Esterházy prince, Nikolaus II, took the trouble to write irascibly from Eisenstadt to remind his Kapellmeister that he was responsible for ensuring that "all the individual members of the band show the proper obedience" and that their "various duties be performed in an exemplary manner"—duties that included "personal appearance, care of uniforms, and other tokens of good behavior," along with music making.³

Such ostensibly menial duties were in many respects continuous with musical performances at court, and even shared their evanescence, since they were not intended to produce property and certainly not capital. Rather—in a logic that was, during this period, violently radicalized in transatlantic slavery—it was the laboring potential of the subject's whole person that the Esterházy contract claimed. To the extent that Haydn's repeated exertions produced more lasting byproducts, these necessarily belonged to his prince. As the 1761 contract had put it,

> The said *Vice-Capel-Meister* shall be under permanent obligation to compose such pieces of music as His Serene Princely Highness may command, and neither to communicate such new compositions to anyone, nor to allow them to be copied, but to retain them wholly for the exclusive use of his Highness; nor shall he compose for any other person without the knowledge and gracious permission [of his Highness].⁴

This rule was to change along with a revised set of contractual conditions in the late 1770s, as a generation of music sellers in Vienna and beyond sought to tap Haydn's uncapitalized musical labor. But, even then, the bulk of Haydn's labor was used up within the Esterházy court—at least until the London trips of the 1790s.

Haydn certainly reflected on the meaning of work. His mature retellings of his biography noticeably cleaved to an enlightened ideal of ethical self-fashioning—a conception of unstinting application that was more frequently denoted by a word such as *Fleiß* rather than *Arbeit* (work).⁵ *Fleiß* is sometimes translated as "industry"—though in the early modern sense of the English word, since *Fleiß* did not connote urban mass production—but one might also render it as "application" or "diligence," both of which capture its connotations of prudence, as well as allegiance to a principle of conduct.⁶ Haydn would profess to Griesinger late in life that he had advanced in his profession only "through much Fleiß."⁷ "Young people can see from my example that something may still come from nothing," he told Dies, around the same time.⁸ And in the autobiographical sketch that Haydn provided to *Das gelehrte Oesterreich* in 1776, he explicitly contrasted the self-depleting scourge of wage labor—"many geniuses run aground because of their need to earn their daily bread," he ruefully observed—with the more productive kind of Fleiß by which he had flourished: a "zeal for composition [*Compositions Eyfer*]" compelled him to produce music "well into the night."⁹ This was less

a Weberian work ethic than a principle of dedication appropriate to dynas-
tic politics—the principle elaborated in Karl von Eckartshausen's *Sittenlehren für alle Stände der Menschen zur Bildung junger Hertzen*, a popular guide
to everyday ethical instruction that sat on Haydn's bookshelf.[10] In his own
teaching, Haydn regularly voiced views on the moral necessity of Fleiß in the
straightforward, earnest style of Eckartshausen: "With application and effort
[*mit Fleiß und Mühe*] he can become a distinguished man yet," he informed
the father of one of his charges in 1804.[11]

Subversions and inversions of such solemn court hierarchies had for centuries been the premise of comedy, not least in the clownish servant roles of
the commedia dell'arte, which in turn populated the topsy-turvy world of Italian comic opera—a carnivalesque of interchanging masters and servants that
was signaled, as in Pergolesi's *La serva padrona*, even in the names of the century's most frequently performed and debated examples. It was doubtless this
species of comic inversion that Haydn had in mind when, in 1790, he wrote to
Marianne von Genzinger describing his chastening return to a drab and dis-
orderly Eszterháza following weeks of celebrity-level pampering amid the Viennese beau monde over the Christmas period: "Nothing could console me,
my whole house was in confusion," he wrote. "I could only sleep very little,
even my dreams persecuted me; and then, just when I was happily dreaming
that I was listening to the opera *Le nozze di Figaro*, that horrible North wind
woke me and almost blew my nightcap off my head." To this soundtrack of
comic opera, Haydn went on to recall, Leporello-like, Vienna's many tempting delicacies, comparing them unfavorably with the offerings in the Eszterháza mess hall: "instead of that delicious slice of beef, a chunk of cow 50 years
old; instead of a ragout with little dumplings, an old sheep with carrots." And
Haydn conceived of this transformation from grand Kapellmeister into flus-
tered buffo character explicitly in terms of sovereignty and servitude: "I found
everything at home in confusion, and for three days I didn't know if I was
Chapel Master or Chapel Servant [*CapellMeister oder Capelldiener*]."[12]

Liberty, Work, Stress

Within a year of sending this letter, Haydn's status had changed beyond recognition. His prince, Nikolaus I, was no more, the Esterházy orchestra was
disbanded, and Haydn was feted on all sides in London—hailed as a "great
Sovereign of the tuneful art" in a grandiloquent poem of welcome published
by Charles Burney.[13] Only months into his English excursion, however, following his inaugural season in London and several weeks of travel in the

English provinces, the newly crowned musical sovereign wrote to von Genzinger about work once again—not to puzzle over his status as master or servant but to bemoan the unending burden of Arbeit.

> Oh, my dear and gracious Lady, a certain freedom tastes sweet indeed. I had a
> good Prince but was at times subordinate to base souls. I often sighed for re-
> lease, and now I have it to some extent. And I recognize the benefit of all this,
> even if my mind [Geist] is burdened with more work [Arbeith]. The awareness
> of being no bonded servant [kein gebundener Diener] compensates for all the
> effort [Mühe]. As dear as this freedom is, I nevertheless gladly long to be once
> again in the service of Prince Esterházy, only for the sake of my poor family.[14]

This was a notable admission to the wife of Nikolaus I's former personal phy-
sician; perhaps Haydn thought that his friend would understand his feelings
especially well. Now that his daily habits were no longer explicitly regulated
by the reciprocal principles of mastery and servitude but ostensibly by the
forms of liberal self-governance appropriate to London's musical marketplace, Haydn began to describe a distinctively modern psychosocial predicament, which would plague him throughout his years in England: stress.[15]
Haydn had come to interpret his prior situation at the Esterházy court as a
set of constraints and his London experiences as newfound freedom. But this
freedom meant work.

When he wrote this letter, in the early fall of 1791, Haydn had no conception that the coming London season would be the most exposing professional
challenge he had yet faced. At the end of the year, his former student Pleyel
joined the rival Professional Concert. Maintaining cordial relations despite
the constant hype of the press, master and pupil engaged in several semipub-
lic rituals of hierarchy and mutual respect, enough to put Haydn at ease. But
time was short, and Haydn began to conceive of his vanishing hours and days
in terms of productivity. In January 1792, he wrote again to von Genzinger,

> I am tormented, here in London, by having to attend all sorts of private con-
> certs, which cause me a great loss of time; and by the vast amount of work
> [Arbeithen] which has been heaped on my shoulders, you would, my gracious
> Lady, have the greatest pity on me. I never in my life wrote so much in one year
> as I have here during this past one, but now I am almost completely exhausted
> and it will do me good to be able to rest a little when I return home. At present
> I am working [ich arbeithe] for Salomon's concerts, and I am making every
> effort to do my best.

"I, or rather my brain, is indeed exhausted," he added.[16]

By early March, the situation had deteriorated. If he had previously considered a return to his Esterházy service on account of his family, Haydn now

professed to long for escape, as his freedom revealed its dependence on a new kind of servitude:

> There isn't a day, not a single day, in which I am without work [*ohne Arbeith*], and I shall thank the dear Lord when I can leave London—the sooner the better. My labors [*Arbeithen*] have been augmented by the arrival of my pupil Pleyel, whom the Professional Concert have brought here. He arrived here with a lot of new compositions, but they had been composed long ago; he therefore promised to present a new piece every evening. As soon as I saw this, I realized at once that a lot of people were dead set against me, and so I announced publicly that I would likewise produce 12 different new pieces. In order to keep my word, and to support poor Salomon, I must be the sacrificial victim and work [*arbeithen*] the whole time. But I really do feel it. My eyes suffer the most, and I have many sleepless nights.[17]

Within the bounds of the Esterházy court, Haydn was an affective laborer. But now the loyal service of the court Kapellmeister had become the toil of the service worker.

The Work of Comedy

On the surface, the ambience of the music that Haydn exerted himself to produce, rehearse, and perform during these months barely matches the desperate mood of his letters. The very day that Haydn complained of aching eyes and sleepless nights to von Genzinger concluded with the premiere of his grand and comical Symphony no. 98: "The new Symphony in B-flat was given, the first and last Allegros encort," Haydn proudly recorded in his notebook.[18] Its long and rambunctious concluding Allegro, though not appreciably strained or strenuous, nonetheless gives the impression of a musician wildly running through all the strategies he knew to serve the paying public—a translation of the social relations that newly mediated Haydn's music into an aesthetic, an adaption of the Italianate comic register that had long shaped his music to London's concert scene. As in several of the London symphonies, the Allegro lurches between various species of genial pastoral, an exhortative maestoso register, and the nervous rhythmic-melodic repetitions redolent of operatic ensembles. Here, though, the contrasts are acute: the opening 6/8 gigue tune, carried by the strings and a solo oboe, is answered by a grand tutti with trumpets and drums. Then, creeping onstage with comic hesitancy—the violins test and retest the gigue's characteristic two-note upbeat and staccato downbeat before continuing—a brief transition leads to a clattering rustic dance, with *forzato* offbeats and sliding half-step pitch bending in the winds and strings. And there is more: a short, entreating solo in the oboe, which is swept away in a forthright cadence.

The music that follows is more or less all about syntactic closure, with all manner of detours and interventions on the way. It begins with a cumulative passage in the violins, its series of repeating melodic tags arranged as questions and answers—a device straight from the world of comic opera. The passage repeats, gathering in force, the questions and answers having now acquired a quirky chromatic embellishment; this time around, an oboe joins in with the answers, and a pair of bassoons provide background offbeats. This increasingly madcap musical context gives the brassy tattoo that suddenly intervenes a mock-heroic aspect—particularly when the response involves, once again, the violins' becoming awkwardly snagged on the way to a cadence: twice they try out the same gesture, only to land on a pitch a half step too high. And even amid the concluding cadential flourishes and fanfares that follow, a dramatic unison passage in the strings is gently tripped up by a syncopated lunge toward the flattened sixth scale degree.

Tuneful rather than thematically knotty, the bold characterizations of the finale are achieved in large part by the demarcation of distinct instrumental characters, which support the movement's broad physical comedy.[19] The development section is accordingly concerned less with devices that sound like thematic manipulation than with exaggerating the foregoing gestural and timbral contrasts. To start with, a colorful unprepared modulation—up by a third—announces a solo violin carrying the repeating melodic tags from earlier, over a simple oompah accompaniment.[20] It is important to remember that this would have been a specific violinist: Salomon, "in the hollow of the piano" at which Haydn was seated, "on a high platform," as Charlotte Papendiek recalled it.[21] So when Salomon's part too—in the most harmonically ambiguous moment of the movement—gets snagged on the two-note upbeat and staccato downbeat from the gigue tune (fig. 4.1), the running joke would have been balder still. The development section consists of three of these violin solos (the second combined with flute) divided by stormy orchestral modulations. On the third, the violin's hesitations are the most dramatic yet, hovering on a pair of fermatas before turning once again to the two-note upbeat and staccato downbeat derived from the gigue. The broken repetitions of this melodic fragment are by now predictable, but on this occasion, they feel their way toward a full reprise of the gigue tune, now played by the solo violinist alone.

The abbreviated recapitulation ends by declining its energetic drive toward closure and grandly announcing a long coda. First, as if exhausted from the perpetual testing of successive musical tactics to entertain and amuse, the strings present a quiet statement of the gigue marked *Più moderato*, with

FIGURE 4.1. Johann Salomon gets "stuck" during his solo (third stave down). The development section of the finale of the Symphony no. 98, in Salomon's quintet arrangement, first violin part. From *Haydn's Grand Symphonies, Composed for Mr. Salomon's Concerts and arranged for five Instruments* (London: Robert Birchall, 1800).

a chromatic staccato variation. This slackening of tension only increases the power of the sudden orchestral eruption that elides with the last cadence of the tune's eight measures—violins racing downward in sixteenth notes before settling into an expansive cadential pattern, prominent horns adding an ebullient pastoral character. But this turns out to be a buildup to the entrance of a solo keyboard. This would, of course, have been Haydn himself. Until this stage, the composer would have been providing unobtrusive continuo. But what turns out to be the final statement of the gigue is now coupled with the conspicuous tinkling of music-box arpeggios high up in the piano. And this is the last gambit of the piece: with the end of the gigue tune, the symphony sweeps to a brassy conclusion.

Haydn's culminating insertion of himself into his symphony was the apogee of the movement's incessant impulse to please—a moment, moreover, in which it displayed its author busily at work. The overall impression, especially in this passage, is of zaniness—surely the most appropriate word, given the long association of the zany with service labor. Sianne Ngai's excavation of the zany aesthetic, with its origin in the *zanni* servant roles of the commedia dell'arte, emphasizes its "stressed-out, even desperate quality," balanced precariously at the "politically ambiguous intersection between cultural and occupational performance, acting and service, playing and laboring"—more or less where Haydn was positioned during his surprise piano solo, and indeed throughout his stressed-out periods of overwork in London.[22] In this respect, Haydn's London music might recall the behavior of that quintessential eighteenth-century musical zany, Rameau's nephew, Denis Diderot's comic creation, whose pathological cycling through an immense repertoire of mismatched sociomusical performances—"singing, shouting, waving about like a madman, being in himself dancer and ballerina, singer and prima donna"—appears, as Roger Grant observes, to escalate the stylistic estrangements and self-conscious commentaries of Italian comic opera to the point of grotesque.[23] But where the nephew's desperate social climbing appears to have provoked his unhinged version of the affective labor of the court musician, the zaniness of Haydn's London music seems to have been, in part, a reaction to the increasing absorption of this affective labor by the marketplace.[24] To produce his promised twelve new symphonies, Haydn drew upon a vast reservoir of musical resources, honed by decades of court service, yet in London's concert scene, his work served nobody in particular—or, rather, anybody who was able and willing to pay. And, in the music's all-hands-on-deck desperation to please, the result is frequently an absurdist vein of musical comedy, even amid a tone of solemnity and grandeur. As Adorno once mused, "Music has become comic in the present phase primarily because something so completely useless is carried on with all the visible signs of the strain of serious work."[25]

Haydn's evanescent performance of musical labor was not wholly amenable to reproduction, it seems, whether in performance by others or as notation. In the piano quintet arrangement of the Symphony no. 98, created and published by Salomon, the status of the zany piano solo evidently proved troublesome, in part because it was not yet fully thinkable apart from Haydn's embodiment of it in the Hanover Square rooms, nor from the most up-to-date English piano he had played there, with its extra notes (compared to most contemporary instruments) tinkling at the top of the keyboard. Salomon's solution was to place the relevant passage at the foot of the page (fig. 4.2) with a special instruction (which also amounted to an advertisement for the latest

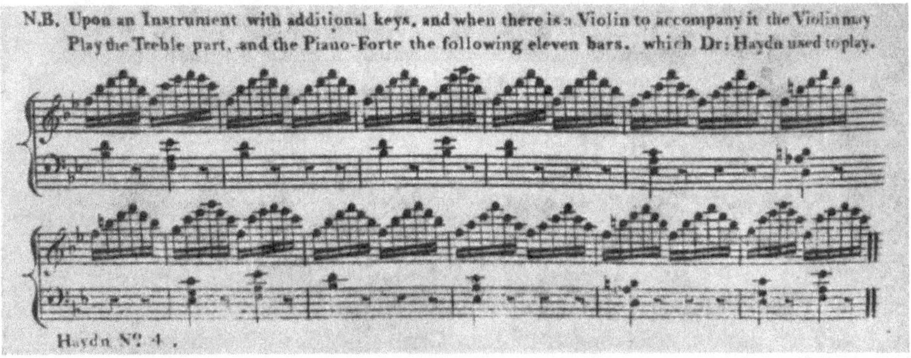

FIGURE 4.2. The marginal trace of Haydn's Hanover Square performance in Salomon's quintet arrangement of the finale of the Symphony no. 98.

piano technologies): "Upon an instrument with additional keys [i.e., the extra high notes], and when there is a Violin to accompany it, the Violin may Play the Treble part [i.e., the tune] and the Piano-Forte the following eleven bars, which Dr. Haydn used to play." In this passage, the work was not yet fully detachable from the musical worker.

Work, Property, Works

On April 14, 1791—six weeks or so after the premiere of the Symphony no. 98—Haydn was deposed before the Court of Exchequer in Westminster Hall (with Salomon acting as interpreter) as a witness in a dispute between Longman & Broderip and William Forster over the ownership of three piano trios (Hob. XV:3–5) that Haydn had sent to London in the 1780s. A contract from 1786, almost certainly produced as evidence in the case, shows that Forster had paid the substantial sum of £70 for a wide selection of musical works.[26] In the meantime, Longman & Broderip had independently been importing music engravings to London via Artaria, in the process revealing not only the fragile legal basis upon which Haydn had declared Forster "the sole proprietor of the said works" but also that two of the piano trios published in London were by none other than Pleyel, whose work Haydn had claimed as his own.[27] Yet these early legal tangles did not prevent Haydn from endorsing similar contracts with Salomon at the end of his London visits. In 1795, he granted Salomon "exclusive rights" to the first six London symphonies, and the next year he signed a contract declaring Salomon the "sole owner and proprietor" of the second six, promising to make "no other but personal use of them." One might consider these legally enshrined relationships, as well as the printed transcriptions, excerpts, and performance parts that appeared in London over next decade, as the technologies by which Salomon continued to extract value from work that Haydn had performed years before.[28]

"Labour is a commodity like any other," pronounced Edmund Burke in 1795.[29] Earlier in the century, such a belief would have been far from self-evident—and radicals such as William Cobbett continued to dispute it well into the nineteenth century.[30] By the time of Haydn's London visits, the distinctively English association of work, property, and liberty was a commonplace of popular patriotism, celebrated in Hogarth's series *Industry and Idleness* and in such songs as Henry Green's ode to British naval prowess, "The Wooden Walls of Olde England," which glorified the relation between freedom and work that Haydn came to experience with such ambivalence: "Liberty rewards the toil / Of Industry, to labour prone."[31]

Governing such popular notions was a Lockean conception of property—part of the old legal covenants of the English Restoration. In the primordial scenario imagined by Locke, property was produced as if from the metabolic interaction of two separate but otherwise compatible natures, the laboring body and the natural world in which it resides. "The *labour* of his body, and the *work* of his hands, we may say, are properly his," reasoned the canonical passage from the *Second Treatise of Government.* "Whatsoever then he removes out of the state that nature hath provided, and left it in, he hath mixed his *labour* with, and joined it to something that is his own, and thereby makes it his *property*."[32] Throughout the eighteenth century, however, which materials counted as natural resources and which kinds of labor successfully produced property from them were in a permanent state of renegotiation. The legal strictures that helped to produce musical property, which Haydn personally encountered in Westminster Hall, had only recently begun to regulate the behavior of English booksellers, and there remained widespread skepticism of the notion that any single person could claim ownership of something as spectral as a gathering of musical or literary ideas—the kind of property, moreover, that plainly owed its existence to the unending collaboration of peers and precursors.[33] Linking authorship with ownership along orthodox Lockean lines thus involved recasting the creative process as an improbable form of agriculture. The East Anglian Unitarian minister William Enfield was one of many pamphleteers who appropriated the Virgilian georgic image of husbandry in his 1774 *Observations On Literary Property*: "It is not more evident that the corn which the husbandman gathers into his barn is the fruit of his labour in manuring the ground, sowing the seed, and gathering in the harvest; than that a train of ideas and words, not to be found in any other work, hath been the result of genius and understanding industriously employed."[34] In the year that this polemic was published, the decision in *Donaldson v. Beckett* supported, in English law, a concept of literary property founded upon authorship—though it would be misleading to regard this decision as either a watershed or wholly conclusive.[35] Three years later, Johann Christian Bach's successful suit against the music seller James Longman meant that, in England, published music was, notionally at least, to be subject to the same legal rules as printed books, as opposed to the engraving of pictures and maps.[36]

The dispute between Longman & Broderip and Forster that centered on Haydn thus tested some of the latest developments in English law. Still, to most eighteenth-century thinkers, the printed media that music sellers exchanged was hardly the paradigmatic form that musical labor took. Even Adam Smith, who adopted the broadly Lockean stance that all "vendible commodities" were nothing more than "a certain quantity of labour stocked and stored up to be employed, if necessary, upon some other occasion," counted music making among the "unproductive" forms of labor, unsuited to the usual mechanisms of storage and exchange. The "declamation of the actor, the harangue of the orator, or the tune of the musician, the work of all of them perishes in the very instant of its production," he pronounced—these would never congeal into conservable forms, would dissipate before they could be absorbed within a system of exchange.[37] Given Smith's examples, his claim might appear to be primarily about texts versus acts, or technological mediation versus some early conception of liveness. But his was an argument about the production and reproduction of economic value, and his distinction between unproductive and productive labor accordingly echoed the contrast, experienced personally by Haydn, between performative musical service, of the kind described in his 1761 Esterházy contract, and the carefully priced work cataloged in his 1786 contract with Forster. This is to say that, to Smith, service—the forms of labor that Michael Hardt and Antonio Negri once called *immaterial*—still lay outside of the domain of capital altogether.[38] On the same assumption, Marx, in the *Grundrisse*, would endorse Smith's division of unproductive from productive labor, and with recourse to the same musical model: the piano maker, but not the pianist, he argued, generates and reproduces capital.[39] As the Lockean terms of Hannah Arendt's *The Human Condition* would have it, musical production continued to occupy the uncertain space between the "labor of bodies" and the "work of hands"—*labor* that is consumed in the very process of sustaining itself and *work* that fabricates the more lasting furniture of human civilization, forever positioned against the inevitable decay of an imagined nature.[40] From this perspective, even the equivocal, marginal reappearance of the zany piano solo "which Dr. Haydn

used to play" in Salomon's quintet version of the Symphony no. 98 is not only
the mark of a particular historical event on a text. It is the residual trace of
transient musical labor on a more lasting work.

The Creation Concept

Lasting works became Haydn's main preoccupation upon his return to Vienna. Between 1796 and 1801, Haydn and the music antiquarian Gottfried
Baron van Swieten collaborated on *The Creation* and *The Seasons*, Handelian
oratorios that were self-consciously conceived and received as masterworks.

By and large, music scholarship has described the recovery and persistence of musical works in late eighteenth-century urban centers via the paradigm of "canon formation"—as a question of increasing historical awareness and ideologies of the "classic," ultimately guaranteed by the immaterial
metaphysic of the work concept.[41] But to reconsider the work concept via
the concept of work—as labor that has been "stocked and stored up to be
employed, if necessary, upon some other occasion," to recall Adam Smith's
formulation—is to be reminded not only that economic conceptions of work
and the noneconomic conceptions of the masterwork have shared origins but
also that what we call canons are produced and sustained by an immense
investment of human energies, a tangle of practices and materials.[42]

Among the many things that Haydn brought back from London to Vienna
in 1795, when he nominally resumed his service with the Esterházy family,
was a conception of the musical work derived from English legal frameworks.
In 1796, he signed a potentially lucrative contract with Frederick Augustus
Hyde—a Londoner connected with Clementi and his associates—in which
Hyde promised to purchase any "new and Original Compositions" that
Haydn produced over the next five years, up to the value of £150 per year,
and Haydn in turn pledged to send all such compositions to Hyde before
any of his competitors.[43] The contract listed the advance prices of a range of
genres: £60 for three piano sonatas or six Italian songs, £75 for three string
quartets or six English songs, £100 for three symphonies.[44] In the event, being
otherwise occupied with the late masses and the two late oratorios, Haydn
produced a scant quantity of music in these genres between 1796 and 1801.
Even so, the contract made thinkable the future expenditure of his energies as
a prepackaged series of works, listed and priced as pure potential—equivalent
units of authorial labor, which Haydn had yet to discharge.

Even the late eighteenth-century English reinvention of the Handel oratorio, which crucially shaped van Swieten and Haydn's vision of *The Creation*,
might be conceived less as a newly historicist or monumentalizing aesthetic

than a reconfigured bundle of technologies and institutions.[45] These included principles of association (the Concert of Antient Music and the Handel festivals in Westminster Abbey), formats such as the keyboard transcription (the 1790s witnessed an avalanche of publications of Handelian excerpts by music sellers who also worked closely with Haydn), places of ritual veneration (such as the 1738 statue of Handel by Louis François Roubiliac in Vauxhall Gardens, which Haydn recorded seeing in his London notebooks),[46] and relatively new genres, such as the musician biography (John Mainwaring's *Memoirs of the Life of the late George Frederic Handel* was one of the earliest examples).[47]

Van Swieten, along with such music-loving patrons as Prince Joseph Schwarzenberg, had sought to foster similar institutions in Vienna. "Every year he gives some grand and magnificent concerts, where only pieces by the old masters are performed," wrote Johann Ferdinand von Schönfeld of van Swieten in his 1796 musical yearbook. "His great love is for the Handel style from which great choruses are often performed."[48] Van Swieten was the founder of the Gesellschaft der Associierten Cavaliere (a society that sponsored musical performances in the 1780s and 1790s with an antiquarian bent) and was also involved with the Tonkünstler Societät—the Musicians' Benevolent Society, with its tradition of Lenten and Advent choral concerts. Both of these societies guaranteed that, to the extent that there was a public concert scene in Vienna in the late eighteenth century, its musical character was markedly Handelian. In the late 1780s, van Swieten had commissioned Mozart to produce a series of reorchestrations of works by Handel—*Messiah, Judas Maccabaeus, Alexander's Feast*, the *Ode to St. Cecilia*, and *Acis and Galatea*—and these sonically weightier versions remained standard in Vienna and elsewhere well into the nineteenth century.[49] Even the original poem of *The Creation*—which was presented to Haydn in London, and which van Swieten turned into a bilingual libretto—was a relic of the English Handel tradition, having reportedly been intended for Handel himself.[50] Van Swieten's leaner poem retained the basic ingredients of the earlier one: biblical phrases from Genesis and passages adapted from Milton's *Paradise Lost*—which is to say that the poem reproduced excerpts from two of the most reprinted books of the eighteenth century.[51]

The materials of the Handelian tradition upon which *The Creation* drew—its texts and publications, its institutions and associational practices—were more than agents of "canon formation," then. Like the contracts that Haydn signed with Salomon at the end of his London trips, they were new mechanisms for extracting value from the labor of the dead.[52] In the years following his return from England, Haydn became increasingly sensitive to the idea that his music was destined to outlive him. In a reply to the 142 musicians of the Parisian Concert des Amateurs, who had sent him a medal following the French premiere of *The Creation*, Haydn wrote, "I have often doubted whether my name would survive me; but your kindness inspires me with confidence, and the token of esteem with which you have honored me justifies my hope that perhaps I SHALL NOT WHOLLY DIE."[53]

Haydn's *Creation* thus plied between the contrasting yet entwined worlds of economic and cultural capital.[54] In England, before so much as a measure of Haydn's new oratorio had been heard, it sparked another round of legal disputes: Salomon, who had helped to procure the poem, threatened Haydn with a lawsuit as soon as he heard that his friend was setting it—doubtless with the aim of receiving a cut of the profits that this valuable piece of Handelian real estate would generate, at the very least by securing the opportunity to present its London premiere.[55] In Vienna, by contrast, *The Creation* entered commercial arenas more obliquely. It was rehearsed before a select group of musicians and noblemen in the Schwarzenberg Palace on April 29, 1798, and received a premiere in front of a barely less exclusive group in the palace the next day. "Prince Schwarzenberg," recalled the Swedish diplomat and Haydn fanatic Fredrik Samuel Silverstolpe, "was so utterly enchanted by the many beauties of the work that he presented the composer with a roll containing one hundred ducats, over and above the 500 that were part of the agreement": this gesture of patronage—of aristocratic gift exchange—recast Haydn's work as, once again, a species of court service.[56] Similarly exclusive concerts were staged on May 7 and 10, and in the Lobkowitz and Schwarzenberg Palaces the next year. It was March 19, 1799, before *The Creation* was presented to a more mixed, paying public in the Burgtheater, when the streets were reportedly thronged by a crowd numbering in the hundreds. The *Allgemeine musikalische Zeitung* reported that the theater earned "a sum that has never been taken in by any Viennese theater," partly because of a hike in the price of a box.[57]

Haydn's *Creation* burst upon these aristocratic and commercial scenes with nothing less than a theatrical performance of his authorial labor—his musical creation of light. Following the oratorio's fractured overture, the C minor "Representation of Chaos," the divine injunction "let there be light" in the chorus—words that had been the epitome of the biblical sublime ever since Longinus, and which Handel had previously set in his oratorio *Samson*—provokes a sudden blast of brass and drums in C major, which banishes the foregoing minor-mode darkness.[58] At the rehearsal of April 29, this passage was reportedly greeted with rapture, the performers having to wait several minutes before they could resume playing. Haydn had evidently been planning to maximize the effect of his surprise: not even van Swieten had been forewarned. "I think I see his face even now, as this part sounded in the orchestra," recalled Silverstolpe. "Haydn had the expression of someone who is thinking of biting his lips, either to hide his embarrassment or to conceal a secret. And in that moment when light broke out for the first time, one would have said that rays darted from the composer's burning eyes."[59] Though the aesthetic of this supernatural instant of creation is worlds apart from the sudden, zany tinkling of Haydn's piano solo in the Symphony no. 98, both moments share an unusually self-conscious theatricality.[60] In both Hanover Square and the Schwarzenberg Palace, Haydn organized his music in such a way as to reveal the author at work. In the oratorio, however, Haydn's act of creation presented itself in the theological guise of "gift, superfluity, and gratuitous gesture," to use Eagleton's words—the divine musical analog of Schwarzenberg's gracious bestowal of an extra hundred ducats.[61] As in Mauss's theories of the gift, the performative act of giving suspends economic exchange, becomes a sui generis action, equivalent to no other.[62] To the extent that this was evanescent musical labor, then, it sought to elude the logic of equivalence.

But this opening instant of transient "labor" thus produces, ex nihilo, the ensuing "work" (to use Arendt's distinction)—a work that not only resisted the degeneration of nature but presented itself as a self-organizing second nature. "Our master has now cultivated and harvested another field," breathed Carl Friedrich Zelter in his reverential 1802 review.[63] This georgic trope of quasi-divine husbandry—central to eighteenth-century theories of genius popularized by essayists such as Edward Young—served to displace the Lockean encounter of the earth's bounty and the body's labor to a realm now encompassed by the musical master, and indeed the musical masterwork.[64] The formal plan of *The Creation* described this very conceptual displacement in its stylized transition from musical chaos, via the creation of light, to a stable opening aria—a "new world," as Zelter heard it.[65] This formal simulacrum of the progression from undeveloped fantasy into organized musical utterance appeared to incorporate a putatively natural exterior into a self-sufficient, autotelic musical work.[66] As Zelter punned in an earlier 1801 report on *The Creation*, "It is its own creation, of its own kind and its own free play of Art, which serves the master's hand in the modeling of a new garden, a new Eden."[67]

The outpouring of celebratory verse that accompanied the early reception of *The Creation* tended without exception to elaborate upon the obvious parallel between Haydn the creator and the divine creator himself. Gabriele von Baumberg's "An den grossen, unsterblichen Haydn" (To the great, immortal Haydn), which was distributed as a broadsheet inside the Burgtheater before the 1799 public premiere, began its second stanza with an exultant apostrophe:

> Jüngst schuf *Dein* Schöpferisches WERDE!
> Den Donner, durch den Paukenschall;
> Und Himmel—Sonne—Mond—und Erde,
> Die Schöpfung ganz—zum Zweitenmal.
> [Now you have created *your* LET THERE BE!
> The thunder, through the drum's clangor;
> And heaven—sun—moon—and Earth,
> The entire creation—for a second time.]

And lest its apotheosis was not explicit enough, the conclusion spelled it out:

> So huld'gen wir im Aug die Thränen
> Dem Kunstwerk deiner Phantasie
> Der Allmacht deiner Zaubertöne
> Und Dir, dem Gott der Harmonie![68]
> [So we pay homage with tears in our eyes
> To the artwork of your imagination
> To the omnipotence of your magic sounds
> And to *you*, the god of harmony!]

Two years later, Christoph Martin Wieland published a poetic tribute to the oratorio in the *Allgemeine musikalische Zeitung*, which concluded with an echo of the words "Achieved is the glorious work" ("Vollendet ist das große Werk"), the grand B-flat chorus with fugue that concluded part 2 of the oratorio, and the six biblical days of creation:

> O jedes Hochgefühl, das in den Herzen schlief,
> Ist wach! Wer rufet nicht: wie schön ist diese Erde,
> Und schöner, nun der Herr auch dich ins Daseyn rief,
> Auf daß sein Werk vollendet werde![69]
> [O every exaltation that slept in our hearts
> Is roused! Who does not call out: how beautiful is this Earth,
> Nay, more beautiful, now that the Lord has summoned you into existence,
> To complete his work!]

With the glorious work complete, Haydn had transformed from affective laborer into deity, from service worker into divine creator.

The chorus "Achieved is the glorious work"—the oratorio's most self-conscious celebration of its own musical achievement—staged one of the most blatant encounters between Handelian past and Haydnesque present, not only in its choral weightiness and concluding turn to a festive learned

FIGURE 4.3. *Fortspinnung* in the chain of suspensions that begin "Vollendet ist das große Werk." *Die Schöpfung: ein Oratorium von Joseph Haydn im Clavierauszug* (Vienna: Mollo, 1799).

style but also on the level of musical syntax. Its opening musical paragraph, stated as an introduction in the orchestra and repeated in the chorus, unfolds, following a triadic flourish and declamatory stepwise head motif, into an open-ended sequence of 7-6 suspensions (essentially a passage built on a descent through the octave in a succession of 6/3 chords)—the kind of *Fortspinnung* that Wilhelm Fischer once took as native to "baroque" phrase structure (fig. 4.3).[70] If Haydn's opening creation of light embodied the sublime of overwhelming power and inconceivable scale—the species of sublime experience theorized by Burke and Kant—"Achieved is the glorious work" returned to a sublime of an older, Longinian sort, one shared by more or less all of the choruses in the oratorio: the sublime as an elevated rhetorical register, a Handelian tone of voice.[71]

Lawrence Kramer has pointed out that neither the sublime obscurity of the "Representation of Chaos" nor the instantaneity of its banishment can be sustained but can only be recollected and supplanted by the grandiose, prosaic, or beautiful numbers that follow.[72] Even greater than the distance between the sublime creation of light and the festive Handelian tone of "Achieved is the glorious work" is the radical contrast between the otherworldly mystery of chaos and the all-too-worldly blatancy of "Strait opening her fertile womb," whose cartoonish musical imitations catalog with absurd clarity the newly created creatures of the earth, from the lion to the worm. In Scott Burnham's terms, *The Creation* moves from an opening performance of the "process of nature," which underpinned nineteenth-century organicist aesthetics, to a depiction of the "products of nature"—and so to the strategies of musical mimesis, which frustrated even Haydn's most forgiving exegetes.[73] While the creation of light from chaos strove to confound representational distance and physical performance, by far the greater portion of *The Creation* revealed that Haydn was, as Johann Karl Friedrich Triest wrote in the *Allgemeine musikalische Zeitung*, "forced to continual descriptions of objects," which "pass by us as in a magic lantern [show]"—the kind of popular optical entertainment that, as Deirdre Loughridge has shown, mediated the oratorio's arresting audiovisual language.[74] Even Zelter, who otherwise claimed to appreciate the "succession of paintings" that made up the poem, confessed that "the eagle's flight and the dove's cooing" left him cold.[75] And yet the lofty Handelian utterances and prosaic "descriptions of objects" that constituted *The Creation* were, in Zelter's view, transformed in advance by a metaphysically prior mimesis—one that, as Derrida once showed, covertly shaped the anti-mimetical orientation of Kantian aesthetics: the imitation of the divine act of creation itself.[76] The fantastical opening of *The Creation* transfigured the music that followed. "It is the true fantasy of a great mind, which should, and does, represent to the inner spirit those mixed-up, vast forces that progressively yield to order," wrote Zelter. "And in this spirit I view the whole work."[77] Regarded as the culmination of an entire process of creation—one set in motion by the sublime opening—"Achieved is the glorious work" placed a worthy Handelian seal on a self-contained work.

Zelter's focus on the whole, from whose unfolding the diverting moments in *The Creation* were theoretically inseparable, was not merely an organicist philosophical conceit. It was expressed in the distinctive media protocols that the earliest public performances and publications of *The Creation* sought to teach. A poster advertising the premiere of the oratorio in March 1799 gave advance warning to any excitable concertgoers hoping for the usual on-the-spot encores and assumed that any applause would be directed at Haydn rather than the hardworking performers: "If in case there arises the opportunity for applause, it will be permitted him to receive it as a much appreciated mark of satisfaction, but not as a request for the repetition of one or the other individual piece; for otherwise the true connection between the various single parts, from the uninterrupted succession of which should proceed the effect of the whole, would be necessarily disturbed."[78] A similar preoccupation with the whole informed Haydn's luxurious subscriber-funded publication of the oratorio, which, unusually for the time, appeared in score rather than parts: "The work is to appear in three or four months, neatly and correctly engraved and printed on good paper, with German and English texts, and in full score, so that, on the one hand, the public may have the work in its entirety, and so that the connoisseur may see it *in toto* and thus better judge it; while on the other, it will be easier to prepare the parts, should one wish to perform the work anywhere."[79] So commonplace did such attitudes become in the nineteenth century that it is easy to overlook that this constituted a new theory of the musical text—one that would be restated by Breitkopf & Härtel around the same time, in their announcement of a complete works edition.[80] In score, Haydn indicated, the whole of *The Creation* could be both possessed and grasped synoptically, even while retaining the potential to marshal the labor of a performance.

The Creation entered a new century leading the double life that was the lot of the nineteenth-century masterwork: an ideal version of itself permanently coexisted with the reality of its multiple modes of material existence. After all, most music lovers came to know *The Creation* primarily through printed chamber adaptations and keyboard reductions, where it was more easily divided into detachable episodes and passages, and where its reception was more intermittent and synecdochal.[81] In the early keyboard reductions that appeared in London and Vienna, the sublimity of Haydn's musical light was less dazzling and more plainly reproducible than before, while the series of miniatures that constituted a number such as "Strait opening her fertile womb" appeared more than ever to lurch zanily between registers in order to delight and entertain: the balletic leaping of the tiger yielding to the tremolo buzzing of insects and, at the end, the chromatic slither of the worm (fig. 4.4).

Even greater transgressions on the oratorio's sublime whole were Joseph Woelfl's three sonatas for violin and piano, published in 1801—superb novelties, each based on a patchwork of unrelated themes from *The Creation*. Playing through these elegant sonatas, one could hardly pretend that Haydn's musical creations could not be productively extracted from the unfolding of a musical whole and sold on. In the bizarre Largo introduction to the third sonata, even the solemn eternity of the oratorio's opening chaos is packed into a concise sixteen measures before the recycled creation of light intervenes, with strenuous double-stops in the violin—though the resolution of its formerly colossal cadence is now cut short by a brief reversion to chaos before the introduction turns absentmindedly to an Allegro moderato based on "In native worth and honour clad" (fig. 4.5). In the context of this madcap potpourri, the performative gesture that once posed as the constitutive outside of a sublime whole appears as just another delectable passage, equivalent to all the other musical bits and pieces. And, to that extent, what was formerly divine creation is audible once again as labor, sublimity as zaniness, the masterwork as hard work.

The Industry Concept

Van Swieten and Haydn began work on *The Seasons* in the midst of the unprecedented success of *The Creation*. Yet the published reception of *The Seasons* expanded on the few negative notes that had already crept into the reception of the earlier oratorio. Nearly all reviewers, including the ever loyal Zelter and Haydn's colleague Griesinger, had harsh words for van Swieten's text, which was a drastic compression of Barthold Brockes's midcentury translation of James Thomson's poem, reprinted and excerpted in abundance throughout

FIGURE 4.4. Zany swerves between buzzing insects and the slithering worm in Muzio Clementi's piano reduction, *The Creation: An Oratorio, Adapted for Voices and Piano Forte* (London: Longman, Clementi, Banger, Hyde, Collard, & Davis, c. 1801).

FIGURE 4.5. Haydn's sublime creation of light becomes zany in the opening Largo from Joseph Woelfl's Sonata for Piano and Violin, op. 14, no. 3, one of three sonatas based on themes from *The Creation* (Leipzig: Breitkopf & Härtel, 1801). Staatsbibliothek zu Berlin—Preußischer Kulturbesitz, Musikabteilung mit Mendelssohn-Archiv. Used by permission.

the century.[82] Even though Zelter, in his 1804 review, claimed to appreciate, albeit with a certain defensiveness, that "the whole of *The Seasons* is like looking at a gallery, a suite of paintings,"[83] others were less enthused by what one report of an early Leipzig performance described as its "vulgar imitation of nature in details, unworthy of a great artist"—a fatal deviation from the process of nature toward its mere products: "For that very reason, [it] creates no whole," concluded the reviewer.[84] It hardly helped matters that, late in 1801, the German writer Johann Gottlieb Karl Spazier published, in his *Zeitung für die elegante Welt*, excerpts from a note to the arranger of the piano version, the Leipzig musician August Eberhard Müller, in which Haydn disparaged the tone paintings in *The Seasons*—he requested that the orchestra's imitation of croaking frogs at the end of "Summer" be excised altogether—and appeared to blame the worst excesses of musical mimesis on van Swieten: "'This whole passage'—he writes—'with its imitation of a frog, did not come from my pen. I was forced to write down this French trash. With the whole orchestra, this wretched idea disappears pretty soon, but it can't remain in a piano reduction.'"[85] This report caused a temporary breach between Haydn and van Swieten and was presumably one of the reasons that Griesinger claimed that Haydn was less inspired by the worldly picture gallery of *The Seasons* than the divine mystery of *The Creation*.[86]

The distinction between the celestial and the worldly has long since structured the popular perception of Haydn's two late oratorios—the austere biblical sublime of *The Creation* versus the sentimental pastoral of *The Seasons*. But, as James Webster noted, part 3 of *The Creation*, depicting the Garden of Eden, partakes of the pastoral mode as much as any section of *The Seasons*—and no contemporary publication described *The Seasons* as a pastoral in any case.[87] Like Thomson's poem, Haydn's *Seasons* is georgic rather than pastoral: by and large, the oratorio does not associate nature with retreat or repose, fantasy or desire, but instead explicates humanity's union with nature, primarily through the image of husbandry.[88] Work is the abiding subject of *The Seasons*, represented in every season other than "Summer"—cultivation in "Spring," harvesting in "Autumn," and spinning in "Winter." Indeed, the first solo aria of the oratorio, "Schon eilet froh der Ackersmann," depicts the cheery labor of the husbandman, whistling as he goes about his work. The orchestra soon lets the audience know that the tune he whistles is none other than the theme of the Andante from Haydn's *Surprise*, the violins weaving their scrap of diegetic music through the wider musical environment. If, as Gerber put it, Haydn had a knack for producing tunes that appeared *bekannt*, or already known, then he here redoubled the illusion by reprising a melody that was already well known to music lovers in Vienna, London, and elsewhere.[89] In a number about cultivation—the collaboration of nature and culture through work—Haydn portrayed his own music as somehow both given and made.

But the apogee of the musical georgic in *The Seasons* is without question the trio and chorus celebrating Fleiß—"industry" in the equivalent section of Thomson's poem—in "Autumn": "So lohnet die Natur den Fleiß." The earliest reviewers were almost universally skeptical about this number, at least with respect to its words. "A song of praise is dedicated to noble Fleiß," wrote Zelter in his 1804 review. "But in all these matters the poet remains endlessly behind the composer. Since, not only does he load the composer with pointless things that don't at all suit an interesting portrayal, but he also burdens him with a completely unreasonable number of prosaic words, which would surely have embarrassed any other composer."[90] Others argued that this uninspiring concreteness had been ineptly combined with its apparent opposite, excessive abstraction: "Industry, allegorically described, is too abstract for musical composition," complained a 1801 report on *The Seasons* in the *Journal des Luxus und der Moden*.[91] Part of the problem lay in the form of van Swieten's verse, the major part of which consists of an apostrophe to industry before unspooling into a litany of its various products, without much in the way of poetic elaboration:

> Von dir, o Fleiss, kommt alles Heil.
> Die Hütte, die uns schirmt,
> Die Wolle, die uns deckt,
> Die Speise, die uns nährt,
> Ist deine Gab', ist dein Geschenk.
> [From thee, O Industry, come all blessings.
> The hut that shelters us,
> The wool that clothes us,
> The food that nourishes us,
> Is thy bestowal, is thy gift.]

This is doubtless what Spazier, in the *Zeitung für die elegante Welt*, was referring to when he cited the "wretched and dry texts" at the beginning of "Autumn": an infelicitous blend of the too abstract and the too prosaic.[92] It may have been this critical reception that prompted Haydn's sheepish exchange about the *Fleiß* chorus with Griesinger: "When he came to the place *O Fleiß, o edler Fleiß, von dir kommt alles Heil!*, he remarked that he had been an industrious man all his life, but that it had never occurred to him to set industry to music."[93]

In Viennese and other predominantly German-speaking environments, the problem may also have been the word *Fleiß* itself, which lacked the English philosophical connotations of *industry* or *labor*. As with all the numbers in the oratorio, van Swieten had, in the *Fleiß* chorus, truncated an extended passage from Thomson almost to the point of blankness. The corresponding section in Thomson's poem begins with an image of ripening corn and a similar apostrophe to industry, before unfolding into a hundred lines or so that describe humanity's ascent from a state of nature to the apex of civilization, represented by the city of London. Husbandry is the foundational metaphor—the primordial georgic scene that turns into the foundation of human history, ultimately begetting the luxuries of the urban world that so eagerly consumed Thomson's poem.

> These are thy blessings, Industry, rough power!
> Whom labour still attends, and sweat, and pain;
> Yet the kind source of every gentle art
> And all the soft civility of life:
> Raiser of human kind!

Humanity in the state of nature—"Materials infinite; but idle all"—is taught by industry, in Lockean fashion, to "dig the mineral," "chip the wood, and hew the stone," and to load its table with "wholesome viands." And this in turn produces polite manners and "decent wit," and thence "science, wisdom," the law and the public realm, and commerce, emanating from its global center, London.

> Nurse of art, the city reared
> In beauteous pride her tower-encircled head.
> Then Commerce brought into the public walk
> The busy merchant; the big warehouse built;
> Raised the strong crane; choked up the loaded street
> With foreign plenty; and thy stream, O Thames,
> Large, gentle, deep, majestic, king of floods!

Ending this immense historical chain is the arts: "The canvas smooth, / With glowing life protuberant, to the view / Embodied rose." Though humble in appearance, industry turns out to be sublime to contemplate: a single, simple principle of limitless fecundity.[94]

This was the sweeping and deindividualized vision of historical and geographical interconnection promoted by the concept and genre of landscape, and the attendant idea of industry as a universal force, which would produce the modern discipline of political economy.[95] A similarly overwhelming list of industry's incalculable products opened *The Wealth of Nations*, in which Adam Smith's contemplation of the division of labor unravels as ordinary an item as a woolen coat into an ever-expanding number of actors that ultimately "exceeds all computation": "The shepherd, the sorter of the wool, the wool-comber or carder, the dyer, the scribbler, the spinner, the weaver, the fuller, the dresser" depend on the "merchants and carriers . . . ship-builders, sailors, sail-makers, rope-makers." Even a humble pair of sheep shears require "the miner, the builder of the furnace for smelting the ore, the seller of the timber, the burner of the charcoal to be made use of in the smelting house, the brick-maker, the workmen who attend the furnace, the mill-wright, the forger, the smith," and so on.[96] Thus does even the most modest work unspool into the improbable parataxis of endless workers and thence into the near-mystical substance of labor itself, which binds the world together.

With its frugal inventory of shelter, clothing, and nourishment, van Swieten's *Fleiß* chorus responded only weakly to Thomson's dizzying landscape of labor. But Haydn's music added some of the activity and variety that the text excised, moving sequentially or circling energetically during the list of industry's products and giving *Fleiß* more expansive and elevated treatments at points of resolution. Following a modulation in the course of the

FIGURE 4.6. Listing the blessings of industry in the piano reduction of *The Seasons* by Ferdinand Ries. *Die Jahreszeiten von J. Haydn* (Bonn: Simrock, c. 1803).

opening bass solo, the tenor and soprano enter with a lyrical apostrophe to industry ("Von dir, o Fleiß, kommt alles Heil"). The litany ("Die Hütte, die uns schirmt," etc.) then unfolds as a rising formula—an instance of the gambit that Gjerdingen, after Riepel, calls a Monte—and concludes in a tender cadential melody on "ist deine Gab, ist dein Geschenk" (fig. 4.6).[97] Later on— back in C major, and once the chorus has been introduced—the soloists will present the litany as a squarely repeating turn figure over a tonic pedal, coming to the words "ist deine Gab, ist dein Geschenk" in a lyrical cadence.

The idea of industry becomes sublime, however, in the culmination of the movement: a C major fugue with brass and drums in the Handelian high style. Here, the immensity and profusion of the music begins to overwhelm the words altogether—although, in the course of the fugue, the litany crops up once more, again in the form of the repeating turn figure over a root-note pedal. The chorus is now paired exclusively with the sublime ideal of industry, interjecting lustily on the words "o Fleiß" while the soloists enumerate industry's products. Especially in this closing fugue, Haydn presages the concluding double chorus of the entire oratorio—also in a majestic C major—which envisions the eternal glories of heaven. The subject of the oratorio's concluding fugue noticeably shares with the *Fleiß* fugue an emphasis on the flattened seventh scale degree characteristic of the chromatic maneuver theorized in published partimenti by Zingarelli (the stock move that we followed across Europe in chapter 1—the schema that Robert Gjerdingen calls the Quiescenza).[98] That these choruses have so much in common strongly implies that industriousness is next to godliness (figs. 4.7 and 4.8).

Fugue was a marker of the Handelian sublime—just as it was in "Achieved is the glorious work." But as an audibly complex musical technique, it was notably antithetical to the kind of naturalness represented by the *Surprise*

FIGURE 4.7. Fugue subject from the *Fleiß* chorus, with its distinctive flattened seventh.

FIGURE 4.8. Fugue subject from the culminating chorus of *The Seasons*, also with a distinctive flattened seventh. *Die Jahreszeiten, nach Thomson* (Leipzig: Breitkopf & Härtel, 1802).

tune in the opening aria of *The Seasons*: especially in its fugue, the *Fleiß* chorus bore the traces of considerable authorial labor and sounded appropriately busy. Eighteenth-century writers who inveighed against the obscurantism of the learned style frequently coupled laboring and counterpoint: "All the jargon of different parts, of laboured contrivance," as Burney dismissively wrote in the course of his tour through Italy and France.[99] This may explain why Zelter—an antiquarian who was otherwise committed to the learned styles of an earlier generation—granted so much space in his reviews of Haydn's last oratorios to a defense of their fugues. His second essay on *The Creation* concluded with an expression of gratitude that Haydn was "not ashamed to adorn his works with contrapuntal beauties." He stressed, however, that Haydn was able to produce fugues "with a certain lightness, looseness, or exuberant freedom," and that, while this required "many years of long dedication" to master, the result, in Haydn's case, was learned but not labored.[100] Similarly, he deemed the *Fleiß* chorus "a true masterpiece of dignity, clarity, and genius," in spite of its prosaic words.[101]

And while the fugue does not pose as an artless musical second nature, one could say that its deindividuated performance of teeming musical Fleiß gave sonic form to the synoptic, depersonalized landscape perspectives of eighteenth-century political economy. Neither labored nor zany, the audible industriousness of Haydn's fugue provided a musical analog for that ubiquitous yet sublime principle that brought unity to multiplicity—work.

Working Concepts

For some time now, musicologists have treated the work concept as an ethically compromised ideological construct, mostly because of the work that it occludes and excludes. From this perspective, the work concept recasts the labor of artists as improbable Promethean creativity even as it obscures the collective labor of many other actors and collaborators: the creative genius is rewarded, even as his myriad cocreators are short-changed. The main theoretical solution to this inequity has been to turn art into art worlds and to reclaim all of its participants as workers and all measurable exertions as forms of labor.[102] In the wider political sphere, this move motivated the concept of affective labor itself, through which a generation of activists sought to acknowledge the value-creating activities that have traditionally existed (or have appeared to exist) outside of capital.[103] This was one of the triumphs of Euro-American feminism in the twentieth century, from Silvia Federici to Arlie Hochschild.[104]

But, as a later generation of feminist and postcolonial thinkers has observed, this theoretical and political tactic served to reinscribe the primacy of labor, and especially wage labor: "The social role of waged work has been so naturalized as to seem necessary and inevitable, something that might be tinkered with but never escaped," despairs Kathi Weeks.[105] To note that the rays that Silverstolpe imagined darting from Haydn's eyes in the instant that he created musical light both relied upon and obscured a hardworking infrastructure—the musicians and singers performing in the Schwarzenberg Palace, most obviously—is to haul Haydn before the Court of Exchequer once again, this time to adjudicate whose labor produced his valuable musical property, and so to clock in a previously unseen shift of musical workers. That the first performance of *The Creation* took place in a court milieu that was to an extent sheltered from the encroaching relations of capitalist wage labor may make us think twice, however. Bringing "our definition of musical/ sonic labor closer to the types of labor typically considered radically distinct from it," as Jim Sykes recommends, may also mean reducing a diversity of sociomusical scenarios to an implicitly econometric principle, one with historically and geographically local origins.[106]

In today's increasingly posthuman humanities, however, scholars have begun to confer the status of value-creating laborer on ever wider collections of actors. In the era of ecological disaster, theorists are less inclined to regard nature as a passive Lockean "resource" than as a teeming collection of coworkers—a "collective, distributed undertaking of humans and non-humans acting to reproduce, regenerate, and renew a common world," according to

Alyssa Battistoni's thoroughly collaborative definition.[107] The lists of people and things that increasingly populate today's network-focused sociologies, not least the zany ontological catalogs of hardworking objects that Ian Bogost has called "Latour litanies," seek in part to give credit where credit is due in the laborious production of worlds—to recognize and reward "worms, or electricity, or various gadgets, or fats, or metals, or stem cells," to call upon a characteristic litany by Jane Bennett.[108] And there is no question that even contemporary published commentaries on Haydn's late oratorios at times invite perspectives that might temper the relentlessly author-focused vision of Haydn's most deferential reviewers and instead invite us to unravel masterwork into network. Joseph Richter's *Eipeldauer Briefe*—comic letters about current events written in the voice of a local rustic—described the 1799 public premiere of *The Creation* in a way that gave pride of place to human and animal viscera and so drew out otherwise submerged relationships between the animal bodies that mediated the music and the animal kingdom that the oratorio depicted. "For the life of me I wouldn't have believed that human lungs and sheep gut and calf's skin could create such miracles. The music all by itself described thunder and lightning and then, cousin, you'd have heard the rain falling and the water rushing and even the worms crawling on the ground." In this account, Haydn the Promethean author disappears behind the climate, the animal skins, and the worms.[109] It is tempting to invoke such descriptions to legitimize a revised and expanded musical organicism, of the kind articulated by Holly Watkins—*The Creation* as the simulacrum of a profuse, self-organizing system, minus the anthropocentrism and single creative genius.[110]

I suspect, though, that expanding Richter's list of mediators into a full-blown Latour litany may involve substituting the sublime of Haydn's work with the speciously ethical sublime of the network, whose limitlessness is substantiated by the supposed smallness, marginality, and animality of the many actors that work to produce it—a sublime web of relations, gesturing toward the liberal promise of a total inclusivity, always just beyond the horizon of our methodological perception. The actors who populate such a landscape count as worthy of recognition only once the theorist has interpellated them as (net)workers: just as Haydn musicalizes the worm within the synoptic God-vision of *The Creation*, so Bennett (via Charles Darwin and Latour) envoices "worms as vibrant material actants" in her sweeping theoretical vision of the eternally thrumming ecopolity.[111] More than two centuries on, and worms continue to serve their old aesthetic function, as a pleasing symbol of the marginal, lowly, and excluded. It seems to me, moreover, that this is all uncomfortably close to the late capitalist "network morality" decried by

Boltanski and Chiapello: everyone and everything must be active, must have an impact, if they are to be worthy of acknowledgment.[112] That Latour litanies resemble, in their penchant for zany juxtaposition and paratactic rhetoric, the sublime lists that illustrate the division of labor at the start of *The Wealth of Nations* is, I think, no accident: in contrasting ways, both rely on the poetics of the eighteenth-century landscape view, a sociological georgic that claims to trace the (net)working of innumerable actors across previously unthinkable expanses of space and time.[113] If this is the case, the grand sonic analogs of works and working in *The Creation* and *The Seasons* are not the opposite of a less hierarchical, less anthropocentric view of collaborative social labor. Rather, they are compelling musical expressions of one of its foundational aesthetic premises: the vibrant landscape of labor. Unseat the overpromoted authors and demote even humanity itself—but everything is still perpetually at work.

The reader who has followed the argument of this book up to this point will not be surprised by the main argument of this chapter—namely, that the musical work concept and the economic concept of work have shared intellectual and political origins. On this premise, I have sought to question much of the contemporary published commentary on Haydn's late oratorios, which otherwise appears to chart the rise of a now familiar set of Romantic values: the lasting artwork as an implicit rebuke to the transient values of the market, and artistic labor as a supernatural way of creating something from nothing—a species of work wholly distinct from other more prosaic forms of labor. But if, as Scarry (Elaine) has observed, Marx taught generations of thinkers "to recognize human labor in successive circles of self-extension," I wonder if the correct inference to draw from this is that, as Scarry (Richard) once said, "Everyone Is a Worker."[114] Haydn was not always, was not even usually, a worker—that quintessentially modern political agent, who either retains control of his labor or is forced to sell it to others. As chapel master and chapel servant, successful entrepreneur and stressed-out freelancer, beneficiary of aristocratic patronage and recipient of public acclaim, Haydn illustrates what the ethnographic study of musical livelihoods has long insisted—that the interactions between musicians and the formal and informal economies of labor they inhabit are frequently too complex, textured, and ethically confounding to be arranged along the same old liberal axis of freedom versus constraint, masters versus servants.[115] By the start of the nineteenth century, Haydn had experienced and witnessed many kinds of exertion, collaboration, loyalty, and remuneration, and this shaped the often contradictory depictions, performances, and aesthetic transmutations of work in his later music. He had passed into and out of England's incipient musical labor market, into and out of full-time service to the Esterházy family, and had lived out the contrasts between court service and affective labor, the busy work of the theater musician and the measurable outputs of the service worker, the prestigious duties of the Kapellmeister and the divine inspirations of the Romantic genius. Haydn's career contradicts at every turn the Romantic fantasy of the artwork as something beyond the instrumentalized realm of exploitative economic relations. And yet, as with even the most everyday forms of cultural production, perhaps, Haydn's surviving compositions, a series of not-quite-works by a not-quite-worker, seem to give evanescent shape to forms of human flourishing that cannot be described merely in terms of work.

Epilogue

Value (1808)

The world is too much with us; late and soon
Getting and spending, we lay waste our powers
WILLIAM WORDSWORTH (1802)[1]

Of Time and Fashion

In the course of an obituary for Luigi Boccherini in the *Berlinische musika-lische Zeitung* of 1805, Johann Friedrich Reichardt took the opportunity to compare his musical contemporaries with a generation past—a generation that, to Reichardt, now included Haydn.[2] Mozart and Haydn, wrote Reichardt, were "heroes of art": "Their pure, perfected works endure, and remain valid, no matter that time and fashion and their slaves may pursue thousand upon thousand diversions in total confusion."[3] Zelter had used similar language in his extended think pieces on *The Creation* and *The Seasons* in the Leipzig *Allgemeine musikalische Zeitung*: "Despite all the changes and accidents of time and fashion," Haydn's works "will remain immortal as long as music is an art," he wrote in 1802.[4] Two years later, he concluded that *The Seasons* "will last for the duration of all times. In its quality it stands out among the oratorio-works of all times, and of its kind has nothing above it, save Handel's *Messiah*."[5] To the present-day reader, such pronouncements, especially when they accumulate at the overdetermined historiographical threshold "around 1800," seem to reveal the hardening of various idealist tropes, now almost banal in their familiarity: the caprice of fashion versus the eternal truths of art, tainted diversions versus pure works, slaves of time versus the free appreciators of timeless value, the value of commodities versus the value of art.

These distinctions were made thinkable in part by the media forms in which they were articulated. Reichardt and Zelter articulated their thoughts in the midst of a musician obituary and an in-depth review of a printed musical score—both relatively new genres. Since the second half of the eighteenth century, a generation of music journals, most of them published in cities some way north of Vienna, had gathered up and repackaged musical works with historically divergent functions and institutional origins, and in such a way as to enable new kinds of comparative technical evaluation and long-range diachronic storytelling. These journals took up positions both within and against the lively print markets of the German cities that fostered them, their very titles signaling newness, newsiness, and the passage of historical time, as well as, in the English fashion, their status as elevated artistic warehouses (the primary connotation of the word "magazine"): the *musikalisches Kunstmagazin*, the *Magazin der Musik*, the *Berlinische musikalische Zeitung*, the *Allgemeine musikalische Zeitung*, the *Zeitung für die elegante Welt*, the *Journal des Luxus und der Moden*, and so on.[6] These were printed stores of miscellanies, catering to the whim of the times, and also austere preservers of timeless value. At the same time, both Reichardt and Zelter helped to create and sustain new concert-giving societies—high-end musical storage units with which the latest generation of music journals were in dialogue. In 1783, Reichardt introduced the Parisian format of the Concert Spirituel to Berlin, which cultivated the music of Handel and Haydn in particular, while Zelter, at the time he published his reviews of Haydn's late oratorios, had recently been appointed director of Berlin's antiquarian Sing-Akademie.[7] These were the latest institutional mechanisms for producing the musically eternal.

These institutions appeared in Vienna somewhat later, but when they did, Haydn was at their heart. "Music lovers in the capital have long desired to see the creation of a musical institution which would perform the works of great masters to perfection," reported the *Pressburger Zeitung* in its announcement of the Liebhaber Concerte in 1807, echoing the statutes of the newly formed institution itself, which had declared "the performance of significant and decidedly excellent musical works" to be its primary mission.[8] The climax of the first subscription concert sponsored by the Liebhaber Concerte was a gala performance of Haydn's *Creation*, in Carpani's Italian translation, in the University Hall on March 27, 1808. Held in honor of Haydn's approaching seventy-sixth birthday, the event was widely expected to be the composer's last public appearance: Haydn was by this time too weak to leave his house unaided and was carefully conveyed to the hall in a carriage supplied by Prince Esterházy. There he was feted with many of the honors usually reserved only for the nobly born—a man now divided, like a monarch or a hero, between the symbolic and the material realm. "Haydn, accompanied by many noble Viennese friends of art, was brought with the sound of trumpets and timpani to an easy chair in the middle before the orchestra," recalled Griesinger.

> Sitting between his adored Princess Esterházy and several artistic ladies, surrounded by artists, pupils, gentlemen and ladies of the highest rank, and an extremely numerous company from cultivated society, Haydn received from

all who could get near him the sincerest proofs of high esteem, of tender so-
licitude for his weak old age, and of joy that it was permitted him to live to
see this day.[9]

Noting that Haydn wore the handsome medal presented to him by the Parisian Concert des Amateurs, the French ambassador Count Andréossy reportedly told the old man that he deserved "all the medals awarded in the whole
of France."[10]

As in the Burgtheater premiere of *The Creation* nearly a decade earlier,
festive poetry mediated the event as it happened—a sonnet by Carpani and
an ode by Heinrich von Collin, who, within weeks, would be enlisted as a
state propagandist upon the founding of the Austrian conscription army, the
Landwehr.[11] By now, the trope of the artist as divine creator had hardened into
orthodoxy. "With a single motion of his powerful eyelashes / Out of nothing
he brings forth all living things and the universe [*A un muover sol di sue pos-
senti ciglia / Trar dal nulla i viventi e l'Universo*]," began Carpani's sonnet.[12]
Von Collin opened his ode with an apostrophe to this earthly god of music:
"You have borne the world in your breast [*Du hast die Welt in deiner Brust
getragen*]."[13] A longer retrospective verse by von Collin about the concert,
published a year after his death in 1812, recalled Haydn's creation of light,
which became, yet again, the emblematic moment of the oratorio and of the
entire occasion:

> "Licht werd' es," scholl's! Licht ward's! dem Rufe beben
> Die dunklen Schatten, reißen, schwinden, fliehen! -
> Ein Jubelruf: "Hoch soll der Meister leben!"
> Da weint der Greis, und seine Wangen glühen;
> Begeistert streckt zum Himmel er die Hände:
> "Nicht ist es Frucht von menschlichem Bemühen,
> "Gott gab mir's ein, daß ich es recht vollende!"
> ["Let there be light," it resounded! There was light!
> The dark shadows quake at the call, and are rent, fade, and flee!—
> A cheer: "Long live the Master!"
> Then the old man weeps, and his cheeks are burning;
> Inspired, he extends his hands to heaven:
> "It is not the fruit of human effort,
> "God had me complete it!"][14]

Similar scenes can be found in Haydn's early biographies. "At the words
'And there was light' thunderous applause interrupted the performance and
Haydn, the tears streaming down his pallid cheeks and as if overcome by the
most violent emotions, raised his trembling arms to Heaven, as if in prayer to

the Father of Harmony," recalled Carpani.[15] Griesinger's version of the story described how, following the re-creation of light, the audience "as usual broke into the loudest applause. Haydn made a gesture of the hands heavenward and said, 'It comes from there!'"[16] The members of the Liebhaber Concerte had, it seems, built a conduit between heaven and earth.

Romantic Infrastructures

These days, most scholars in music studies—even those inspired by the anthropologists of the ontological turn—would be unlikely to take seriously the idea that Haydn's musical light came from heaven. I suspect that most would treat this sort of thing as an expression of the most insidious and corny nineteenth-century ideologies, which have long since served to conceal the reality of a hardworking infrastructure—the material world that, when the clear-eyed historian or media archaeologist finally attends to it, automatically disenchants the discursive pretentions of musical Romanticism.[17]

Yet few in the University Hall, whether in the orchestra, chorus, or audience, whether Carpani, von Collin, or Griesinger, would have been under the illusion that the re-creation of Haydn's musical light required no materials, no human energies. Indeed, building the infrastructure capable of mediating between heaven and earth had been hard going. The Liebhaber Concerte, as the name indicates, was a coalition of wealthy amateurs and musicians, nobles and professionals. Though most music historians would reasonably regard it as a sort of public concert series, it is not clear that this is precisely what it was. The organization was known by several names, each of which signaled a distinct infrastructural status: Freunde der Tonkunst, Gesellschaft von Musikfreunden, Musikalisches Institut.[18] Haydn's March 27 gala event, supported by this institute, society, or association of friends, was not only a concert but an elaborate civic ritual of the kind that was fast becoming routine in wartime Vienna: a self-conscious multimedia event, designed to be historic—a new Napoleonic genre, even, in which Haydn and his masterwork were paraded as priceless monuments of Habsburg culture.[19] Notably, the one surviving illustration of the occasion, by the miniaturist Balthasar Wigand, was painted on the lid of a beautiful stationary box presented to Haydn by Princess Marie Hermenegild Esterházy—a dinky depiction of the event that was at once an aristocratic favor and a sentimental souvenir (fig. 5.1). None other than Reichardt, recently released from a short-lived stint as Kapellmeister in Kassel and now on the road, was shown the box when he paid Haydn a visit toward the end of the year—he arrived in Vienna too late to witness the concert itself—and his published memoir describes the "old hero"

FIGURE 5.1. 1909 copy of Balthasar Wigand's picture of the performance of *The Creation* in the University Hall on March 27, 1808 (original lost). Wien Museum 33860/2.

calling for the box and revealing the luxurious black and gold autograph book inside, signed by Haydn's most eminent patrons and supporters.[20]

Wigand's picture—whose representation of the well-known musicians and patrons present has been painstakingly researched by Theodor Albrecht—inevitably drew attention to aristocratic hierarchies and relationships of prestige: Haydn is seated in the center, and the three most prominent figures standing in the foreground to his left are Princess Marie Esterházy (offering the elderly composer her shawl), Prince Lobkowitz (leaning on his cane), and Prince Nikolaus Esterházy (who, a late arrival, was probably not even present while Haydn was in attendance; too weak to endure the whole performance, Haydn was carried from the hall before the second part of the oratorio began). Behind Haydn's chair, scroll in hand, stands the venerable court Kapellmeister Antonio Salieri, who directed the performance. The poet von Collin is among a selection of notable figures in the foreground, farther from Haydn's chair.[21]

This covers the *Freunde der Tonkunst*—and perhaps the musical *Gesellschaft*—but Wigand's picture also depicted less prominent people, objects, and technologies that were necessary to the creation of something more like an *Institut*: the performing musicians, instruments, and printed parts, of course, as well as the singers (the soprano Therese Fischer, in white, is seated next to the piano, while the bass Carl Weinmüller stands on her right) and the hierarchies of political authority and musical knowhow that installed Salieri as director, the virtuoso Franz Clement as band leader (he is shown standing at his music desk on the right of the platform), and Michael Umlauf, deputy Kapellmeister at the Kärntnertortheater, at the keyboard.[22] Though the orchestra mixed professionals and amateurs, the latter designation had as much to do with noble rank (that is, that one did not need to work for a living) as musical skill. The corps of professionals incorporated some major figures in European music, in any case: the violins alone included, behind Clement, the impresario Joseph Würth and the composer Conradin Kreuzer. And one must not forget, as a crucial part of this new institute, the performance space that surrounded them, the ornate and spacious Aula of the university—a cavernous chunk of midcentury French baroque designed by Jean Nicolas Jadot de Ville-Issey that, during this period, hosted a range of official functions. After only one performance, the Liebhaber Concerte decided to relocate to the university because of unusually high audience figures: over 1,300 people were expected to show up to the season's opening concert in the Mehlgrube ballroom.[23]

The question of audience numbers implicates other, less visible structures that organized Wigand's scene, including the rules that governed access. As with a similarly short-lived concert series led by the violinist Würth between 1803 and 1805, the Liebhaber Concerte was funded entirely by advance subscriptions rather than any direct aristocratic sponsorship: a selection of seventy or so nobles were nominated to purchase bundles of tickets, which they distributed at their discretion.[24] The audience was thus exclusive but somewhat more anonymous than attendees at older court-focused events, extending the high-minded musical tastes associated with such organizations as van Swieten's Gesellschaft der Associierten Cavaliere (which had been supported by direct aristocratic patronage) to a wider Viennese constituency. These older music-making bodies were a further infrastructural precondition for the March 27 event, also invisible in Wigand's picture—Viennese institutions that had created paths on which the music making of the Liebhaber Concerte depended, paths beaten by many of the same patrons and performing personnel.[25] By 1808, *The Creation* would have been nothing less than thoroughly well known to all of the evening's performers and listeners. Outside of the opera, Haydn's two late oratorios were without question the most frequently repeated works in Vienna during the early years of the nineteenth century, staples of the court-supported concerts of the Tonkünstler Societät and regular attractions in the Theater an der Wien, where, before his rapid decline in health, Haydn had once directed *The Creation* himself. *The Creation* had been the Advent offering of the Tonkünstler Societät in 1807, only months before the gala performance in the University Hall—an occasion that incorporated many of the Liebhaber Concerte performers, including Weinmüller. The Lenten concerts of the society in 1808, barely two weeks after the finale of the Liebhaber Concerte, featured *The Seasons*. And already on April 17, *The Creation* was performed yet again at a charity concert in the Burgtheater, with more or less the same soloists and section leaders who had featured on March 27.[26]

Despite all this work, the infrastructure of the Liebhaber Concerte remained fragile, to say the least. The ill-fated Austrian assaults on French forces in early 1809 did not help. The second occupation of Vienna followed, and a disastrous financial collapse, which put paid to the patronage of several music-loving nobles, including the extravagant Prince Lobkowitz. It turned out that the gala performance of *The Creation* was the culmination of the one and only season of the Liebhaber Concerte. It had lasted for a mere twenty concerts.[27]

Haydn Recalled

Only months before the 1801 premiere of *The Seasons* in the Schwarzenberg Palace, one of Haydn's most celebrated pupils was busily negotiating with publishers. In a letter to the Leipzig music seller Hoffmeister, Beethoven lamented that musicians should have to deal with money at all and proposed a utopian solution: "I wish things were different in the world. There ought to be in the world a *Magazin der Kunst* to which the artist would only bring his artworks in order to take what he needed; as it is, one must be half businessman, and how can one be reconciled to that!"[28] This Magazin der Kunst was no journal. Rather, Beethoven literalized a metaphor derived from print media to envision a market-resistant art store. While Haydn pursued most of his career oblivious to such Romantic fantasies yet lived to see his music absorbed by the new guardians of musical value, from music journals to concert societies, Beethoven was surrounded by these proliferating infrastructures even before he reached professional maturity. To Beethoven, the serious artist was forever divided between art and the market, the Magazin der Kunst and the music seller, the inner realm of feeling and the world of material exchange. *Homo economicus* and *Homo aestheticus*—those eighteenth-century twins, in Haydn's story—were, to Beethoven, unrelated, even permanently antagonistic.

Beethoven was in the audience on March 27, 1808. Albrecht suggests that he is depicted in the foreground of Wigand's picture, standing alone with his back turned to the viewer, third from right.[29] This conjecture is not merely a fantasy of present-day scholarship still disproportionately preoccupied with encounters between great men, amid the throng of lesser-known contemporaries. Beethoven's presence on March 27 and his bearing toward Haydn were noted by several witnesses and even merited a few florid lines in von Collin's 1811 memorial poem (the poet knew the composer well, and Beethoven had lately supplied the overture to von Collin's *Coriolan*, which had been performed more than once in the Liebhaber Concerte series).[30]

> Sieht weinend man ihm Gegenküsse senden:
> Beethoven's Kraft denkt liebend zu vergehen,
> So Haupt als Hand küßt glühend er dem Greise:
> Da wogte sich mein Herz vor Lust und Wehen
> [Weeping, one sees him returning kisses:
> Beethoven lovingly takes care to hold back his strength
> As he glowingly kisses the old man on head and hand:
> My heart surged with tremors of joy.][31]

The impression—self-consciously performed by Beethoven and his peers in the Aula—of a generational shift, and perhaps even a handover of authority, had been reinforced by the previous nineteen concerts of the Liebhaber Concerte. In these performances, Haydn's music had featured five times, while works by Mozart, Cherubini, and Beethoven had each appeared more than twice as often.[32] What is more, *The Creation*, though widely acknowledged as the period's exemplary masterwork, was sole evidence of the view, which had once dictated the musical selections of such organizations as van Swieten's Gesellschaft der Associierten Cavaliere, that the Handelian oratorio was music in its highest form.[33] To be sure, choral music remained prominent in the Viennese musical landscape, in festive and liturgical contexts, as well as the concerts of court-sponsored associations such as the Tonkünstler Societät. Yet, aside from the occasional solo vocal piece, the performances of the Liebhaber Concerte had consisted almost exclusively of concertos, overtures, and symphonies: "excellent musical works" here meant large-scale instrumental compositions.

In these compositions, as Mark Ferraguto has shown, Beethoven had, since 1806 or so, embarked on a project of emulating Haydn with ever greater overtness—a kind of "commemoration" inspired in part by publishers' and reviewers' skepticism about the gargantuan *Eroica* but also by the decision of the Leipzig music sellers Breitkopf & Härtel to issue selected Haydn orchestral works in miniature score (Beethoven had recently acquired the new small-format scores of several Haydn symphonies produced by Pleyel in

Paris).[34] Beethoven's allegiance to his old teacher had long been appreciable in matters of musical detail, of course: the climax of the coda of the first movement of his Second Symphony had practically quoted a striking harmonic progression from the end of "The Heavens Are Telling," the C major chorus that concluded part 1 of *The Creation*.[35] But the Fourth Symphony, from 1806, was more explicit yet in its renewed Haydnesque, not least in its shadowy minor-mode Adagio introduction—a theatrical, Cherubini-inflected spin on the slow introductions in all but one of Haydn's London symphonies (perhaps especially no. 102, also in B-flat), as well as the murky "Chaos" from *The Creation*.[36] Just as the earliest generation of miniature scores now presented large-scale works, old and new, in a format amenable to the synoptic view of the concertgoing collector, so, within a concert infrastructure such as the Liebhaber Concerte, these pieces were redisplayed side by side as substitutable units of musical experience, as if in dialogue: Beethoven's Second was featured on the opening concert in the Mehlgrube on November 12, 1807, and again in the University Hall on February 22, 1808; his Fourth was performed on December 27, 1807; and one of Haydn's symphonies in B-flat opened the concert of February 28, 1808.[37]

Beethoven staged the grandest concert of his career nine months after Haydn's gala celebration, in the Theater an der Wien on December 22, 1808. The word that Beethoven chose to describe the concert—fairly conventional at the time—established its own set of relationships to the coalescing institutions of Viennese music: *Akademie*—that is, an association of learned people. One of the many misfortunes that befell this Akademie was a clash with the first of the two Advent concerts of the Tonkünstler Societät (neither party was inclined to reschedule). Still, it made for a pointed contrast. As usual, the Tonkünstler Societät was presenting an oratorio, though this time it was neither *The Creation* nor *The Seasons* but a work by Haydn that even more explicitly linked him to an earlier musical tradition: his Italian oratorio *Il ritorno di Tobia*, produced for the society in 1775. In 1784, Haydn had revised the piece for a repeat performance by the Tonkünstler Societät—and now, a quarter of a century on, another of Haydn's former students, Sigismund Neukomm, stepped in to revive and reorchestrate the creaking old masterpiece once again, doubtless as part of his own bid to represent and perhaps succeed his aged mentor (Neukomm's Fantasy for Orchestra appeared alongside the first part of the oratorio on December 22).[38] Beethoven left his mark on the second of the Tonkünstler Societät concerts, on December 23: his Third Piano Concerto was paired with the second part of *Il ritorno di Tobia*.[39]

Though unable to call on the services of many of the most experienced performers in Vienna, who were already contractually committed to the

Tonkünstler Societät, Beethoven's Akademie was an ambitious summation of his achievements in every major musical genre and consisted exclusively of his own music: the Gloria and Sanctus of the Mass in C Major, a solo piano fantasy, the Fourth Piano Concerto, the early operatic scena "Ah! perfido," the Sixth and Fifth Symphonies (which, in this order, opened each half of the program), and, to conclude, the Choral Fantasy, by which Beethoven presumably aimed to bring together all of the evening's genres and performers. By all accounts, the standard of performance was shambolic: with barely any rehearsal time for so many new and challenging works, Beethoven had fallen out with the orchestra and singers, Beethoven's piano playing and hearing were not what they used to be, and the Choral Fantasy had been a last-minute addition. Seated in a box next to the loyal Prince Lobkowitz (and too close to the performers to attempt a discreet departure) was, yet again, Reichardt, who was one of several audience members to describe how the concluding Choral Fantasy came apart altogether and had to be restarted.[40] That there was no heating in the Theater an der Wien for a four-hour stretch only increased the audience's discomfort. "There we continued, in the bitterest cold, too, from half past six to half past ten, and experienced the truth that one can easily have too much of a good thing—and still more of a loud," recalled Reichardt, who expressed his sorrow that this had been Beethoven's only chance to earn some extra income all year.[41] Thus do infrastructures become most perceptible when they cease to work.[42]

Yet neither Reichardt nor Lobkowitz could have missed Beethoven's myriad allusions to proximate masterpieces by Haydn. The Mass in C Major was a recent commission from the Esterházy court and invited direct comparison with Haydn's masses, the most recent large-scale works that he had produced. More striking, however, were the relationships between the instrumental works on the concert and Haydn's late oratorios. Eighteenth-century aestheticians had long described the symphony as an instrumental species of chorus—as an orchestral translation of the choral aesthetic of sublime collective expression.[43] Beethoven's Fifth and Sixth Symphonies made this parallel explicit, and were plainly in dialogue with *The Creation* and *The Seasons*—the works that had dominated Vienna's early nineteenth-century concert scenes. The *Pastoral* responded above all to the bucolic episodes in *The Seasons*. The merry dancing of countryfolk in the third movement, the theatrical interruption of the thunderstorm, and the concluding pseudo-choral *Hirtengesang* (shepherd's song) together described a trajectory from turbulent nature to choral celebration that, as Richard Will has argued, restated the storm and evensong from "Summer" of *The Seasons* in the generic terms of the symphony.[44] And the Fifth would surely have recalled the re-creation of light from *The Creation* in the dazzling C minor–to–C major transition to its blazing march finale—one of several passages that, as Deirdre Loughridge has shown, exploited the pervasively audiovisual aesthetic of Haydn's oratorio.[45]

The trope of formless musical darkness expunged by light—and C minor by C major—occurred once again in the grand finale of the concert, the Choral Fantasy. Performing the parallel between composer and divine creator, which had been central to the reception of Haydn's *Creation* ever since its Burgtheater premiere, Beethoven devised a finale that opened with a solo keyboard improvisation—a fantasy beginning in C minor, as inchoate as Haydn's chaos, but here emerging as if directly from the imagination of the musical genius.[46] The improvisation effected a transition to C major and introduced a series of variations on a tune from Beethoven's early song "Gegenliebe," which ultimately unfolded into a choral finale on the self-referential subject of spiritual renewal through music:

> Wenn der Töne Zauber walten
> Und des Wortes Weihe spricht,
> Muss sich Herrliches gestalten,
> Nacht und Stürme werden Licht.
> [When the magic of tones reigns
> And speaks the sacred Word,
> Glory must emerge,
> Night and tempests turn to light.]

The relationships between the works on Beethoven's 1808 Akademie and Haydn's late oratorios amounted to more than a collection of near quotations, stylistic allusions, or generic translations. They were audible traces of a larger social performance of substitution, one that would enact and reproduce the major institutions of nineteenth-century music: Beethoven's *Seasons* and *Creation*, Beethoven's chaos and creation of light, Beethoven's chorus in praise of a glorious work achieved. As in the awkward processes of social substitution that Joseph Roach once called "surrogation," Beethoven's performance simultaneously sustained and covered up a relation to the musical past.[47] And Haydn was accordingly absorbed into the very infrastructure of Viennese music history, joining the network of things that are partially "displaced in the focus on the matter they move around," as Brian Larkin has put it.[48] In this context, Haydn was not precursor or predecessor but part of the platform upon which Beethoven's music was staged.[49]

Gold Is a Mighty Thing

Six years after Haydn's 1808 gala concert, Carl Weinmüller, who had been a soloist that evening, took up the role of the jailer Rocco in the successful revival of Beethoven's *Fidelio* in the Theater an der Wien. Rocco's only solo number was the so-called Gold aria—a terse comic song in act 1, which served to illustrate the small-minded materialism of the folk who harbored the disguised heroine Leonore. The simple song alternates between a plodding 2/4 meter, which describes the miseries of a penniless existence, and a tripping 6/8 dance, which celebrates the joyful rolling and jangling of coins; each verse ends back in 2/4 with Rocco lecturing his daughter Marzelline in the form of repeated tagline: "Es ist ein mächtig Ding, das Gold!" (Gold is a mighty thing).[50] When the Leipzig Hegelian Amadeus Wendt reviewed the score of *Fidelio* in the *Allgemeine musikalische Zeitung* a few months after its Viennese revival, he did not conceal his disdain for the Gold aria, whose musical ordinariness and "money morality [*Geldmoral*]" were, he thought, too much in keeping with the spiritually barren world of the opera's *bürgerlich* (that is, bourgeois or mercantile) opening. Beethoven's music, especially in conjunction with the heroic rescue and liberation that end the whole opera, "elevates this bürgerlich scene with magic power into a stronger and more Romantic world," he concluded.[51] To Wendt, Beethoven's music was manifestly the opposite of the bürgerlich, and *Fidelio* was a masterwork precisely because it described in miniature the purpose of all truly Romantic art: to obliterate and transcend the world of petty materialism.

Beethoven certainly professed to belong to the kind of spiritual aristocracy that spurned the values of the merely bürgerlich—no matter that he was perpetually forced to be "half businessman" as well as artist. In 1819, in the course of legal wrangles over his nephew Carl, the Austrian *Landrecht* discovered that the Flemish "van" in Beethoven's name was not an aristocratic German "von," as he had quietly allowed many people to believe.[52] Beethoven claimed to have told the court, "I had *never* worried *about my nobility*"—and Anton Schindler, with greater poetic license, recalled that Beethoven pointed to his head and heart and announced, "My nobility is *here* and *here*." Thus did a generation of nineteenth-century artists incorporate and spiritualize the ancient protocols of aristocratic distinction.[53]

These days, it is more or less an ethical imperative to be skeptical of such beliefs, as the insidious spectralization of elitism, exclusion, and hierarchy—as the unwelcome haunting of "bourgeois culture" by the "phantom of aristocratic values," to use Jean Baudrillard's hyperbolic wording.[54] We are also equipped with theoretical tools—Pierre Bourdieu's sociologies of taste in

particular—that can easily reveal nineteenth-century institutions as mechanisms for reproducing social distinction, for converting financial capital into
"cultural capital" and back again.[55] Like the theatrical scene of the art auction
theorized by Baudrillard, the Aula of the university or the Theater an der
Wien can be recast as a "crucible of the interchange of values," ceaselessly
converting exchange value into "sign value"—the principle of "aristocratic
exchange" that reproduced hierarchies within the semiotic domain of culture.[56] And yet these analyses, as their main concepts display, often work by
triumphantly translating the terms of culture into those of the market: *value,
capital, exchange.* This is all too easy in the case of early nineteenth-century
institutions, such as the Liebhaber Concerte or Reichardt's music journals,
because, as we have seen, they were premised on a new conception of "cultural value" that, as John Guillory once showed, was thinkable only via the
equally new economic conceptions of value that it came to oppose: the "thousand upon thousand diversions" versus enduring masterworks, monetary
value versus aesthetic value.[57] The Magazin der Kunst was only ever divided
from the actual marketplace of art by the most fragile ideological membrane.

Any victory over these Romantic habits of thought would be hollow, to say
the least, were it merely to confirm that gold is, after all, a mighty thing—that
capital is always art's reality principle, whatever any German idealist might
imply to the contrary. Granted, this book has been premised on the claim
that Haydn's music charted the drastic reordering of material relationships
over the course of the eighteenth century, and I have argued that his distinctive late aesthetic openly harnessed ways of interacting with and conceiving
of music that were unthinkable without the rapid growth of urban music
markets. But the utopianism of many musicians of Beethoven's generation
was not merely a delusional or ideological insistence on the value of art in
the face of the market realities that Haydn's generation had once acknowledged and even celebrated. It was openly cultivated and enacted through
new nineteenth-century infrastructures—concert societies, universities and
conservatories, and even new publication formats—that sought to function,
in part, as bulwarks against what one might as well call capitalism (and so
frequently depended upon paths laid down by the political authority, physical
fabrics, wealth, and associational practices of courts).[58] Haydn survived to see
many of his works absorbed into these infrastructures, but his music was by
and large not created for them. If it is nowadays easy to identify with Haydn's
openness to the music markets he encountered in Vienna and London, this
is not because of a happy coincidence between the outlook of today's market-
saturated societies and those of the late eighteenth century but because the
kind of music-related infrastructures that coalitions of musicians, business-

men, and patrons painstakingly constructed toward the end of Haydn's career have, especially since the late twentieth century, been progressively eroded by the logic of capital.

These days, puncturing the aristocratic pretensions and profaning the sacred pieties of art has never been easier or more attractive, and has never provoked less outrage. And it must be granted that, should scholars truly want to incorporate a greater diversity of musics, technologies, and sounds into their histories, then they cannot pursue the feeblest version of a politics of inclusion and strive merely to host more people and things within inherited intellectual infrastructures.[59] The promise of the upheavals of the present, as in the fast-changing music scenes of late eighteenth-century London and Vienna, is that the old infrastructures of musical knowledge and pleasure might be radically reordered, even dismantled altogether. Yet Haydn's experience of the excitable, productive, and catastrophic disruptions of his time shows that, once everything that is solid has melted into air, the residue is never the flat, networked, vibrational world of liberal (and, nowadays, neoliberal) fantasy—a world that is always less exploitative, less exclusive, less politically hierarchical than the one it supplants. To deregulate is always merely to push the infrastructure upon which we depend deeper into the shadows and so to make those who control it less accountable. This is one of the things that the economic history of Haydn's music has to tell us. An infrastructure is not a self-organizing gathering of matter. It is built by people with particular values and political purposes, and always at tremendous cost. As in Haydn's earlier age of new media, new economies, and new fantasies of global connectivity, the question is not whether old aesthetic and political hierarchies can be erased. There is no doubt they can be. It seems to me more important to ask what new hierarchies are replacing the old, and who gets to choose what they are.

Acknowledgments

I was introduced to the ideas that eventually turned into this book around twenty years ago, in one of the most thrilling classes I took in graduate school, Eighteenth-Century Aesthetics, with Neil Saccamano. I still think about the density, intensity, and shared purpose of that seminar whenever I run one of my own. As it happens, during that same semester, a handful of students had persuaded James Webster to meet informally every week simply to listen to Haydn's *Creation* all the way through, stopping to talk about each number in turn. It was a semester of total immersion in detail. It dawned on me then how much time it takes not just to say something of value but to listen.

But, as always, the lion's share of inspiration, as well as intimidating scholarly standards, has come from my colleagues in the Music Department at Berkeley. I love and admire them all very much. My dear friend Mary Ann Smart is a model thinker and reader. She responded to all of the manuscript, even when it was in a muddle, and saw things that no one else could have. I've spent much of the time since my previous book trying (vainly) to be more like James Davies, who writes and conjures worlds like nobody else. Having such a friend down the hallway for more than a decade has shaped my work more than any other factor. My newest colleague Lester Hu took on a respondent role in a symposium based around this book, read the whole thing, and showed me how to approach the material from entirely new perspectives. Over many conversations, Delia Casadei generously gave me access to her profound mind, committed intellectual outlook, and bibliographic obsessions. Emily Zazulia's precision of thought and quietly subversive stance toward our discipline have been a constant influence ever since she arrived at Berkeley. Gavin Williams read and heard about bits of this book as it was being written and offered concrete ideas, corrections, and reformulations, all of which I gratefully accepted. Ben Brinner and Jocelyne Guilbault were asked to read a version of the book early on and gave the sort of detailed feedback that fundamentally altered its course. Richard Taruskin has been an encouraging, trenchant, and funny walking companion this past year, and I'm lucky to have been exposed to his experience and insight so often. I'm grateful, too, for conversations about the discipline and much more besides with Maria Sonevytsky and T. Carlis Roberts.

Many others at Berkeley beyond the Music Department have been a source of surprising new thinking and sound advice. I've treasured the opportunity to talk about music with Tom Laqueur, who always came equipped with big ideas and historical tidbits, as well as writerly tips to boost morale. Ian Duncan, Amanda Goldstein, Tim Hampton, Tom McEnaney, Kent Puckett, and Andrea Roth gave me things to read and mind-bending perspectives from other disciplines. Susan Moffat, the executive director of the Global Urban Humanities Initiative at Berkeley, has been a dynamic and supportive presence and prompted me to collaborate on an urban studies seminar with Nicholas de Monchaux. I learned a lot that semester. Sections of this book were hammered out during a year as a fellow at the Townsend Center for the Humanities; my thanks to the other fellows and, in particular, the former director Alan Tansman. Thanks must also go to Jean Day and the members of the editorial board of *Representations*: over the past few years, I've been educated, energized, and amused on a regular schedule by witnessing (and now and again joining in with) its conversations.

My intuition is that this is a moment—either in institutional history or my personal history (maybe both: can't tell yet)—in which collaborating with graduate student colleagues, reading their recommendations, and (over)hearing their thoughts is more important than ever. I mean to imply a good deal more than the usual pieties about learning from one's students when I say that I've learned a vast amount from a series of graduate seminars, viva voce exams, and conversations with Susan Bay, Virginia Georgallas, Ryan Gourley, Peter Humphrey, Edward Jacobson, Alessandra Jones, Amalya Lehmann, Gabrielle Lochard, Jonathan Meci, Edmund Mendelssohn, Sarah Plovnik, Kim Sauberlich, Desmond Sheehan, Saraswathi Shukla, Danielle Simon, Jon Turner, John Walsh, Parkorn Wangpaiboonkit, and Rosie Ward.

Several colleagues in music studies read more or less all of this book in advance of its publication. A grant from Berkeley's Institute of International Studies allowed me to share a nearly complete draft at a symposium in March 2020 with three scholars I especially admire: Roger Grant, Deirdre Loughridge, and Gavin Steingo. They did an immense amount of work (and even Conor Loughridge did more than his share by providing the book's title a couple of weeks later). They left town barely hours before the you-know-what started, and for the next year or so, I held fast to the memory of those couple of days as something close to my ideal vision of the generous, warm, intellectually gregarious, intensely serious, and always fun interactions that strike me as among the greatest privileges of doing this job. In Ellen Lockhart I've been fortunate to have these sorts of interactions on tap: she was available to be interrupted to talk about ideas and books (and a few other things) while I was writing and read the manuscript from beginning to end with her characteristic intellectual x-ray vision. David Yearsley read the whole book with meticulous care: his knowledge, iconoclasm, and journalistic nous led to a series of important revisions, in detail and structure.

Others read and responded to shorter sections of the book as I wrote them. Ever since grad school, Emily Dolan has been my first port of call for scholarly orientation and reassurance, and she always made time to discuss impasses with me and immediately put her finger on the problem, even though she's a bit busier these days. Dean Sutcliffe has been a supportive colleague and friend for many years now, and I have been one of many scholars to profit from his exacting standards, anti-factional outlook, and sense of style. I had several long and illuminating conversations with my old friends Roger Moseley and Ben Walton, who each read bits of the book in the form of talks and articles. Ben Piekut has been a bracing person to argue with; he read an early version of chapter 2, and his feedback compelled some crucial changes. Elaine Sisman also kindly took the time to read an early version of that chapter. Joy Calico was a supportive and brilliant editor when an earlier version of chapter 2 appeared as "Interesting Haydn: On Attention's Materials," *Journal of the American Musicological Society* 71, no. 3 (2018): 655–701. It is reprinted here by permission of the University of California Press.

Without the opportunity to share work in conferences and colloquies conceived by others I would not have been able to complete this book. These include Emily Green and Catherine Mayes's Consuming Music, Commodifying Sound at Yale University; Mary Hunter and Richard Will's volume *Engaging Haydn*; Stephen Hinton's Haydn—Patronage and Enlightenment at Stanford University; Carmel Raz and James Grande's Sound and Sense in Britain, 1770–1840 at Columbia University's Heyman Center for the Humanities; and Carmel Raz (again) and Fran Brittan's *JAMS* colloquy Attention, Anxiety, and Audition's Histories. I was extremely lucky to have been included in these projects. I also had the opportunity to propose and defend several of the arguments in this book via talks at the Australian National University, Cornell University, Dalhousie University, Duke University, King's College London, Stanford University, the University of Melbourne, the University of Toronto,

Yale University, the American Musicological Society annual conference, and the International Music Society congress. At these events and others (and over email too, of course) esteemed colleagues gave me valuable criticism and encouragement, shared their own works in progress, and pointed out books and scholars unknown to me. My thanks to Tom Beghin, John Bender, Anna Maria Busse Berger, Karol Berger, Mark Evan Bonds, Kate Bowan, Erica Buurman, Jim Chandler, Chris Chowrimootoo, Sarah Collins, Jamie Currie, Oskar Cox Jensen, Michael Denning, Emma Dillon, Steve Feld, Martha Feldman, Mark Ferraguto, Matthew Gelbart, Robert Gjerdingen, Dana Gooley, Yoel Greenberg, Thomas Grey, Kate Guthrie, Katherine Hambridge, Julia Hamilton, Matthew Head, Erin Helyard, Jim Hepokoski, Sarah Hibbard, Jo Hicks, Stephen Hinton, Mary Hunter, Thomas Irvine, David Irving, Estelle Joubert, Brian Kane, Gundula Kreuzer, George Lewis, Birgit Lodes, Aoife Monks, Fabio Morabito, Adeline Mueller, Kate van Orden, Roger Parker, Paul Pickering, Alex Rehding, Annette Richards, Emanuele Senici, Ben Steege, Martin Stokes, Anicia Timberlake, Gary Tomlinson, Bettina Varwig, Jacqueline Waeber, Jim Webster, Emily Wilbourne, Richard Will, David Wyn Jones, and Anna Zayaruznaya.

Not having access to archives in the latter stage of this project was nothing less than a massive bummer. Most problems were overcome or alleviated by accommodating and creative librarians. My thanks to the curators and archivists at the Rare Books and Music Reading Room of the British Library, the reading room of the Bishopsgate Institute, the Music Department of the Staatsbibliothek zu Berlin, the State Library of Mecklenburg-Vorpommern Günther Uecker, the Music Department of the Austrian State Library, Stanford University Libraries, the Houghton Library at Harvard University, the study room of the Yale Center for British Art, and Berkeley's Jean Hargrove Music Library—especially John Shepard.

Marta Tonegutti and Dylan Montanari at the University of Chicago Press have made starting and completing this project a pleasure rather than a chore. I am hugely grateful to them and to the anonymous readers who provided substantial and invigorating engagements with the manuscript. At the end of the process, Matthew Perez was a stylish and exacting copyeditor.

It seems to me that the tumult in the world beyond this book needs no more acknowledgment than it has already received or doubtless will receive. It is enough to say that friends and family have for some time been badly missed yet badly needed. I owe special thanks, then, to Sezi Seskir, always rapturous, intensely musical, and very funny to talk to. And to Anna Goldsworthy, whose absurd list of talents extends to correspondence. Merritt and Schuyler Oliver repeatedly supplied a change of view out of the window when we all desperately needed one; the spade work on this book was completed on their watch in the middle of Oregon. My sister Jenny and brother-in-law Chris gamely showed up in London whenever I was doing research there, then gamely stayed in touch when showing up in person was no longer an option. This book is dedicated to my dad, who knows quite a lot about both music and economics. Last, and most importantly, my love and thanks to Penny, Felix, and Fraser. They have, needless to say, been close by lately.

Notes

Abbreviations

cc: Haydn, Joseph. *The Collected Correspondence and London Notebooks of Joseph Haydn*. Edited and translated by H. C. Robbins Landon. London: Barrie and Rockliff, 1959.
gb: Haydn, Joseph. *Gesammelte Briefe und Aufzeichnungen*. Edited by Dénes Bartha. Kassel: Bärenreiter, 1965.

Introduction

1. "To MR. URBAN, on his completing the 53rd Volume of THE GENTLEMAN'S MAGAZINE," *Gentleman's Magazine* 53, no. 1 (1783): ii.

2. See Robbins Landon, *Chronicle and Works*, 2:478. Translation adapted from Wyn Jones, *Life of Haydn*, 107.

3. See Wyn Jones, 106–7.

4. Letter of September 29, 1782: *CC*, 38; *GS*, 119. Haydn's request for full weight currency reflects contemporary anxieties about coin clipping in Austria at this time, when the value of coinage was still ostensibly established by metal content.

5. See the letter of March 14, 1791: *CC*, 115; *GS*, 255.

6. *CC*, 293, 306; *GS*, 353–54, 553.

7. R. Williams, *Culture and Society*, 35.

8. See, inter alia, Eagleton, *Ideology of the Aesthetic*; and Ferry, *Homo Aestheticus*.

9. This is the sociological tradition of Pierre Bourdieu. See especially Bourdieu, *Distinction*; and Bourdieu, *Rules of Art*. With respect to the history of modernism, see Huyssen, *After the Great Divide*. In connection with German musical cultures of the late eighteenth century and early nineteenth century, see, inter alia, De Nora, *Construction of Genius*; and Gramit, *Cultivating Music*.

10. See Rowlinson, *Real Money and Romanticism*. In music studies, see Zaslaw, "Working Stiff"; and Chua, "Mozart, Money, Music."

11. In music criticism, the canonical Frankfurt school essay in this vein remains Adorno, "Fetish Character in Music."

12. Ngai, *Our Aesthetic Categories*. See also Jameson, *Postmodernism*, esp. 5–6.

13. See Guilbault, "Roy Cape's Labour"; Stokes, "Marx, Money, and Musicians"; Steingo, *Kwaito's Promise*; Sykes, *Musical Gift*.

14. See Lynch, *Economy of Character*; Gallagher, *Body Economic*; Poovey, *Credit Economy*;

Woodmansee, *Author, Art*; and the essays gathered in Osteen and Woodmansee, *New Economic Criticism*. More recent studies have developed this body of research in a broadly new materialist spirit, by articulating connections between literature, political economy, and the natural sciences. See, e.g., the essays collected in Barney and Montag, *Systems of Life*.

15. See Caygill, *Art of Judgement*, 38–102; Guillory, *Cultural Capital*, ch. 5; and Poovey, "Aesthetics and Political Economy." Moreover, as more recent studies have argued, these discourses were once grounded in a shared vitalist conception of the world that confuses present-day conceptions of new (Lucretian) and old (Marxist) materialisms. See Goldstein, *Sweet Science*; and Barney and Montag, *Systems of Life*.

16. See Schabas, *Natural Origins of Economics*.

17. Robbins Landon, *Chronicle and Works*, 2:712. On Haydn's changing perception of his public, see Sisman, "Haydn's Career"; and Fuhrmann, *Haydn und sein Publikum*.

18. Griesinger, *Two Contemporary Portraits*, 23.

19. Polanyi, *Great Transformation*.

20. This prevailing view has been revised and resisted in work by Birgit Lodes. See the essays collected in Lodes, Reisinger, and Wilson, *Beethoven und andere Hofmusiker seiner Generation*.

21. *Lady's Magazine*, February 1791, 108. See also Geiringer, *Haydn*, 107.

22. Kittler, "City Is a Medium."

23. See Wood, *Origin of Capitalism*, ch. 5. See also Wallerstein, *Historical Capitalism*.

24. As argued in classics of urban studies, such as Jacobs, *Cities and the Wealth of Nations*.

25. Harvey, *Rebel Cities*, 5.

26. Here, I have been inspired by the urban studies turn within scholarship on literary Romanticism, such as Chandler and Gilmartin, *Romantic Metropolis*.

27. C. Burney, *Present State of Music*, 205.

28. See Morrow, *Concert Life*, esp. ch. 3. On London's concert life in the same period, see McVeigh, *Concert Life in London*.

29. *Morning Chronicle*, December 30, 1790, reprinted in Robbins Landon, *Chronicle and Works* 3:31. See also McVeigh, *Concert Life in London*, ch. 2–4.

30. See Robbins Landon, 3:160–61.

31. Florida, *Rise of the Creative*; and Florida, *Cities and the Creative*.

32. See Robbins Landon, *Chronicle and Works* 3:124. On the regulation of urban noise in this period, see Cockayne, *Hubbub*, ch. 5.

33. Cited in Greig, *Beau Monde*, 64.

34. On "scenes," especially as they have been theorized in popular music studies, see, inter alia, Straw, "Scene Might Be."

35. See Robbins Landon, *Chronicle and Works* 2:454–45. Gotwals, *Two Contemporary Portraits*, 33. Scholarship that emphasizes Haydn's stylistic responses to these new markets includes Wheelock, *"Ingenious Jesting with Art"*; Sisman, "Haydn's Career"; Somfai, "London Revision"; Schroeder, *Haydn and the Enlightenment*; and Fuhrmann, *Haydn und sein Publikum*.

36. On Haydn and the attention economy, see Mathew, "Attention Economy."

37. E. Thompson, *English Working Class*, 9.

38. In the case of Marx, this case has been made convincingly by Goldstein in *Sweet Science*, "Coda." It is also among the premises of the essays collected in Barney and Montag, *Systems of Life*. Among all new materialist writers, Jane Bennett has been clearest that she belongs to a tradition of "Democritus-Epicurus-Spinoza-Diderot-Deleuze" more than the (more historically bunched-together, one should note) "Hegel-Marx-Adorno." See Bennett, *Vibrant Matter*, xiii.

39. Roach, *It*, 12–21.

40. This includes studies as varied as Chapman, *The Jazz Bubble*; Green and Mayes, *Consuming Music*; Guilbault and Rommen, *Sounds of Vacation*; Steingo, "Musical Economies"; Sykes, *Musical Gift*; and T. Taylor, *Music and Capitalism*.

41. That the Enlightenment was "an event in the history of mediation" is the foundational claim of Siskin and Warner, "Form of an Argument." See also Siskin and Warner, "If This Is Enlightenment." In this sentence, I have used Siskin and Warner's rubric of "cardinal mediations" (formats and genres, principles of association, protocols and laws, and infrastructures). See Siskin and Warner, "Form of an Argument," 12–15. I will remain sensitive to these categories throughout this book, though I will not always deploy this vocabulary.

42. With respect to music from this period, see, inter alia, Gramit, *Cultivating Music*; S. Rose, *Musical Authorship*, ch. 4; Weber, *Musician as Entrepreneur*. Two recent studies have treated some of these questions from a philosophical-theoretical perspective: Currie, *Politics of Negation*; and Waltham-Smith, *Music and Belonging*.

43. In this emphasis, I have been inspired by the work of Emily Dolan and Deirdre Loughridge in particular. See Dolan, *Orchestral Revolution*; and Loughridge, *Haydn's Sunrise, Beethoven's Shadow*.

44. May 2, 1792: *CC*, 281.

45. Robbins Landon, *Chronicle and Works* 3:160–61.

46. Davison, "Musical Genius."

47. See Guillory, "Media Concept," 323n4.

48. The importance of the question *in what?* explains why this book makes no distinction between examples and figures: insofar as possible, I have tried to resist the idea that one should distinguish between relatively transparent versions of The Music in modern editions and the now noticeable mediacy of historical editions or transcriptions. Several recent publications crucially contribute to our understanding of music printing and selling in this period. See, for example, the essays in Rasch, *Music Publishing in Europe*; and Rasch, *Circulation of Music*. Rupert Ridgewell has published a series of important and detailed studies of the Viennese music industry, especially Artaria. See Ridgewell, "Economic Aspects"; Ridgewell, "Inside a Viennese *Kunsthandlung*"; Ridgewell, "Mozart's Publishing Plans"; and Ridgewell, "Artaria's Music Shop." Meanwhile, there have been several important contributions to our knowledge of music selling in England; see, e.g., the essays in Kassler, *Music Trade in Georgian England*. Anyone writing about London and the emerging institution of the public concert remains indebted to the continuing work of Simon McVeigh. See McVeigh, *Concert Life in London*.

49. See Devine, *Decomposed*, esp. 165–89.

50. Gotwals, *Two Contemporary Portraits*, 131.

51. Gitelman, *Always Already New*, 154.

52. My inspirations here include sound-focused media archaeologies, such as McEnaney, *Acoustic Properties*.

53. On this claim, see Mathew, "Listening(s) Past."

54. Ridgewell, "Economic Aspects," 89. See van Orden, *Music, Authorship*.

55. Adrian Johns has argued that authority, unity, and permanence were not in any sense the inevitable consequences of a monolithic "print culture" but rather became the ideological companions of certain books and their political uses. See A. Johns, *Nature of the Book*. The point is reargued in connection with the paradigm of interaction by the group of academics who have called themselves the Multigraph Collective in *Interacting with Print*. On the diverse social uses of musical print in an earlier period, see van Orden, *Materialities*; and the essays collected in van Orden, *Cultures of Print*.

56. Examples include the essays in Bijsterveld, *Soundscapes*; Williams, "Voice of the Crowd"; and Dillon, *Sense of Sound*.

57. See Ochoa, *Aurality*. On colonial technologies of music transcription in this period, see also Goodman, "Music Transcription."

58. On the politics of music versus noise in eighteenth-century London, see Cockayne, *Hubbub*, 121–30. On the politics of music as noise in the context of European and non-European contact, see Irvine, *Listening to China*, esp. ch. 2.

59. Steingo and Sykes, "Remapping Sound Studies." See also M. Thompson, "Whiteness and the Ontological."

60. See also Mathew, "Listening(s) Past," esp. 151–53. While I am on the subject of sound studies, this may be the moment to say something about *Noise: A Political Economy of Music* by the French columnist, social theorist, businessman, and civil servant Jacques Attali. I have read this book several times over the years: as an undergraduate, when it was still relatively new in translation and had been promoted amid the ambience of 1990s disciplinary change; at graduate school, when it was a residual presence on syllabuses introducing the discipline of music history; and a number of times since—during the dim early coalescence of this book, as well as during the more coherent phases that followed. My persistence with *Noise* was prompted in part by the small renaissance that it has enjoyed in recent years, anthologized in a generation of sound studies readers, as this relatively young subdiscipline cast around for authoritative disciplinary forebears. Each time, I have been disappointed to rediscover that its mode of argumentation and central claim—that music is a herald of radical sociohistorical and economic transformations—strike me as schematic and glib, not to mention highly improbable, predicated on a simplistic metaphysic of sound and a dubiously avant-gardist theory of historical change. To the extent that *Noise* is cited nowadays, it is usually out of duty, with its high-handed formulations pressed into relevance through special pleading or vague conceptual homologies. Eric Drott's account of how Attali's publications of the mid-1970s were shaped by the contemporary predicament of the French left (see Drott, "Rereading Attali's *Bruits*") has only increased my suspicion that the former prominence and occasional recrudescence of *Noise* in English-language musicological scholarship since then is the consequence of historical accident as much as the resonance or depth of its arguments. And that *Noise* is one of around sixty works trotted out at some speed by Attali on subjects ranging from nomadism and mathematics to children's literature and global governance makes me wonder whether this one early essay deserves the scholarly care that even the skeptical Drott devotes to it. It is as if, several decades from now, scholars working in North American departments of environmental design were regularly citing a slim, speculative volume on architecture by a former Downing Street special adviser. That said, I am still open to being talked round: Susan McClary advances several persuasive reasons to value *Noise* in her passionate preface to the latest English-language edition, while Michael Denning has since made a version of Attali's central thesis seem convincing in his inspiring *Noise Uprising*. But any conversion on my part will come too late for this project—and this explains why, despite the promise of its title, *Noise* is, from this point on, absent from my book.

61. On the problem with "contexts," see Felski, *Limits of Critique*, esp. ch. 5. Felski responds to the sociological methods of Bruno Latour, who gives a usefully concise account of his actor-network-theory (ANT) in Latour, *Reassembling*. Within music studies, Benjamin Piekut has been the most loyal advocate of Latour's work. See Piekut, "Actor-Networks"; and Piekut, *Experimentalism Otherwise*. I have also taken inspiration from Leo Cabranes-Grant's intercultural perspective, which uses ANT "as a springboard, not as a dogma." Cabranes-Grant, *From Scenarios to Networks*, 31.

62. On the limits of relational ontologies of movement and circulation in contemporary South African musical scenarios, see Steingo, *Kwaito's Promise*, ch. 4; and Steingo, "Actors and Accidents."

63. Bennett, *Vibrant Matter*; Tsing, *Mushroom*, 23, 24; Cabranes-Grant, *From Scenarios to Networks*, 31. Cabranes-Grant notably argues that his musical-intercultural networks will "sound more like Elliot Carter than Franz Schubert," because he understands the voices in Carter to be organized less hierarchically and implies that there is something politically suspect about "traditional melodies." I can think of few less inclusive, less professedly intercultural spaces than Carter's high modernist chamber music.

64. Pocock, "Mobility of Property," 109. On the relation of music, early modern fantasies of global connection, and European colonial violence, particularly in the French context, see Bloechl, *Native American Song*, esp. ch. 1.

65. Tsing, *Mushroom*, 24.

66. Walton, "Quirk Shame," 127.

67. Chakrabarty, *Provincializing Europe*.

68. On the relation of "value" and "values" in culture and economics, see Appadurai, "Politics of Value"; Graeber, *Anthropological Theory of Value*; and Spivak, "Scattered Speculations." See also the essays gathered in MacDonald, *Values of Literary Studies*; and Steingo and Moreno's introduction to their special issue of *boundary 2*.

69. On the relation of values to art and attachment, see Felski, *Hooked*, ch. 1, esp. 31–38.

70. See Garratt, "Haydn and Posterity"; L. Kramer, "Kitten and the Tiger"; and Sutcliffe, *Instrumental Music*, esp. 31.

71. This tendency is plain not only in recent publications by Dolan and Loughridge but in decades of creative and innovative research by Tom Beghin, Caryl Clark, James Currie, Matthew Head, Mary Hunter, W. Dean Sutcliffe, Annette Richards, Thomas Tolley, Gretchen Wheelock, and Richard Will—as well as the foundational Haydn scholarship of Wye J. Allanbrook, Elaine Sisman, László Somfai, and James Webster.

Chapter 1

1. Raynal, *Philosophical and Political History*, 6:347.

2. Anon., "Importation of Haydn; or, The Commerce of the Arts," *European Magazine and London Review*, March 1791, 230.

3. Young, *Conjectures*, 12.

4. I am using the term "bioeconomic" here after Gallagher, *Body Economic*, 3 and passim. Also, in terms that owe more to Foucauldian biopolitics, see Barney and Montag, *Systems of Life*, 1–33 (the introduction). On Smith's vitalism, see Packham, *Eighteenth-Century Vitalism*, esp. ch. 2; and Packham, "System and Subject."

5. South, *Twelve Sermons*, 438; S. Johnson, *Dictionary*, s.v. "Commutation."

6. Hume, *Treatise of Human Nature*, 317.

7. L. Sterne, *Sentimental Journey*, 8.

8. Gotwals, *Two Contemporary Portraits*, 120.

9. See M. Head, "Haydn's Exoticisms," 80.

10. For two insightful discussions of contemporary German musical conceptions of sympathy, *Mitleid* and *Mitgefühl*, see Head, "Benevolent Machinery"; and R. Kramer, *Cherubino's Leap*, 189–91.

11. Knight, *Progress of Civil Society*, 53, 135–36. On eighteenth-century revisions of the great

chain of being, see K. Goodman, *Georgic Modernity*, 56. On notions of self-organization in this period and Knight's *Progress*, see Sheehan and Wahrman, *Invisible Hands*, esp. 271–77.

12. Pocock, "Mobility of Property," 109.

13. Clarke, *Statistical View of Germany*, 54.

14. Mattheson, *Der vollkommene Capellmeister*, bk. 2, ch. 4, para. 15–19. On Mattheson and *Vorrath*, see Allanbrook, *Secular Commedia*, 98–99. On Haydn and *Der vollkommene Capell-meister*, see Gotwals, *Two Contemporary Portraits*, 10.

15. Adelung, *Grammatisch-kritisches Wörterbuch*, s.v. "Vorrath."

16. Locke, "Some Thoughts on Education," 202. On the "package logic" of much eighteenth-century thought, see also Franzel, "Metaphors of Spatial Storage," 328–52.

17. Knight, *Progress of Civil Society*, 5. Gallagher, *Body Economic*, 3–4 and passim. On circulation metaphors with respect to the trading nation, see also Lynch, *Economy of Character*, 43, 207–13.

18. See, for example, his work on the "Betrachtung des Neuen Finanz-Wercks" (a pamphlet on the South Sea bubble) and "The Wealth and Commerce of *Great-Britain* Consider'd," cited in Cannon, *Johann Mattheson*, 173–74, 190.

19. On Mattheson's warehouse notion of the musician and attendant view of authorship, see Rose, *Musical Authorship*, esp. 41, 76–77.

20. Gotwals, *Two Contemporary Portraits*, 17 (translation amended).

21. Letter of May 27, 1781: *CC*, 28; *GB*, 97.

22. Letter of February 9, 1790: *CC*, 96–97; *GB*, 228–29.

23. See the essays in Strohm, *Eighteenth-Century Diaspora*.

24. Letter of July 6, 1776: *CC*, 19; *GB*, 77. See also Diergarten, "Haydn's Partimento Counterpoint," 53–75; Gjerdingen, "Partimento," esp. 89.

25. On "contact zones," see Pratt, *Imperial Eyes*, 1–12; Greenblatt, "Mobility Studies Manifesto," 251.

26. See C. Burney, *General History of Music*, 2:959. The extensive manuscript collections of Prince Paul Anton also put Haydn newly in touch with French music at a time when Gluck was producing French operas for the imperial court theater.

27. See Clark, "Haydn in the Theater," 176–99; and Heartz, *Mozart, Haydn*, 329–41. For a detailed example of how Haydn engaged with imported operas, see Rice, "*Montezuma* at Eszterház."

28. On partimento technique as constitutive of Italianate styles of the period, see Gjerdingen, "Partimento"; Gjerdingen, *Galant Style*; and Sanguinetti, *Art of Partimento*.

29. Allanbrook, *Secular Commedia*, 26.

30. See Sisman, "Haydn's Theater Symphonies," 292–352; on the Symphony no. 59, 342–43. The 1774 performance was almost certainly responsible for the symphony's nickname, "Das Feuer." See Robbins Landon, *Chronicle and Works*, 3:279–80.

31. See Gjerdingen, *Galant Style*, ch. 13.

32. Gjerdingen, *Galant Style*, 6; Grant, *Peculiar Attunements*, 10; Mirka, "Topics and Meter," 374. On formula in late eighteenth-century instrumental music, see also Sutcliffe, *Instrumental Music*, ch. 3.

33. Mirka, *Oxford Handbook*, 2. Emphasis in original. See, for example, Derrida, "Signature Event Context," 1–23.

34. On the original as a function or product of the copy, see J. Sterne, *Audible Past*, esp. ch. 5.

35. See Grant, *Peculiar Attunements*, ch. 2, esp. 68–81.

36. On eighteenth-century music in the tradition of opera buffa as a *speculum mundi*, see Allanbrook, *Secular Commedia*, ch. 3. For a critique of this musical mirror as a potentially more insidious form of world making, see Currie, *Politics of Negation*, ch. 1.

37. See the damning critique of the "topic" concept in Rumph, *Mozart and Enlightenment Semiotics*, ch. 3.

38. Pirated editions of Haydn symphonies had appeared in France and the Netherlands by the middle of the 1760s. On Haydn, copyists, and piracy, see Robbins Landon, *Chronicle and Works*, 2:602–5. On piracy as a condition for the circulation of knowledge in this period, see Johns, "Piratical Enlightenment," 301–20.

39. Letter of October 7, 1787: *CC*, 71; *GB*, 180.

40. See Meci, "Afterlives."

41. Letter of 1768 (no other date): *CC*, 11; *GB*, 60. See also Sisman, "Haydn's Career," 8–9.

42. This was surely a symptom of his heightened awareness of the division of sound and source. Rapidly changing media regimes arguably make the fact of this division—conceptually essential to the coherence of any sounds—appreciable in new ways, as in R. Murray Schafer's anxieties about "schizophonia," prompted by what he called the "electronic age" (see Schafer, *Soundscape*, 90–91). This may also explain why the earliest generation of "mobile music" studies have disproportionately focused on such technologies as the Walkman, iPod, and smartphone and in some cases overstate the fact of global dispersion that is so much a part of the digital-era media imaginary. See, for example, the essays in Gopinath and Stanyek, *Oxford Handbook*, 2 vols.

43. H. C. Robbins Landon, writing of the spread of Haydn's music in the 1780s, described a "grand dissemination." See Robbins Landon, *Chronicle and Works*, 2:588–605. There is a parallel here with Jean Christophe Agnew's discussion of the changing market conditions of eighteenth-century writers, which contrasts "the private circulation of handwritten manuscripts within close courtly circles" with "the public distribution of printed volumes before a new and anonymous readership." Agnew, *Worlds Apart*, 166.

44. James Webster showed this some time ago in *Haydn's "Farewell" Symphony*.

45. Tracing the interaction between related principles of (digital) musical reproducibility via changing technologies and media forms is partly the object of Roger Moseley, *Keys to Play*, esp. key 2.

46. Ridgewell, "Economic Aspects," 91–92. On the range of things that Artaria sold and made, see Ridgewell, "Inside a Viennese *Kunsthandlung*."

47. They contracted out the expensive, complex, and messy business of printing until the early 1790s; see Ridgewell, "Economic Aspects," 95.

48. For a concise discussion of the possible range of new contracts in the 1770s, see Wyn Jones, *Life of Haydn*, 101–2.

49. I am explicitly summarizing these changes in terms of what Siskin and Warner call "cardinal mediations": infrastructures, genres and formats, protocols, and associational practices. See Siskin and Warner, "Invitation," 12–15.

50. There is a parallel here with Jonathan Sterne's argument that a range of existing cultural techniques and competencies allow new technologies to be perceived as "working." In his examples—late nineteenth-century telephony and phonography—the success of public demonstration was guaranteed in part by what he calls the "clichéd and conventionalized language" that these technologies were typically required to reproduce, the kind of thing "that the audience either already knew or could readily understand." J. Sterne, *Audible Past*, 250–51. It is a nice irony

that Sterne draws on the concept of the cliché here, which, like the stereotype, derives from early nineteenth-century technologies of print reproduction (on which, more below). Barbara Johnson has characterized the stereotype as the "already-read text"; see *Critical Difference*, 3.

51. On the relationship between paper, genre, and credit, see Poovey, *Credit Economy*.

52. Letter of August 10, 1788: *CC*, 77; *GB*, 191.

53. Letter of October 26, 1788: *CC*, 79; *GB*, 195.

54. Letter of March 29, 1789: *CC*, 82–83; *GB*, 202. On the fantasia as commodity, see Fuhrmann, "Originality as Market-Value."

55. See Price, *Handbook of London Bankers*, 71.

56. Cited in Roscoe, "Haydn and London," 207. Emphasis in original.

57. *New Music Published in London, and imported from different Parts of Europe, in the Year, 1781* (London: Longman & Broderip, 1781).

58. *A Complete Register of all the New Musical Publications imported from Different Parts of Europe by Longman and Broderip* (London: Longman & Broderip, 1786).

59. See Wyn Jones, "From Artaria," 109.

60. See Mace, "London Music Sellers."

61. Woodfield, "John Bland."

62. Cited in Woodfield, "John Bland," 213.

63. See Robbins Landon, *Chronicle and Works*, 2:718.

64. Woodfield, "John Bland," 238–44.

65. McKendrick, "George Packwood."

66. *CC*, 251; *GB*, 481.

67. See Robbins Landon, "Four New Haydn Letters," 213–19.

68. *Morning Chronicle*, January 3, 1791; see Robbins Landon, *Chronicle and Works*, 3:31.

69. Busby, *Concert Room and Orchestra*, 1:269.

70. Robbins Landon, *Chronicle and Works*, 3:73.

71. See Komlós, "Miscellaneous Vocal Genres," 170–72.

72. See Pohl, *Mozart und Haydn*, 118–19. Mary Blair (née Johnson) was married to the Scottish-born industrialist Alexander Blair, who had made a fortune in soap and lead making in the Black Country. They lived in a new mansion at 28 Portland Place.

73. Robbins Landon, *Chronicle and Works* 3:75–76.

74. Letter of October 13, 1791: *CC*, 120; *GB*, 263–64 (translation slightly amended). On the changing meanings and functions of credit in this period, see Finn, *Character of Credit*, esp. ch. 1 and 2.

75. Robbins Landon, *Chronicle and Works*, 2:753, 3:27–28, 35.

76. Kittler, "City Is a Medium," 725.

77. Letter of January 8, 1791. *CC*, 113; *GB*, 252 (translation amended).

78. Robbins Landon, *Chronicle and Works*, 3:129.

79. *CC*, 289; *GB*, 531.

80. Cited in Nex, "Longman & Broderip," 63.

81. See King, "Music Circulating Libraries."

82. See R. Head, "Corelli in Calcutta," 550. Tolley, "Music in the Circle"; Woodfield, "Haydn Symphonies in Calcutta"; and Woodfield, *Music of the Raj*.

83. Robbins Landon, *Chronicle and Works*, 3:415.

84. See Haydn's long notebook entry on the Macartney Mission, *CC*, 299–300; *GB*, 544. On music and the mission, see Irvine, *Listening to China*, ch. 4; and Lindorff, "Burney, Macartney."

85. On the eighteenth-century ivory trade, see Feinberg and Johnson, "West African Ivory Trade"; and Alpers, *Ivory and Slaves*.

86. One could consider the piano here in the context of what Jacob Smith has called "eco-sonic media"—though I do not think that I am in a position to adjudicate which sound technologies were the most environmentally virtuous. See J. Smith, *Eco-Sonic Media*. Also Dawe, "Materials Matter." The ivory trade doubtless had a significant and measurable environmental impact in the eighteenth and nineteenth centuries. See, for example, Håkansson, "Human Ecology."

87. See *The Times*, November 12, 1790, 2. On this delegation, see Power, *Art of the Cherokee*, 71.

88. On this song in particular, see Pisani, *Imagining Native America*, 53–59. Part of Pisani's aim is to discriminate whether this song is any way (authentically) Cherokee, and to what extent. From a political and historical perspective, this may be a defensible goal, though it contradicts recent approaches in the humanities and social sciences that would not seek to disentangle the products of what used to be called "cultural encounter" but rather to regard such artifacts as productive of distinctively European conceptions of cultural difference.

89. Anne Hunter's husband, the surgeon John Hunter, was to commission pictures of members of the 1790 Cherokee party. William Bowles, meanwhile, was painted by Thomas Hardy in 1791, shortly before Hardy produced his portrait of Haydn.

90. The "Death Song" could be situated in the process that Steven Feld described as "schizophonic mimesis"; see Feld, "Pygmy POP." Glenda Goodman has argued that notation is an inherently colonial technology in these cases, which necessarily cannot capture the "ineffability of the aural," which "eludes empire's grasp" (see G. Goodman, "Music Transcription," 43, 40). I would, however, caution against the dubiously commonsense notion that may be implied by these claims: that printed notation is self-evidently less transparent than later forms of sound reproduction and accordingly requires musicologists to inquire into questions of authentic style and origin (as Pisani does in *Imagining Native America*) in ways that phonograph recordings do not (even Goodman writes of music alienated by notation "from its culture of origin"; "Music Transcription," 44). First, as Paula McDowell has shown, "orality" by no means describes the unsullied condition in which European technologies of notation and phonography encountered previously unrecorded sonic practices but was itself an eighteenth-century European invention—"a back-formation of print" (*Invention of the Oral*, 287). Second, I would prefer to say that a phonograph recording produced in London and a printed score produced in London are both European media forms, each with a potentially extractive imperial logic, each producing and making knowable an ostensible "original." On colonial extraction and inscription, see also Ochoa, *Aurality*, esp. ch. 1. Brian Hochman argues that the racial fantasies of early ethnographies—and in particular their documentation of "vanishing" peoples—crucially shaped beliefs about the media technologies they used (not least that these technologies preserve or archive the real). One could imagine extending this argument to encompass the commerce in music prints, and especially early prints that documented supposedly non-European music; see Hochman, *Savage Preservation*.

91. Busby, *Concert Room and Orchestra*, 1:127.

92. Robbins Landon, *Chronicle and Works*, 3:65. Emphasis in original.

93. *CC*, 289, 291, 292, 297; *GB*, 532–35. Haydn visited the Portsmouth Dockyard in the summer of 1794, though, as a foreigner, he was forbidden from entering the dockyard itself.

94. The piece probably remained unfinished because the earl became embroiled in a scandal that led to a prison sentence early in 1795. The text of the *Invocation*—an eccentric assertion of Britain's dominion of the sea, which had been heard in London ten years earlier in a version by

Friedrich Hartmann Graf—derived from verses that prefaced Marchimont Nedham's translation of John Selden's 1635 *Mare Clausum*, an arcane legal treatise advancing the contested idea
that the ocean could be privately owned. See Mikusi, "New Light."

95. On these martial and maritime compositions, see Mathew, "Heroic Haydn," esp. 13–15.

96. Sloterdijk, *World Interior of Capital*, 122–23.

97. Gotwals, *Two Contemporary Portraits*, 149–50. Dies's story sees the captain sail to America, Carpani's to Calcutta. Carpani, *Le Haydine*, 225–27.

98. See *CC*, 275; *GB*, 511.

99. On the Hastings trial, see Musselwhite, "Trial of Warren Hastings"; Carnall and Nicholson, *Impeachment of Warren Hastings*; and Pitts, *Turn to Empire*, esp. 64 –71.

100. See Olleson, *Journals and Letters*, 34.

101. *CC*, 254; *GB*, 486. On Burney, Hastings, and Haydn, see Woodfield, *Music of the Raj*,
218–21.

102. Cited in Pitts, *Turn to Empire*, 74.

103. Burke, *Philosophical Enquiry*, 41. See Horwärthner, "Joseph Haydn's Library," 421.

104. Cited in Pitts, *Turn to Empire*, 74. On Smith, sympathy, and distance, see Forman-
Barzilai, "Sympathy in Space(s)"; Paganelli, "Moralizing Role of Distance"; and Marshall, *Figure
of Theater*, 180.

105. See Musselwhite, "Trial of Warren Hastings," 92–94. On Burke's rhetorical tactics, see
also Aravamudan, *Tropicopolitans*, 224–29. On sympathy and abolitionist rhetoric, see Boulukos, "Capitalism and Slavery"; Harding, "Commerce, Sentiment"; Meneley, "Acts of Sympathy";
and Waters, "Sympathy, Nerve Physiology."

106. Fairclough, *Romantic Crowd*, 52. On the "communication of sentiments," see Hume,
Treatise of Human Nature, 412. "The enabling condition of mediation," writes John Guillory, "is
the interposition of *distance*"—an observation that applies equally well to eighteenth-century
conceptions of sympathy; Guillory, "Genesis," 357.

107. A. Smith, *Theory of Moral Sentiments*, 111. See also Marshall, *Figure of Theater*, 171. Incidentally, Haydn owned the 1793 edition of *The Theory of Moral Sentiments*; see Horwärthner,
"Joseph Haydn's Library," 420.

108. Letter of April 12, 1792: *CC*, 280; *GB*, 519.

109. Hume, *Treatise of Human Nature*, 414.

110. Richards, *Free Fantasia*, ch. 5. On the division of self within eighteenth-century conceptions of sympathy, see Marshall, *Figure of Theater*, 175–77.

111. Festa, *Sentimental Figures of Empire*, 24. On affect and mobility, see also Burgess, "On
Being Moved" and "Transport."

112. On character and "character," see Lynch, *Economy of Character*, 38; Oakleaf, "Marks,
Stamps, and Representations"; and, in the French (but musical) context, Stevens, "Meanings and
Uses." For an example of the eighteenth-century use of the term "musical character" to refer to
inscription, see Hawkins, *General History*, passim.

113. Festa, *Sentimental Figures of Empire*, 20.

114. On the prints that Haydn acquired in London, see Tolley, *Painting the Cannon's Roar*,
207–42. On Hastings, Haydn, and *The Judgement of Britannia*, see Tolley, "Comic Readings,"
169–70.

115. Festa, *Sentimental Figures of Empire*, 51.

116. Robbins Landon, *Chronicle and Works*, 2:599.

117. Kittler makes this observation in "City Is a Medium," 724.

118. Beghin, *Virtual Haydn.*

119. See, for instance, Somfai, "London Revision."

120. Robbins Landon, *Chronicle and Works,* 3:209.

121. Van Oort, "English Classical Piano Style."

122. Gotwals, *Two Contemporary Portraits,* 61.

123. Beghin proposes that Jansen, with fewer publishing opportunities of her own, would have been more inclined to keep back a new Haydn sonata until she had toured with the piece; see Beghin, *Virtual Haydn,* 251.

124. Tuer, *Bartolozzi and His Works,* 1:23–24.

125. Beghin, *Virtual Haydn,* ch. 6, esp. 231–42.

126. Ratner, *Classic Music,* ch. 23.

127. Allanbrook, *Secular Commedia,* 270.

128. Stephen Rumph has debunked the topic concept's tenuous claims to historical validity in *Mozart and Enlightenment Semiotics,* ch. 3. See also Sutcliffe's skeptical take on topic theory and topical mixture in Sutcliffe, "Topics in Chamber Music," esp. 118–22.

129. A. Smith, *Theory of Moral Sentiments,* 210. See also Caygill, *Art of Judgement,* 85–98.

130. In Guillory's media-historical terms, one could say that the topic announces "a social investment in the medium itself" rather than any content it may seem to convey; "Genesis," 358.

131. Sutcliffe, "Topics in Chamber Music," 120.

132. Twining, "On the different Senses," 74. Emphasis in original.

133. Chandler, *Archaeology of Sympathy,* 12. See also Burgess, "On Being Moved."

134. Eagleton, *Ideology of the Aesthetic,* 368. On Haydn's music from this period, the commodity form, and aesthetic autonomy, see Mathew, "Haydn Hero," esp. 22–23.

135. J. W. N. Sullivan maintained, for example, that the expressive world of Beethoven's early music is marred by its periodic recourse to what he called "stock situations"; see Sullivan, *Beethoven,* 69.

136. See Twyman, *Printing,* 22; Kubler, *New History of Stereotyping;* and, in music, Devriès-Lesure, "Technological Aspects," 86–87. Also Lynch, *Economy of Character,* 221. For the colonial and postcolonial implications of the cliché and stereotype, as technologies and value judgments, see Hofmeyr and Nuttall, "Book in Africa."

137. Benton, "Pleyel as Music Publisher," 126–27.

138. For Allanbrook at her most polemical, see "Once More, with Feeling." See also Gjerdingen, *Galant Style,* introduction.

139. Allanbrook, *Secular Commedia,* 129.

140. This is Currie's important argument in *Politics of Negation,* ch. 1.

141. The phrase "novels of circulation" was coined by Douglas in her essay "Britannia's Rule and the It-Narrative." See also Lynch, *Economy of Character,* ch. 2; Bellamy, *Commerce, Morality,* 119–28; and the essays in Blackwell, *Secret Life of Things.* On music and it-narratives, see Green, "Memoirs"; and Green, "Read a Rondeau."

142. Latour, *Pandora's Hope,* 192.

143. Steingo, "Actors and Accidents," 555.

144. Boltanski and Chiapello, *New Spirit of Capitalism,* 155.

145. E. Thompson, *English Working Class,* esp. ch. 6.

146. See the analogous arguments about "world literature" rehearsed in Apter, *Against World Literature,* esp. the introduction.

147. On the politics of empathy, see M. Nussbaum, *Upheavals of Thought,* part 2; and M. Nuss-

baum, *Political Emotions*. Michael Frazer argues for a direct connection between the eighteenth-century politics of feeling and present-day principles of justice in *The Enlightenment of Sympathy*.

148. See William Cheng's vision of "empathy *as* a resonant form of musicality"; W. Cheng, *Just Vibrations*, 10. See also Gayle Wald's discussion of the aesthetic-political figure of "vibe" in twentieth-century Black musical traditions; Wald, "Soul Vibrations." Roger Grant's *Peculiar Attunements* elaborates the idea that music is the enabling figure of affect theory, in the eighteenth century and today.

Chapter 2

1. Perec, *Species of Spaces*, 50.

2. Many of these newer paradigms have been inspired by the work of Bruno Latour. For a tidy summation of Latour's methods and outlook, see his *Reassembling the Social*. On the New Historicist attitude to the detail and the anecdote, see Gallagher and Greenblatt, *Practicing New Historicism*, esp. ch. 2. On the apparent methodological relationships between Latour's sociological method as applied in music and literary history and New Historicist practice, see Mathew and Smart, "Elephants," 67–68. Annette Richards has demonstrated the importance of the anecdote in early music biography, especially in England, and especially in connection with portraiture: Richards, "Carl Philipp Emanuel Bach," esp. 369–79.

3. *CC*, 270–71; *GB*, 505–7.

4. Fineman, "History of the Anecdote," 61.

5. *CC*, 260, 273, 259; *GB*, 493, 509, 493.

6. Swift, *Letter of Advice*, 19. On this passage, see Allan, *Commonplace Books*, 54. On the concept of the "extended mind," see Clark and Chalmers, "Extended Mind."

7. Locke, *Essay concerning Human Understanding*, 104.

8. See Allan, *Commonplace Books*, ch. 5–7.

9. On the anthology and the commonplace book in the eighteenth century, see L. Price, *Anthology*, esp. ch. 1 and 2.

10. Ngai, *Our Aesthetic Categories*, 47.

11. *CC*, 304–12; *GB*, 551–58. Gotwals, *Two Contemporary Portraits*.

12. Ngai, *Our Aesthetic Categories*, 119.

13. See Borthwick, "Latin Quotations" and "Haydn's Latin Quotations." See also Allan, *Commonplace Books*, ch. 6 and 10.

14. Barthes, "Reality Effect." On the possible relationships between reality (effects) and New Historicist criticism, see Gallagher and Greenblatt, *Practicing New Historicism*, 28–31.

15. Perhaps the most quoted phrase of Derrida's *Of Grammatology*, 158.

16. Latour, "Why Has Critique Run." See also his *Reassembling the Social*, 87–120. On the concept of interest in eighteenth-century politics and culture, see Jost, *Interest and Connection*. Scholarship on music and interest in this period includes Lockhart, "Pygmalion"; and Sutcliffe, *Instrumental Music*, esp. ch. 3. The idea of interest is implicit in, if not central to, Hunter's "'Most Interesting Genre.'" My concern with musical interest here is related to, and inspired by, studies of attention and attentiveness across the humanities; see especially Crary, *Suspensions of Perception* and *Techniques of the Observer*. Recent historical studies of music and attention include Steege, *Helmholtz*, ch. 3; and the colloquy edited by Brittan and Raz, "Attention, Anxiety." On attention and music in the eighteenth century, see Raz, "An Eighteenth-Century Theory"; Riley, *Musical Listening*; and Tolley, *Painting the Cannon's Roar*.

17. Innis, *Bias of Communication*, xxvii. Innis attributed the question to a former philosophy professor.

18. Herder, "Origin of Language," 111; James, *Principles of Psychology*, 1:402. Emphasis in original. Among the recent studies in social psychology to elaborate on James's premise, see Zerubavel, *Hidden in Plain Sight*, esp. ch. 1.

19. Kames, *Loose Hints upon Education*, 156.

20. Lorraine Daston discusses the relationship between note taking and taking note in the context of later practices of scientific observation in her (independently titled) article "Taking Note(s)."

21. One can trace some of the recent scholarship of "scapes" to the "taskscape" theorized by Tim Ingold and the global "scapes" elaborated by Arjun Appadurai. Ingold, "Temporality of the Landscape"; Appadurai, "Disjuncture and Difference."

22. The nomenclature originates with Schafer, *Soundscape*, esp. 9–10. Recent studies of historical soundscapes that continue to use Schafer's language include the essays collected in Bijsterveld, *Urban Past*.

23. *CC*, 261; *GB*, 494.

24. *CC*, 278; *GB*, 516. Peter Hoyt has argued in an unpublished paper that the song was a hymn tune used to satirize religious nonconformism. Hoyt, "Haydn's Rowdy Fellows."

25. Letter of January 8, 1791: *CC*, 112; *GB*, 252.

26. See Shesgreen, *Images of the Outcast*, 102–7; and Cockayne, *Hubbub*, 128–30. See also Barlow, *Enraged Musician*.

27. *The Spectator* 251 (December 18, 1711), reproduced in Morley, *The Spectator*, 2:153–55.

28. J. T. Smith, *Vagabondiana*, vi.

29. See Shesgreen, *Images of the Outcast*, esp. 124–31; and Hitchcock, *Down and Out*, 222–28.

30. Colman's play is discussed by Timothy Erwin in his "*Ut rhetorica artes*," 64–79.

31. See Shesgreen, *Images of the Outcast*, esp. 136–38. Hitchcock points out that "Cries of London" portraits were popular souvenir items for tourists and seem to have shaped the self-presentation of street criers themselves. Hitchcock, *Down and Out*, 223. Haydn was very attentive to contemporary English visual arts and popular prints; see, for example, Tolley, "Caricatures." On contemporary representations of ballad singers in the streets, see Cox Jensen, *Ballad Singer*, esp. ch. 1.

32. Prints of these two songs were included in the Vauxhall Gardens song collections; see, respectively, Hook, *Collection of Favorite Songs* (1793); and Hook, *Collection of Favorite Songs* (1796).

33. See Robbins Landon, *Chronicle and Works*, 3:53, 615. Landon thought that Papendiek might have been thinking of the finale of Symphony no. 104. The musical depiction of London street cries has a long history, going back at least as far as Orlando Gibbons's *Cryes of London*. Haydn's predecessor as Esterházy kapellmeister, Gregor Joseph Werner, had composed an entire cantata based on local street cries. For a description of part of the work, see Loughridge, *Haydn's Sunrise, Beethoven's Shadow*, 72–78.

34. Boswell, *Boswell's London Journal*, 44.

35. Letter of January 8, 1791: *CC*, 112; *GB*, 251.

36. Boswell, *Boswell's London Journal*, 130.

37. Letter of January 8, 1791: *CC*, 112; *GB*, 251.

38. *CC*, 258; *GB*, 491.

39. On this tendency, see Allan, *Commonplace Books*, 242.

40. *CC*, 257, 268, 275; *GB*, 489, 503, 511.

41. *CC*, 253; *GB*, 484.

42. Janowitz, "Artifactual Sublime," 248.

43. *CC*, 251, 277; *GB*, 481, 515. See also Berg, *Luxury and Pleasure*, ch. 5.

44. *CC*, 259; *GB*, 492.

45. Simmel, "Metropolis and Mental Life," 103, 105.

46. Johnson, *Dictionary*, s.v., "To interest" and "Interest."

47. See Homer and Sylla, *History of Interest Rates*, ch. 11. See also Jost, *Interest and Connection*.

48. The cost of things is certainly a motif of Thomas Nugent's four-volume *Grand Tour*, e.g., "The palace of *Altieri* is a very stately structure, the building of which is said to have cost a million of crowns"; Nugent, *Grand Tour* 3:233.

49. *CC*, 276, 272; *GB*, 513, 508.

50. Hume, *Treatise of Human Nature*, 406–14.

51. Hume, 413, 414.

52. Boswell, *Boswell's London Journal*, 68.

53. Hume, *Treatise of Human Nature*, 413. By "work of art" Hume would have meant any product of human handiwork or artifice rather than specifically items of fine art. Hume theorized interest in explicitly economic terms in his essay "Of Interest"; see Hume, *Political Essays*, 126–35.

54. Goux, *Symbolic Economies*; Shell, *Money, Language, and Thought*. See also Foucault's archeology of exchange in *Order of Things*, 166–214.

55. Wu, *Attention Merchants*, 20. See also Mathew, "Attention Economy."

56. Certeau, *Practice of Everyday Life*, 101.

57. Immanuel Kant's most concise statement of his position on taste and interest is in the section "The Liking that Determines a Judgment of Taste Is Devoid of All Interest," in *Critique of Judgment*, 45–46.

58. These distinctions in Kant were deconstructed by Derrida in "Economimesis." Pierre Bourdieu later criticized Derrida, arguing that, even while he unearthed and deconstructed the buried social distinctions in Kant's division of the aesthetic from the economic, he nonetheless upheld the spurious high-status practice of "pure reading." Bourdieu, *Distinction*, 485–500. Given that Bourdieu made this charge at the end of a substantial volume of arcane social science, it is hard to see where this process of intellectual one-upmanship—each writer trying to adopt a position more virtuously impure than the other—could end.

59. A critique of any assumed relationship between broadly Kantian models of disinterestedness and late eighteenth-century instrumental music can be found in Allanbrook, *Secular Commedia*, 79–82.

60. Shaftesbury, *Characteristics*, 416. On the intellectual history of interest and disinterest, see Jost, *Interest and Connection*; Paulson, *Beautiful, Novel, and Strange*, ch. 2; Pikulik, *Ästhetik des Interessanten*; Poovey, "Aesthetics and Political Economy," esp. 83–91; and Woodmansee, *Author, Art*, ch. 1. See also Stolnitz, "Origins of 'Aesthetic Disinterestedness'"; and, among the critiques of this widely read essay, Rind, "Concept of Disinterestedness."

61. See Ngai, *Our Aesthetic Categories*, 5–6 and passim.

62. Hirschman, *Passions and the Interests*. See also the more recent "deep history" of interest by the anthropologist David Graeber in *Debt*, esp. 326–35.

63. Sulzer, *Allgemeine Theorie der schönen Künste*, 2:691: "was eine Angelegenheit für uns ist, und uns einigermaßen zwinget, unsre Begehrungskräfte anzustrengen."

64. Letter of June 14, 1792: *CC*, 284; *GB*, 524.

65. Gotwals, *Two Contemporary Portraits*, 157.

66. In Adam Phillips's psychoanalytic terms, boredom is the "suspended animation of desire." A. Phillips, "On Being Bored," 78. See also A. Phillips, *Attention Seeking*.

67. Simmel, "Metropolis and Mental Life," 105.

68. Spacks, *Boredom*, ch. 2. On the history of eighteenth-century literature and inattention, see N. Phillips, *Distraction*.

69. See Domingo, *Rhetoric of Diversion*.

70. S. Johnson, *The Rambler*, 221. See also Spacks, *Boredom*, 40.

71. Burke, *Philosophical Enquiry*, 29.

72. In the extensive literature on curiosity and curiosities in this period, see Benedict, *Curiosity*; Daston and Park, *Wonders*; Evans and Marr, *Curiosity and Wonder*; Pomian, *Collectors and Curiosities*; and Whitaker, "Culture of Curiosity."

73. Burke, *Philosophical Enquiry*, 29.

74. McVeigh, *Concert Life in London*, ch. 5. This is not to say that an emphasis on newness was a feature of musical commerce only in London, of course.

75. Hook, *Third Collection of Songs*, 11.

76. This was the psychic condition of the nineteenth-century Parisian flâneur, as diagnosed by Walter Benjamin: "Boredom is a warm gray fabric lined on the inside with the most lustrous and colorful of silks." Benjamin, *Arcades Project*, 105.

77. Edgeworth, "Ennui," in *Tales of Fashionable Life*, 1:2–3. On this story, see also Greig, *Beau Monde*, 47–48.

78. Adam Smith, "Of the Nature of That Imitation Which Takes Place in What Are Called the Imitative Arts" (1795), excerpted in Weiss and Taruskin, *Western World*, 250.

79. Quoted in Woodfield, "John Bland," 228. Woodfield surmises that this disaster may have prompted Salomon to purchase Haydn's *Arianna a Naxos*—possibly the "New Cantata" performed by Anna Storace in the third of Salomon's concerts in 1791.

80. See, for example, Somfai, "London Revision"; see also Schroeder, *Haydn and the Enlightenment*.

81. Report in the *Public* advertiser, January 5, 1792, reproduced in Robbins Landon, *Chronicle and Works* 3:121.

82. Letter of January 17, 1792: *CC*, 128; *GB*, 274–75.

83. *Morning Herald*, February 25, 1792, reproduced in Robbins Landon, *Chronicle and Works*, 3:136.

84. The Symphony no. 104 came to be known as the *London* (and as the *Salomon* in Germany), though of course this does not refer to any distinctive musical feature.

85. L. Price, *Anthology*, 7. On miscellanies and discontinuous reading and publishing practices, see also Bannet, *Eighteenth-Century Manners*, ch. 4.

86. It is worth noting that the surprise chord was a relatively late addition to the tune in the autograph; see Robbins Landon, *Chronicle and Works*, 3:528–29.

87. For an account of musical repetition as an aesthetic principle, social mechanism, and psychic compulsion—though with respect to Rossini's operas and their reception—see Senici, "Rossinian Repetitions"; and Senici, *Present Tense*, ch. 2. On the principle of repetition in Haydn, see Sisman, *Classical Variation*, esp. 1–18, 61–62.

88. Gotwals, *Two Contemporary Portraits*, 167–68.

89. Gerber, *Historisch-Biographisches Lexicon der Tonkünstler*, col. 610.

90. On the Ponte schema, see Gjerdingen, *Galant Style*, 197–216.

91. Lynch, *Economy of Character*, 92.

92. A. Smith, *Theory of Moral Sentiments*, 232–33.

93. Quoted in Lynch, *Economy of Character*, 66.

94. See Will's landmark study, *Characteristic Symphony*.

95. This is one of the main strands of Lynch's argument in *Economy of Character*, esp. ch. 1 and 2. Publications in the "Cries of London" tradition commonly described themselves as "characteristic." See, for example, one of the anonymously published volumes popular at the start of the nineteenth century, *New Cries of London, with Characteristic Engravings* (several copies are held in the collection relating to urban street life in the Bishopsgate Institute, London.)

96. Sutcliffe, "Expressive Ambivalence," 85.

97. Sutcliffe, 109.

98. Ashe was mistaken, since his benefit had taken place in 1795 (while the symphony had been composed in 1791 and premiered in March 1792). The program survives in the Bodleian Library, Oxford. It is reproduced in I. Taylor, *Music in London*, 6.

99. For a collation of these various stories, see Robbins Landon, *Chronicle and Works*, 3:150–51.

100. Gotwals, *Two Contemporary Portraits*, 33.

101. *The Oracle*, March 24, 1792, reproduced in Robbins Landon, *Chronicle and Works*, 3:150.

102. Williams, *Country and the City*, esp. ch. 12–14.

103. *Morning Chronicle*, March 3, 1795, reproduced in Robbins Landon, *Chronicle and Works*, 3:295.

104. M. Brown, "Mozart and After," 690–91.

105. *Morning Chronicle*, April 9, 1794, reproduced in Robbins Landon, *Chronicle and Works*, 3:247.

106. *Morning Chronicle*, April 9, 1794, reproduced in Robbins Landon, 3:247.

107. *Morning Chronicle*, May 2, 1794, and *The Oracle*, May 1, 1794, reproduced in Robbins Landon, 3:250.

108. *The Sun*, February 24, 1795, reproduced in Robbins Landon, 3:293.

109. Dolan, *Orchestral Revolution*, 130–33.

110. Dolan, 132.

111. The call is a quotation of a standard *Generalmarsch*; see Monelle, *Musical Topic*, 88.

112. *Morning Chronicle*, April 9, 1794, reproduced in Robbins Landon, *Chronicle and Works*, 3:247.

113. On comparable "interpellating" rhetorical strategies and their political uses in the music of Beethoven and his Viennese contemporaries, as well as the military valences of the concept of "attention," see Mathew, *Political Beethoven*, 145–62. Tim Wu discusses the recruitment posters of the early twentieth century as a parallel instance of military attention as the model for consumer attention. Wu, *Attention Merchants*, ch. 3.

114. See Searle, "Pleyel's 'London' Symphonies."

115. *Morning Herald*, February 14, 1792, reproduced in Robbins Landon, *Chronicle and Works*, 3:132.

116. This is observed in Searle, "Pleyel's 'London' Symphonies," 237–38.

117. Richards, *Free Fantasia*, 106–7.

118. U. Price, *Essay on the Picturesque*, 172.

119. Clune, *Writing against Time*, 3; Burke, *Philosophical Enquiry*, 29. In advertising terms,

Tim Wu describes this phenomenon as a "disenchantment effect"—"when a once entrancing means of harvesting attention starts to lose its charm." Wu, *Attention Merchants*, 23.

120. On this aspect of Haydn's *Surprise*, see Miller, *Surprise*, 33–34.

121. Haydn, *Haydn's Celebrated Grand-Military Symphony*.

122. Bohrer, *Suddenness*.

123. Joseph Haydn, *12 London Symphonies, Live at the Wiener Konzerthaus*, Marc Minkowski and Les Musiciens du Louvre, Naïve V 5176, 2009, 4 compact discs.

124. Kivy, *Authenticities*, passim.

125. Dolan, *Orchestral Revolution*, 130, 129.

126. D. Johns, "In Defence of Haydn."

127. Tovey, *Essays in Musical Analysis*, 346.

128. A. Brown, *Symphonic Repertoire*, 2:258.

129. D. Johns, "In Defence of Haydn," 305–6. On music and parataxis, see Sisman, *Classical Variation*, esp. 7–11.

130. This point is made by Roger Parker (also via Certeau's analysis of urban pedestrianism) in connection with London's musical culture in subsequent decades. Parker, "Two Styles."

131. The adversarial politics of surface and depth has been rehearsed frequently over the past decade or so with respect to music from this period; see, inter alia, Allanbrook, "Mozart's K331, First Movement"; and Currie, *Politics of Negation*, esp. ch. 1.

132. Quoted in Lynch, *Economy of Character*, 147. It is surely not coincidental that critics frequently compared Haydn to Shakespeare during this period; see Sisman, "Haydn, Shakespeare," esp. 23–24.

133. Junker, *Zwanzig Componisten: Eine Skizze*, 64: "ernsthafte, interessirende Laune . . . wie bey den tragischen Gesinnungen eines Schakespear" (translation from Sutcliffe, "Expressive Ambivalence," 85). See Sutcliffe's discussion of this passage in "Expressive Ambivalence," 84–85. To the extent that German-speaking music critics deployed the concept of the *Interessant* in this period, they tended to do so in connection with the instrumental music of Haydn and C. P. E. Bach. In 1782, for instance, Johann Friedrich Reichardt wrote that "even if we only had a Haydn and a C. P. E. Bach, we Germans could already boldly claim that we have our own style, and that our instrumental music is the most interesting of all." Reichardt, *Musikalisches Kunstmagazin* 1 (1782): 205 ("Wenn wir auch nur einen Haydn und einen C. Ph. E. Bach hätten, so könnten wir Deutsche schon kühn behaupten, daß wir eine eigne Manier haben und unsre Instrumentalmusik die interessanteste von allen ist").

134. Schlegel, *Study of Greek Poetry*. Schlegel's treatise adumbrated a Schillerian distinction between the interesting and the beautiful, though it was written without his having read Schiller's famous essay *On Naive and Sentimental Poetry* (composed in 1795–96); see Schlegel, *Study of Greek Poetry*, 97. On Schlegel's interesting as an aesthetic-economic category, see Mieszkowski, *Labors of Imagination*, ch. 1.

135. Ngai, *Our Aesthetic Categories*, 124.

136. Much of the music-historical literature that has borrowed approaches and questions from sound studies has staged, queried, and historicized encounters between the organized sounds that have traditionally been music historians' subject and the more broadly conceived "noises" and vibrations that have largely escaped their purview. Influential for my purposes have been such recent studies as Dillon, *Sense of Sound*; and G. Williams, "Voice of the Crowd." What "materiality" means, from a disciplinary point of view, is a knottier question. On this subject, see J. Sterne, "'What Do We Want?'"

137. This is why it may be worth studying the attachments that art practices afford and instigate; see Felski, *Hooked*, esp. ch. 1.

138. A point made by L. Price at the beginning of *Anthology*, 2.

139. Allewaert envisions the world-making potential of synecdoche in "Toward a Materialist Figuration."

140. Stengers, *Power and Invention*, 82.

141. On Haydn's changing relationships with his audiences during his career, see Sisman, "Haydn's Career." On the musician's relationship to London audiences in particular, see McVeigh, *Concert Life in London*, esp. 73–118.

142. "Selves and their interests are historically conditioned ideas," observes Jean-Christophe Agnew. See Agnew, *Worlds Apart*, 5. For a recent vision of networks in music history inspired by Latour, see Piekut, "Actor-Networks in Music History." See also the networks traced in practice in his book *Experimentalism Otherwise*. It is important to Piekut that his networks represent a methodological approach rather than an ontological claim—that is, that networks are a descriptive means to an end and do not constitute a theory of "the way things really are." Other music scholars have implied or asserted just that. See, for example, Eliot Bates, who warns at the very beginning of his important book that "a false appearance" has obscured the "layering and heterogeneity" of his (and, one assumes, any) study, which, in reality, "is an actor-network." Bates, *Digital Tradition*, xi.

143. Quoted in Mehta, *Liberalism and Empire*, 154.

144. See Vogl, *Specter of Capital*, ch. 2. On early imaginative writing that celebrates social circulation, see Lynch, *Economy of Character*, ch. 2; and Bellamy, *Commerce, Morality*, 119–28. Mary Poovey has made the important point that eighteenth-century writing, ranging from treatises on political economy to popular "it-narratives" about the adventures of banknotes, consistently overrated (or perhaps productively imagined into being) the coherence, vibrancy, and geographical extent of material circulation. For instance, although the various banknote adventures published during the period tend to imagine otherwise, a note issued by the Bank of England, among all the bewildering local varieties of paper currency, rarely ever circulated beyond a small metropolitan area—and for the duration of the eighteenth century, very few Britons would have seen or even known how to recognize such a note. See Poovey, *Credit Economy*, esp. 139–40, 151–52.

145. For a comparison of London and Vienna in the 1790s from Haydn's perspective, see Wyn Jones, "Haydn, Austria, and Britain"; and his *Music in Vienna*, esp. ch. 6.

146. See Mathew, "Heroic Haydn"; Mathew, *Political Beethoven*, 46–58, 143–50; Wyn Jones, "Haydn, Austria, and Britain," 8–20; and Wyn Jones, *Music in Vienna*, ch. 7.

147. Tolley, *Painting the Cannon's Roar*, 259–61.

148. See, for example, Bonds, *Music as Thought*, esp. 33–43.

149. See Bonds, ch. 3.

150. James Webster has provided a persuasive account of the way in which formal and narrative elements of Beethoven's Fifth and the *Eroica* were anticipated by Haydn. Webster, *Haydn's "Farewell" Symphony*, 370–72. On the "interesting" moments of the Fifth Symphony and the audiovisual attachments they instigated, see Loughridge, *Haydn's Sunrise, Beethoven's Shadow*, ch. 5.

151. See Guillory, *Cultural Capital*, ch. 5.

152. This is also the premise of Fuhrmann, "Originality as Market-Value." To be sure, Haydn's correspondence contains many complaints about his need to earn money, but these complaints

never adopt the characteristic position of the Romantic artist, which opposes the purposes of the market and art, the businessman and the artist. One of the most penetrating analyses of this position remains Williams, *Culture and Society*, ch. 2.

153. This is the position explored by Jonathan Lamb in *The Things Things Say*. On things and "thing theory," see the essays gathered in B. Brown, *Things*, and, in connection with this period, in Blackwell, *Secret Life of Things*.

154. Eidsheim, *Sensing Sound*, 20. For a critique of the political impulse to dissolve music into sound into vibration, see Mathew, "Listening(s) Past," esp. 148–51.

155. Barthes, "Structuralist Activity," 215. Emphasis in original.

156. Holly Watkins criticizes the notion of "Letting Sounds Be Themselves" in *Musical Vitalities*, ch. 6.

157. For a more developed critique of this tendency, see Davies, "On Being Moved." Jürgen Habermas's early critique of regimes of scientific knowledge—though ultimately directed against psychoanalytic theory—uses the concept of interest in comparable ways. Habermas, *Erkenntnis und Interesse*.

158. Spivak, "Can the Subaltern Speak?," 292.

Chapter 3

1. Fanon, *Black Skin, White Masks*, 82.

2. Beauvoir, *Second Sex*, 718.

3. *Grove Music Online*, s.v., "Shaw, Thomas." Dies, but no other contemporary commentator, described Mr. Shaw as a member of parliament (see Gotwals, *Two Contemporary Portraits*, 152). No one by the name of Shaw sat in parliament during this period, however. It is possible that Dies imagined or surmised that Haydn's "Mr. Shaw" was Sir James Shaw, who, at his time of writing in 1806, was Lord Mayor of London and a prominent public figure. This Shaw, however, had no daughters (see below).

4. *CC*, 275; *GB*, 512. Translation amended. Dies, it seems, assumed that the pin was the same item as the embroidered ribbon, while Griesinger imagined that they were separate; still, both had seen the cherished ribbon. See Gotwals, *Two Contemporary Portraits*, 26–27, 152–53.

5. See Lynch, "Personal Effects," 345.

6. On the Sternean sentimental object, see Festa, *Sentimental Figures of Empire*, ch. 2.

7. Benjamin, *Arcades Project*, 220–21. See also Lockhart, "Voice Boxes," esp. 275–76.

8. On "sentimental possession," see Festa, *Sentimental Figures of Empire*, 68. On boxes and desire, see B. Johnson, *Persons and Things*, 143.

9. Lynch, "Counterpublics," esp. 233. On the public and private spaces of women's music making in the eighteenth century, see, inter alia, Day-O'Connell, "English Canzonet"; G. Goodman, *Cultivated by Hand*; Green, "Read a Rondeau"; M. Head, *Sovereign Feminine*; Richards, *Free Fantasia*, ch. 5.

10. See the essays in Blackwell, *Secret Life of Things*. On it-narratives in musicology, see Green, "Memoirs"; Green, "Read a Rondeau"; and Poriss, *Changing the Score*, ch. 6.

11. Marx, *Capital*, 1:176–77.

12. Cited in Gikandi, *Slavery*, 84.

13. Gikandi, 6–7.

14. The unsurpassed critique of this project remains Spivak, "Can the Subaltern Speak?" A critique of the automatic equation of voice and personhood is an important theme in recent

voice studies; see Dolar, *Voice and Nothing More*; and the essays collected in Feldman and Zeit-lin, *Voice as Something More*.

15. Leah Price invokes the genre history of the it-narrative as an implicit critique of the envoicing of "material culture" in literary studies; see L. Price, "*History of a Book*." Stephen Best has recently contested the figure of "giving voice" that has shaped histories of slavery; see Best, *None Like Us*, esp. interstice.

16. See Borg and Coke, *Vauxhall Gardens*, 244.

17. See Borg and Coke, 166–73. Also Cudworth, "Vauxhall 'Lists,'" esp. 39–42.

18. On the supper boxes, see Borg and Coke, 69–73 and passim; and Grieg, *Beau Monde*, 77–80.

19. *CC*, 262; *GB*, 495–6. Translation amended.

20. Richards, *Free Fantasia*, 133.

21. Angelo, *Reminiscences*, 2:3. Also Greig, *Beau Monde*, 77.

22. Cited in Borg and Coke, *Vauxhall Gardens*, 282.

23. *CC*, 262; *GB*, 496. Translation amended.

24. Goldsmith, *Citizen of the World*, 2:30. See also Greig, *Beau Monde*, 78.

25. On the history of the Vauxhall Rotunda, see Borg and Coke, *Vauxhall Gardens*, 66–68 and passim.

26. See, for example, "*The Female Auctioneer*," *Composed and Sung by the Orphean Family* (Boston: Oliver Ditson, 1850).

27. The previous "Vauxhall Siren" had been the singer Charlotte Brent. See Borg and Coke, *Vauxhall Gardens*, 244.

28. Karamzin, *Letters*, 415.

29. Borg and Coke, *Vauxhall Gardens*, 154.

30. F. Burney, *Evelina*, 197.

31. The tension between and overlapping of generic and material forms of "containment" is one of the starting points of Susan Stewart's discussion of the miniature in *On Longing*, esp. 37–38.

32. On musical-formal fungibility and iterability in a slightly later repertory, see Senici, "Rossinian Repetitions"; and Senici, *Present Tense*, ch. 2.

33. Borg and Coke, *Vauxhall Gardens*, 198.

34. Goldsmith, *Citizen of the World*, 2:29.

35. "We have been *a shopping*, as Mrs. Mirvan calls it, all this morning." F. Burney, *Evelina*, 28. "Shopping," writes Barbara Johnson, "is a desire structure, not just an economic structure"; see *Persons and Things*, 143.

36. S. Johnson, *Idler*, 463–64.

37. Campbell, *Romantic Ethic*, ch. 4 and 5.

38. She was later to achieve wide recognition as a botanical painter under her second married name, Clara Maria Pope.

39. Kelly, *Joscelina*, 1:195. My thanks to Oskar Cox Jensen for bringing this novel, and this episode in it, to my attention. See Cox Jensen, *Ballad Singer*, 22, 54–55.

40. Kelly *Joscelina*, 1:196.

41. Burke, *Philosophical Enquiry*, 83.

42. Burke, 103.

43. Burke, 104–5, 107. On the "serpentine" line, see Hogarth, *Analysis of Beauty*, 33.

44. Burke, *Philosophical Enquiry*, 111, 112. Hogarth also attempted musical analogies; see, e.g., Hogarth, 76–77.

45. Crotch, preface to *Specimens of Various Styles*, 1:2.

46. See Huhn, *Imitation and Society*, 74–81.

47. Hogarth, *Analysis of Beauty*, 42.

48. Hogarth, 32, 33. Emphasis in original.

49. S. Johnson, *Dictionary*, s.v., "Object."

50. Boswell, *Life of Samuel Johnson*, 238.

51. See the essays collected in B. Brown, *Things*; B. Johnson, *Persons and Things*, 61–65; and Lamb, *Things Things Say*.

52. Martha Feldman identifies voice with "the interstices of encounters, the spaces of transition, the spaces in between." See Feldman, "Interstitial Voice," 658.

53. Matthew Head has explicated this tendency in music criticism in his *Sovereign Feminine*. Though Head's focus is eighteenth-century Germany, he discusses, for example, Burney's valorization of the musically feminine (see p. 35).

54. Wollstonecraft, *Rights of Woman*, 77.

55. Burke, *Philosophical Enquiry*, 104. "The emblematic experience of beauty," writes David Porter, "was that of the learned man of taste looking upon a well-proportioned female form." See Porter, "Monstrous Beauty," 406. On the gendering of the mix of aesthetics and economics in the eighteenth century, see Poovey, "Aesthetics and Political Economy."

56. On Barbauld's "The Mouse's Petition," see Coleman, "Firebrands, Letters, and Flowers," esp. 86–87; and Nash, "Animal Nomenclature," esp. 111–13.

57. Barbauld, *Selected Poetry and Prose*, 70–71.

58. See Harris, *Cute, Quaint, Hungry*, ch. 1; and Ngai, *Our Aesthetic Categories*, ch. 1. On the relation between the cute and the Burkean beautiful, see Ngai, 54–55.

59. Harris, *Cute, Quaint, Hungry*, 4, 8. On cuteness and pliable "soft contours," see also Ngai, 64–65.

60. Wollstonecraft, *Vindication*, ch. 5.

61. Barbauld, *Selected Poetry and Prose*, 123. On the sentimental politics of the "Epistle," see Waters, "Sympathy, Nerve Physiology"; and Meneley, "Acts of Sympathy," 48–49.

62. Barbauld, *Selected Poetry and Prose*, 249.

63. Antisentimental abolitionist politics extends from the lectures of Samuel Taylor Coleridge to twentieth-century histories of antislavery literature by Wylie Sypher and others. On Coleridge's 1795 "Lecture on the Slave Trade," see Carey, *British Abolitionism*, 193–94. Wylie Sypher's 1942 *Guinea's Captive Kings* was scathing about the ethics and achievements of sentimental abolitionist literature. See also Ahern, introduction to *Affect and Abolition*; Boulukos, "Capitalism and Slavery"; Meneley, "Acts of Sympathy"; and Tong, "Pity," esp. 137.

64. Carey, "To Force a Tear," 117.

65. Clery, *Feminization Debate*, 12. On the gender politics of British abolitionism, see Rosenthal, "Contradictions of Racialized Sensibility," esp. 173–79.

66. See Ferguson, "Mary Wollstonecraft."

67. Wollstonecraft, *Vindication*, 155, 154.

68. Barbauld, *Selected Poetry and Prose*, 130–32.

69. Clarkson, *African Slave Trade*, 1:191–92.

70. See Festa, *Sentimental Figures of Empire*, 165.

71. Festa, 164–71.

72. See Borg and Coke, *Vauxhall Gardens*, 109; and Mears, "Silver Service Slavery," esp. 56.

73. Clarkson, *African Slave Trade*, 1:191.

74. Hartman, *Scenes of Subjection*, 22. On the problem of the scene of suffering and the "erot-

ics of pathos," see also Ahern, introduction to *Affect and Abolition*; Dayan, "Amorous Bondage"; and Hinton, *Perverse Gaze of Sympathy*.

75. On Cowper's "The Negro's Complaint," see Carey, *British Abolitionism*, 100–102; Festa, *Sentimental Figures of Empire*, 162–64; Tong, "Pity," 134–37.

76. On Day and Bicknell's "The Dying Negro," see Festa, 160–62; Carey, 75–78.

77. The poem was reprinted in Clarkson, *African Slave Trade*, 1:188–90.

78. Hamilton, "'African' Songs."

79. Clarkson, *African Slave Trade*, 1:190.

80. *The Lady's Magazine*, December 1793.

81. The politics of this domestic role play is Hamilton's main subject in "'African' Songs," esp. 158–64.

82. On Roscoe's abolitionist verse, in particular *The Wrongs of Africa*, see Carey, *British Abolitionism*, 92–96.

83. Nathan, "Negro Impersonation."

84. See Barry, "Charles Incledon"; and Borg and Coke, *Vauxhall Gardens*, 161, 168.

85. See Carey, "To Force a Tear," 118–22; Carey, *British Abolitionism*, 178–79. On the extent of Dibdin's racialized performances across his career, see F. Nussbaum, "Racial Performance."

86. Nathan, "Negro Impersonation."

87. It was a much-reprinted verse; see Disney, "Epilogue to *The Padlock*," *Gentleman's Magazine*, June 1792, 557. See also Carey, "To Force a Tear," 121.

88. This reprieve was not granted in the Richard Steele essay on which Colman and Arnold's opera was based. On this opera and the wider Inkle and Yarico tradition, see Bhattacharya, "Family Jewels"; Carey, "To Force a Tear," 125–28; the essays in Felsenstein, *English Trader, Indian Maid*; and O'Quinn, "Mercantile Deformities."

89. See the announcement in *The Times*, April 3, 1792, 1.

90. Cited in Ahern, introduction to *Affect and Abolition*, 1.

91. Cobbett, "Debate," cols. 45–48. On this passage and the ideological importance of singing among enslaved Africans, see also Carey, *British Abolitionism*, 165–71.

92. Gikandi, *Culture of Taste*, 14. On Sancho and Black or African identity in this period, see also Ellis, *Politics of Sensibility*, ch. 2; F. Nussbaum, *Limits of the Human*, ch. 7. On the presence and representation of African people in the London public before emancipation, see Gerzina, *Black London*.

93. See Hart, "New Light"; and Wright, "George Polgreen Bridgetower," esp. 79–80.

94. Grigson, *Poems of Anne Hunter*, 31.

95. Cartwright, *Journal of Transactions*, 1:271.

96. Wheatley, *Complete Writings*, 13.

97. Hunter, *Essays and Observations*, 1:183–84.

98. This is without doubt an instance of the listening practice that Dylan Robinson has theorized as "hungry." See Robinson, *Hungry Listening*. On the relation of the discipline of human anatomy and the "museum gaze" in this period, particularly with respect to John Hunter's specimens, see Chaplin, "Nature Dissected."

99. Gikandi, *Culture of Taste*. His critique draws on Paul Gilroy's notion of the Black Atlantic as a repressed counterdiscourse of modernity; see Gilroy, *Black Atlantic*.

100. Wheelock, "Marriage à la Mode."

101. The word "canzonett" was an Italianate coinage that, at this time, denoted a range of vocal genres, from simple strophic songs to more elaborate arias in Italian.

102. See tables 1 and 2a–d in Wheelock, "Marriage à la Mode," 361, 363–70.

103. Cited in Wheelock, 372.

104. See table 3 in Wheelock, 392.

105. On verse types in English canzonets, see Komlós, "Haydn's English Canzonettas," 87–94.

106. Parke, *Musical Memoirs*, 1:198.

107. Cited in Robbins Landon, *Chronicle and Works*, 3:285.

108. [Stendhal] Bombet, *Life of Haydn*, 150.

109. A letter survives that accompanied the parcel of stockings that Gardiner sent to Haydn himself. August 10, 1804: *CC*, 233.

110. Wollstonecraft directly related "libertine notions of beauty" to women's desire to marry—"the only way women can rise in the world." *Vindication*, 77.

111. For an account of this well-known residence from the perspective of Anne Hunter's salons, see Grigson, *Poems of Anne Hunter*, 39–49.

112. Green, *Dedicating Music*, esp. ch. 2 and 3.

113. February 8, 1793: *CC*, 279.

114. The inscription on the first book reads "The Gift of the Author to Cecilia Maria Barthélemon."

115. See Robbins Landon, *Chronicle and Works*, 3:169.

116. Cited in Robbins Landon, 3:169. Emphasis in original.

117. As Susan Stewart puts it, "the souvenir substitutes a context of perpetual consumption for its context of origin." *On Longing*, 135.

118. See Green, *Dedicating Music*, 83–96.

119. *Grove Music Online*, s.v., "Hornpipe." By the middle of the nineteenth century, an essay in the *Journal of the British Archaeological Association* on the history of "phonic horns" could refer to "the jocund merriment of our good old English country hornpipe" without the need for further clarification. Cuming, "On Phonic Horns," 132.

120. Crotch, preface to *Specimens of Various Styles*, 1:2. Crotch considered the "ornamental style" to be the sonic analog of the picturesque.

121. See Richards, *Free Fantasia*, 133.

122. M. Head, "Haydn's Exoticisms," 89–91.

123. Mayes, "Eastern European National Music." See also Mayes, "Reconsidering an Early Exoticism."

124. M. Head, "Haydn's Exoticisms," 91.

125. Marx, *Capital*, 1:176–77.

126. See, inter alia, B. Johnson, *Persons and Things*, 20–23, 140–42; Moten, *In the Break*, 8–10; Ngai, *Our Aesthetic Categories*, 61–63.

127. Adorno, *In Search of Wagner*, 74. See also Brian Kane's appropriation of the term (though with much less Marxism) to discuss more recent sound arts in *Sound Unseen*, 97–133.

128. Eagleton, *Ideology*, 84–89.

129. For example, Bohlman, "Ontologies of Music," 30.

130. Agnew, *Worlds Apart*, 185.

131. Crotch, index to *Specimens of Various Styles*, 1:18–21.

132. See Irving, "William Crotch's *Specimens*." On Crotch as a musician, thinker, and pedagogue, see also Irving, *William Crotch*.

133. Day-O'Connell, "English Canzonet" and "Composer, the Surgeon."

134. Allanbrook, *Secular Commedia*, 87.

135. Currie, *Politics of Negation*, 6, also ch. 1, passim. On the contested politics and epistemology of the "surface" in literary interpretation, see Best and Marcus, "Surface Reading."

136. This unproblematic globally oriented legibility is one of Emily Apter's targets in *Against World Literature*. On listening as acquisitive, see also Robinson, *Hungry Listening*.

137. See Wahrman, *Modern Self*, esp. ch. 3. See also Hudson, "From 'Nation' to 'Race.'" Several historians have argued that the transatlantic slave trade was pivotal in the emergence of modern racial taxonomies. See Boulukos, *Grateful Slave*.

138. Fanon, *Black Skin, White Masks*, 84.

139. On the later racial politics of the musical style concept, see Mundy, "Evolutionary Categories."

140. Davies, "'I Am an Essentialist,'" 143.

141. W. Brown, "Freedom's Silences," 84.

142. Lockhart, "Voice Boxes."

143. Best, *None Like Us*, 83–84.

144. Barrett, *Blackness and Value*, 78–79 and passim.

145. Moten, *In the Break*, 1–24.

146. A. Cheng, *Ornamentalism*, 17. Cheng ultimately elaborates the connection between ornamentalism and Black studies partly via Hortense Spillers's famous notion of the "hieroglyphics of the flesh." See A. Cheng, 153; Spillers, "Mama's Baby, Papa's Maybe." On skin and bodily surface as privileged sites of socially circulating emotion, see also Ahmed, "Collective Feelings," esp. 29–30. On racialized sonic surfaces, see also Morrison, "Race, Blacksound"; and Eidsheim, *Race of Sound*.

Chapter 4

1. Arendt, *Human Condition*, 122.

2. Robbins Landon, *Chronicle and Works*, 1:351.

3. Letter of August 14, 1802: *CC*, 207; *GB*, 407–8.

4. Robbins Landon, *Chronicle and Works*, 1:351.

5. See Sisman, "Haydn's Career," 10.

6. Adelung, *Grammatisch-kritisches Wörterbuch*, s.v., "Fleiß": "Die Fertigkeit, alles was man zu thun hat. And Sorgfalt, Aufmerksamkeit, Richtung der Empfindungs- und Verstandeskräfte auf das, was man thut."

7. Gotwals, *Two Contemporary Portraits*, 10. Translation amended.

8. Gotwals, 80–81.

9. Letter of July 1776: *CC*, 19; *GB*, 77. Translation amended.

10. Horwärthner, "Joseph Haydn's Library," 444. For Eckartshausen on *Fleiß*, see, "Lehren eines Richters an seine Sohn," 26.

11. 1804 (no other date): *CC*, 231; *GB*, 448.

12. Letter of February 9, 1790: *CC*, 96–97; *GB*, 228–29.

13. See Robbins Landon, *Chronicle and Works*, 3:34.

14. Letter of September 17, 1791: *CC*, 117–19; *GB* 260–61. Translation adapted from Bonds, "Symphonic Politics," 17.

15. George Fink defines stress as "the condition in which an individual is aroused and made anxious by an uncontrollable aversive challenge"; see Fink, *Stress*, 1:4.

16. Letter of January 17, 1792: *CC*, 128–9; *GB* 274–5.

17. Letter of March 2, 1792: *CC*, 132; *GB*, 280. Translation amended.

18. *CC*, 276; *GB*, 512.

19. Dolan makes this point, especially about instrumental solos, in *Orchestral Revolution*, 148–56.

20. A few years later, Carl Friedrich Zelter would complain, in a letter to the Leipzig *Allgemeine musikalische Zeitung*, that an unprepared third relation at this very formal juncture had become one of Haydn's most imitated devices. See Robbins Landon, *Chronicle and Works*, 4:339.

21. See Robbins Landon, 3:52.

22. Ngai, *Our Aesthetic Categories*, 185, 182. On comedy, music, and labor in the eighteenth century, see also Grant, *Peculiar Attunements*, ch. 2.

23. Grant, *Peculiar Attunements*, 81–85. See also Roach, *Player's Passion*, 122–25; and Ngai, *Our Aesthetic Categories*, 189–97.

24. Diderot, "Rameau's Nephew," 68.

25. Adorno, "Fetish-Character of Music," 314.

26. Contract dated 1786 (no other date): *CC*, 53–56; *GB*, 151–54.

27. *CC*, 55; *GB*, 153. On the legal background to this episode, see Mace, "London Music Sellers."

28. Contracts dated August 13, 1795, and February 27, 1796: *CC*, 146; *GB*, 305–6.

29. Burke, "Thoughts and Details," 122.

30. This is one of Karl Polanyi's main arguments in *The Great Transformation*, esp. ch. 6. On the changing meaning of work in England in this period, see also E. Thompson, "Time, Work-Discipline." On Haydn, work, and time in this period, see Day-O'Connell, "Time and Memory."

31. Green's ode was set as a glee by Thomas Arne and later as a Vauxhall Gardens song by James Hook. See Hook, "The Wooden Walls of Olde England" (London: S. A. & P. Thompson, 1790). On Hogarth's *Industry and Idleness* and the class politics of labor, see Jordan, "Idleness, Industry."

32. Locke, *Second Treatise*, 19. Emphasis in original.

33. M. Rose, *Authors and Owners*, 85–86. Legal historians usually consider the so-called Statute of Anne, dating from 1710, to be the earliest copyright legislation, though the law was not intended to guarantee the claims of authors as much as to regulate the rights of booksellers. See Rose, 36–41.

34. Enfield, *Observations on Literary Property*, 20–21. On the importance of the georgic mode in the invention of literary property, see Siskin, *Work of Writing*, 103–29.

35. See M. Rose, *Authors and Owners*, 111; Siskin, 109–12.

36. On the history of music copyright, mostly in England, see Carroll, "Struggle for Music Copyright"; D. Hunter, "Music Copyright in Britain"; Mace, "British Music Copyright"; Mace, "Charles Rennett"; Rabin and Zohn, "Music as Intellectual Property"; Small, "Development of Musical Copyright." On the relation between the legal regime of copyright and the musical work concept, see Barron, "Copyright Law's Musical Work." And on the relation between copyright and the concept of genius, see Woodmansee, *Author, Art*, ch. 2.

37. A. Smith, *Wealth of Nations*, 430–31. On this passage and its relation to contemporary legal and natural philosophy, see Schabas, *Natural Origins of Economics*, 88–95.

38. Hardt and Negri, *Empire*, 290–94.

39. Marx, *Grundrisse*, 305.

40. Arendt, *Human Condition*, ch. 3 and 4.

41. Goehr, *Imaginary Museum*; Weber, *Rise of Musical Classics*.

42. See M. Head, "Music with 'No Past'?" See also Lynch, *Loving Literature*.

43. See Rosenthal, "Contract." For the later transactions that this contract enabled, see also Rowland, "Clementi as Publisher," 172–76.

44. See Rosenthal, 78–79.

45. Matthew Head makes this point in "Music with 'No Past'?"

46. *CC*, 262; *GB*, 496.

47. Mainwaring, *Memoirs*.

48. Schönfeld, "Yearbook," 319.

49. On Handel and Handelian aesthetics in early nineteenth-century Vienna, see M. Head, "Music with 'No Past'?"; and Mathew, *Political Beethoven*, ch. 3.

50. See Olleson, "Origin and Libretto."

51. One of the most successful early English performances of Haydn's *Creation* highlighted this Miltonic lineage by interspersing the oratorio with readings from *Paradise Lost*. See Temperley, *Haydn: "The Creation,"* 40.

52. Following Benjamin Piekut and Jason Stanyek, one could even describe these Handelian mechanisms as late eighteenth-century "technologies of the intermundane": mediating materials that enabled new forms of exchange and collaboration between the dead and the living. See Piekut and Stanyek, "Deadness."

53. Letter of August 10, 1801: *CC*, 189; *GB*, 376. As with the later technologies of sound production discussed by Jonathan Sterne, fantasies of sonic preservation—and what utterances would survive the speaker—seemed to prompt thoughts of death; see J. Sterne, *Audible Past*, ch. 6.

54. Matthew Head shows how these worlds were entangled in the reception of *The Creation* in "Music with 'No Past'?," esp. 198–200.

55. In the event, Salomon directed *The Creation* in London following three earlier performances, including a premiere at Covent Garden in March 1800. See Temperley, *Haydn: "The Creation,"* 35, 39.

56. Quoted and translated in Robbins Landon, *Chronicle and Works*, 4:318. On the persistence of the aristocratic model of gift exchange in musical life, see Green, *Dedicating Music*, esp. ch. 1 and 2. On Haydn's late oratorios at the center of the unusual blend of "aristocratic patronage and bourgeois reception," see Jen-yen Chen, "Musical Culture and Social Ideology."

57. *Allgemeine musikalische Zeitung*, March 24, 1799, col. 466.

58. On the biblical sublime, see R. Smith, *Handel's Oratorios*, ch. 4. On Handel's and Haydn's musical creations of light, see Sisman, "Voice of God," esp. 161.

59. Quoted and translated in Robbins Landon, *Chronicle and Works*, 4:318.

60. This has prompted Raymond Knapp to describe such musical strategies in Haydn in terms of camp; see Knapp, *Making Light*.

61. Eagleton, *Faith, Reason, and Revolution*, 8.

62. Mauss, *Gift*. See also Derrida's well-known deconstruction of the gift concept in *Given Time I*. It seems to me that Jim Sykes's call to rethink musical creativity in terms of the gift (Sykes, "Anthropocene and Music Studies"), while provocative and energizing, understates the status and meaning of the gift in the Christian theological tradition. It may be that the Christian understanding of gratuity is, from Sykes's perspective, too frequently allied with a hegemonic conception of individual interiority that Sykes characterizes as distinctively European or, deeper still, Judeo-Christian. I would only caution against the implicitly extractive logic by which Euro-American theorists derive supposedly redemptive forms of aneconomic exchange

from non-Euro-American societies—a long history that includes not only Mauss's conception of gift exchange but also the later anthropological and sociological theories of Bourdieu, Lévi-Strauss, and Baudrillard.

63. "Nun hat unser Meister, ein anderes Feld angebaut und befruchtet." Zelter, "Recension. Die Schöpfung," col. 389.

64. Georgic tropes are ubiquitous in Young's *Conjectures*. See, e.g., pp. 12 and 54.

65. Zelter, "Recension: Die Schöpfung," col. 393.

66. This transition from performative *labor* to congealed *work* perhaps recalls something of Haydn's oft-cited account of his creative process to Griesinger: "I sat down [at the keyboard], began to improvise [*phantasieren*], sad or happy according to my mood, serious or trifling. Once I had seized upon an idea, my whole endeavor was to develop and sustain it in keeping with the rules of art." See Gotwals, *Two Contemporary Portraits*, 61.

67. "Es ist eine eigene Schöpfung auf eigene Art, und ein eigenes freyes Spiel der Kunst, die sich der Hand des Meisters zur Aniegung eines neuen Gartens, eines neuen Edens bedient." Zelter, "Briefe an einen Freund," col. 291.

68. Reproduced in Robbins Landon, *Chronicle and Works*, 4:457.

69. Reproduced in Robbins Landon, *Chronicle and Works*, 4:583. On these deifying tropes in Haydn reception, see Mathew, "Heroic Haydn," 21–22; Mathew, "Choral Work Concept," 130–34; and Webster, "Musical Sublime," 96–97.

70. Fischer, "Entwicklungsgeschichte."

71. On the tension between the sublime as a metaphysic and as a rhetorical mode or tone of voice, see Allanbrook, "Musical Topos?"; and Mathew, *Political Beethoven*, ch. 3, esp. 126–30.

72. L. Kramer, "Recalling the Sublime."

73. Burnham, *Beethoven Hero*, 119.

74. "Die Gegenstände wie in einer magischen Laterne vor uns vorüber gehen." Triest, "Bermerkungen über die Ausbildung der Tonkunst in Deutschland," col. 409. Loughridge, *Haydn's Sunrise, Beethoven's Shadow*, ch. 4.

75. "Wenn auch nicht etwa der Flug des Adlers und das Girren der Tauben ein besonderes Wohlgefallen erregen können." Zelter, "Recension: Die Schöpfung," 389, 394.

76. Derrida, "Economimesis."

77. "Es ist die wahre Phantasie eines grossen Geistes, die ein durcheinanderwurken ungeheurer Kräfte, welche sich nach und nach in eine Ordnung fügen, dem inneren Geist darstellen soll und darstellt," "Und in diesem Geiste betrachte ich das ganze Werk." Zelter, "Briefe an einen Freund," col. 292.

78. Reproduced in Robbins Landon, *Chronicle and Works*, 4:453.

79. Reproduced in Robbins Landon, *Chronicle and Works*, 4:471.

80. See M. Head, "Music with 'No Past'?," 194; and Mathew, "Choral Work Concept," 134.

81. On the many chamber transcriptions of *The Creation*, see Thormählen, "Playing with Art."

82. Brockes, *Die Jahreszeiten*.

83. "Das Ganze der Jahreszeiten ist als eine Galerie, als eine Suite von Gemälden." Zelter, "Recension: Die Jahreszeiten nach Thomson," col. 515.

84. "Eine gemeine und dem großen Künstler unwürdige Nachahmung der Natur in Einzelnheiten, und eben darum kein Ganzes bilde." Mann, "Extraconcerte," 63.

85. "Diese ganze Stelle—schreibt er—als eine Imitazion eines Frosches ist nicht aus meiner Feder gestossen; es wurde mir aufgedrungen diesen französischen Q-rk niederzuschreiben. Mit

dem ganzen Orchester verschwindet dieser elender Gedanke gar bald, aber als Klavierauszug kann derselbe nicht bestehen." Spazier, "Die Jahreszeiten von Haydn, in Leipzig," 1263.

86. See Gotwals, *Two Contemporary Portraits*, 38–41.

87. Webster, "Sublime and the Pastoral," 156–58.

88. On appropriations of georgic in the eighteenth century, see K. Goodman, *Georgic Modernity*; and Murdoch, "Landscape of Labor."

89. Gerber, *Historisch-Biographisches Lexicon*, col. 610.

90. "Doch in allen diesen Dingen ist der Dichter unendlich weit hinter dem Komponisten zurückgeblieben. Denn, nicht nur, dass er den Komponisten mit Nebendingen beladet, die sich zu einer interessanten Darstellung so gut als gar nicht eignen, hat er ihm eine ganz ungebührliche Anzahl prosaischer Worte aufgepackt, die jeden andern Komponisten sichtbar genirt haben würden." Zelter, "Recension: Die Jahreszeiten nach Thomson," col. 523.

91. Quoted and translated in Robbins Landon, *Chronicle and Works*, 4:46.

92. "Elende trockene Texte." Spazier, "Die Jahreszeiten von Haydn, in Leipzig," col. 1262.

93. Gotwals, *Two Contemporary Portraits*, 40.

94. Thomson, *The Seasons*, 90–93.

95. See K. Goodman, *Georgic Modernity*, 56–57. On the politics of the landscape, see Murdoch, "Landscape of Labor"; and the essays gathered in Mitchell, *Landscape and Power*.

96. A. Smith, *Wealth of Nations*, 116.

97. Gjerdingen, *Galant Style*, ch. 7.

98. Gjerdingen, ch. 13.

99. C. Burney, *Present State of Music*, 109.

100. "Eine gewisse Leichtigkeit, Schlüpfrigkeit, oder übermüthige Freyheit." Zelter, "Recension: Die Schöpfung," col. 396.

101. "Ein rechtes Meisterstück von Würde, Klarheit, und Genie." Zelter, "Recension: Die Jahreszeiten nach Thomson," col. 523. Vincent Novello, recalling a visit to Vienna, claimed that Haydn had complained that "one fugue alone" in *The Seasons* had "cost him 6 weeks' work—and yet nobody seemed to think anything of it." See Robbins Landon, *Chronicle and Works*, 4:149.

102. This was more or less Becker's strategy in his sociological classic, *Art Worlds*.

103. See Hardt, "Affective Labor." The concept of affective labor was, in Hardt's case, a corrective to and nuance of his and Negri's conception of "immaterial labor."

104. Hochschild, *Second Shift*. A generation of Italian Marxist feminists in particular advocated for the recognition and remuneration of domestic labor. See Federici, *Revolution at Point Zero*; and Dalla Costa, *Power of Women*.

105. Weeks, *Problem with Work*, 7. See also Chakrabarty's postcolonial critique of European conceptions of labor and value in *Provincializing Europe*, 76.

106. Sykes, "Anthropocene and Music Studies," 15.

107. Battistoni, "Bringing In the Work," 6.

108. Bogost, *Alien Phenomenology*, 49 and passim; Bennett, *Vibrant Matter*, 94.

109. Quoted and translated in Robbins Landon, *Chronicle and Works*, 4:455.

110. "What if the problem is not with the thesis that certain musical processes create a semblance of the organic but with the models of the organicism brought in to give content to that semblance?" asks Watkins. See *Musical Vitalities*, 18.

111. Bennett, *Vibrant Matter*, 98.

112. Boltanski and Chiapello, *New Spirit of Capitalism*, 463. On an expanded conception of labor as the basis for a general theory of value, see Graeber, *Anthropological Theory of Value*, 45–46, also 38–39, for a critique of this theory inspired by Marilyn Strathern.

113. Latour at times appears to articulate a labor theory of the social, which surfaces most plainly in his incessant pecuniary metaphors: sociologists should ensure that they are "paying the full cost" of every social connection that they propose—every payoff in the form of real knowledge should be earned by a prose reenactment of the work of all the people and things involved in its production; see Latour, *Reassembling the Social*, 23. For other recurrences of the Latourian "cost" trope, see pp. 11, 22, 25, 35, 50, 66, 70, 115, 122, 131, 165, 174, 175, 177, 180, 183, 184, 188, 190, 192, 220, 229, 230.

114. E. Scarry, *Body in Pain*, 284; R. Scarry, *What Do People Do*, 6.

115. See, inter alia, Guilbault, "Roy Cape's Labour"; Stokes, "Marx, Money, and Musicians"; and Steingo, "Music Economies." Despite a long history of these methodological correctives, even subtly argued studies that focus on musical economies, such as Stahl, *Unfree Masters*, continue to proceed from a freedom-versus-constraint model (as Stahl's very title signals).

Epilogue

1. Wordsworth, *William Wordsworth*, 114.

2. Indeed, Haydn's death had been widely rumored around this time, so persuasively that Luigi Cherubini was moved to compose his premature "Dirge on the Death of Joseph Haydn."

3. "Heroen in der Kunst": "Ihre reinen, vollendeten Werke stehen und gelten bleiben, was auch Zeit und Mode und ihre Sclaven für tausend und aber tausend Späße bunt durcheinander treiben mögen." Reichardt, "Nekrolog," 252.

4. "Sie allen Veränderungen und Schicksaal der Zeit und Mode zum Trotz, unsterblich bleiben werden, so lange die Musik eine Kunst heist." Zelter, "Recension: Die Schöpfung," col. 396.

5. "Im Laufe aller Zeiten bestehn wird. Es ragt, in seiner Qualität, unter den oratorisch-musikalichen Werken aller Zeiten hervor, und hat in seiner Art nichts über sich, als Händels *Messias*.": Zelter, "Recension: Die Jahreszeiten nach Thomson," col. 528.

6. On the "magazine" and the storage principle of German journals, see Franzel, "Metaphors of Spatial Storage," 328–52. On the emerging tension between "elite" and "popular" in German musical environments, see Gramit, *Cultivating Music*, esp. ch. 3.

7. *Grove Music Online*, s.v., "Reichardt, Johann Friedrich"; Eberle, *200 Jahre Sing-Akademie*.

8. Pandi and Schmidt, "Pressburger Zeitung," 225; Wyn Jones, *Symphony in Beethoven's Vienna*, 124.

9. Gotwals, *Two Contemporary Portraits*, 48.

10. See Robbins Landon, *Chronicle and Works* 4:360; Collin, "An Joseph Haydn," 129.

11. See Mathew, *Political Beethoven*, 52–53.

12. Reproduced in Robbins Landon, *Chronicle and Works* 4:361.

13. Reproduced in Robbins Landon, 4:360.

14. Collin, "Haydn's Jubelfeyer," 126.

15. See Robbins Landon, *Chronicle and Works* 4:361–62.

16. Gotwals, *Two Contemporary Portraits*, 49.

17. That infrastructures are by and large the hidden material conditions of music that otherwise appears mendaciously immaterial, and that the theorist can thus bear witness to them (even make them somehow audible), is the premise of such studies as Devine, *Decomposed*, which argues that "the inglorious conditions of commerce" are "art's reality"—"hidden in plain sight" (43). It hardly needs saying that this premise depends on its own (materialist) ontology. See also the essays in Devine and Boudreault-Fournier, *Audible Infrastructures*. On the "ontological turn"

in music studies, see Ochoa, "Acoustic Multinaturalism." See also Mathew, "Listening(s) Past," esp. 149–50.

18. Wyn Jones, *Symphony in Beethoven's Vienna*, 123.

19. On these Napoleonic commemorative events as generic hybrids, see Mathew, "Vienna, 18 October 1814."

20. See Robbins Landon, *Chronicle and Works*, 4:174.

21. Albrecht, "Balthasar Wigand's Depiction," 124.

22. March and Olsen carefully describe an institution as a "relatively enduring collection of rules and organized practices, embedded in structures of meaning and resources that are relatively invariant in the face of turnover of individuals and relatively resilient to the idiosyncratic preferences and expectations of individuals and changing external circumstances." See "Elaborating the 'New Institutionalism,'" 3.

23. See Wyn Jones, *Symphony in Beethoven's Vienna*, 124. It is likely that, on March 27, in addition to the area visible in Wigand's picture, the vast crowd also occupied the large vestibules either side of the main performance space.

24. Wyn Jones, 124.

25. On "path dependency" in institutions, see Levine, *Forms*, 59–60.

26. See Morrow, *Concert Life*, 346, 349, 350.

27. See Wyn Jones, *Symphony in Beethoven's Vienna*, 123–29. In spite of this, between 1809 and the end of the Congress of Vienna, there was an appreciable strengthening of institutions within Vienna that supported musicians, music making, and public musical performance, culminating in the founding of the Gesellschaft der Musikfreunde in 1814, by many of the same personnel behind the Liebhaber Concerte.

28. January 15, 1801: Beethoven, *Letters of Beethoven*, 1:48. Translation adapted from Solomon, "Beethoven's *Magazin der Kunst*," 195.

29. Albrecht, "Balthasar Wigand's Depiction," 125.

30. On the relationship between Beethoven and von Collin, see Ferraguto, *Beethoven 1806*, ch. 6, esp. 180–81.

31. Collin, "Haydn's Jubelfeyer," 127.

32. Wyn Jones, *Symphony in Beethoven's Vienna*, 126–28.

33. M. Head, "Music with 'No Past'?," 209–11; Mathew, "Choral Work Concept," 128–29.

34. Ferraguto, *Beethoven 1806*, ch. 4, esp. 146–47.

35. See Webster's discussion of this passage in "Musical Sublime," 83–88.

36. See Ferraguto, *Beethoven: 1806*, ch. 4, esp. 115 and 129–33. On the comparison between the slow introduction of Beethoven's Fourth and Haydn's "Chaos," see also Solomon, "Some Images of Creation."

37. Wyn Jones, *Symphony in Beethoven's Vienna*, 126–27.

38. Morrow, *Concert Life*, 352.

39. Beethoven had wanted his Fourth Concerto performed at this concert, which he had premiered himself the day before, but neither pianist he nominated was able to learn the piece in time. See Thayer, *Thayer's Life of Beethoven*, 450.

40. For a compilation of these reports, see Thayer, 448–49.

41. Quoted and translated in Thayer, 448.

42. See Mathew, "Listening(s) Past," 148.

43. See Mathew, *Political Beethoven*, 126–30.

44. See Will, *Characteristic Symphony*, ch. 4, esp. 181.

45. Loughridge, *Haydn's Sunrise, Beethoven's Shadow*, ch. 5.

46. On the Choral Fantasy as an improvisatory performance of interiority, and contemporary criticism that interpreted it in this way, see Mathew, *Political Beethoven*, 162–63; Richards, *Free Fantasia*, 223–26; Whiting, "Zu Funktion und Programm."

47. Roach, *Cities of the Dead*, 2. Kim Sauberlich has discussed more dispersed processes of musical surrogation by which Haydnesque memories were sustained and erased in Europe's colonies. Sauberlich, "Haydn's Spirits."

48. Larkin, "Poetics and Politics," 329. My thanks to John Walsh for drawing my attention to the anthropology of infrastructure.

49. I borrow the term "platform" from Siskin and Warner, who propose that the political and artistic statements we broadly know as Romanticism happened on the "platform" of the multifarious media forms that had been the Enlightenment—at the moment of saturation, when these interlocking media forms became "load bearing." See Siskin and Warner, "What Is Romanticism?," 285. On proliferation and saturation, see also Multigraph Collective, *Interacting with Print*, esp. ch. 15.

50. On this song and its reception, see Mathew, "Out of Circulation."

51. Wendt, "Gedanken über die neuere Tonkunst," col. 410.

52. See Solomon, "Nobility Pretense."

53. July 19, 1819: Beethoven, *Letters of Beethoven*, no. 953; Schindler quoted in Solomon, "Nobility Pretense," 53.

54. Baudrillard, *Political Economy*, 119.

55. Bourdieu, *Distinction*.

56. Baudrillard, *Political Economy*, 112, 121 and passim.

57. Guillory, *Cultural Capital*, 317.

58. The persistence and transformation of "early modern models" of social relation is one of the major themes of Green, *Dedicating Music*, esp. ch. 1 and 2.

59. Alejandro Madrid argues against "perpetuating the delusional idea that everything is alright and we just need to add some 'new spices to the dish we have'"; see Madrid, "Diversity, Tokenism, Non-Canonical Musics," 126.

Works Cited

Adelung, Johann Christoph. *Grammatisch-kritisches Wörterbuch der hochdeutschen Mundart*. 4 vols. Vienna: Bauer, 1811.

Adorno, Theodor. *In Search of Wagner*. Translated by Rodney Livingstone. New York: Verso, 1981.

———. "On the Fetish Character in Music and the Regression of Listening [1938]." In *Essays on Music*, edited by Richard Leppert, 288–317. Berkeley: University of California Press, 2002.

Agnew, Jean-Christophe. *Worlds Apart: The Market and the Theater in Anglo-American Thought, 1550–1750*. Cambridge: Cambridge University Press, 1986.

Ahern, Stephen, ed. *Affect and Abolition in the Anglo-Atlantic, 1770–1830*. Farnham, UK: Ashgate, 2013.

Ahmed, Sara. "Collective Feelings, or, The Impressions Left by Others." *Theory, Culture, and Society* 21, no. 2 (2004): 25–42.

Albrecht, Theodor. "The Musicians in Balthasar Wigand's Depiction of the Performance of Haydn's *Die Schöpfung*, Vienna, 27 March 1808." *Music in Art* 29, no. 1 (2004): 123–33.

Allan, David. *Commonplace Books and Reading in Georgian England*. Cambridge: Cambridge University Press, 2010.

Allanbrook, Wye J. "Mozart's K331, First Movement: Once More, with Feeling." In *Communication in Eighteenth-Century Music*, edited by Danuta Mirka and Kofi Agawu, 254–82. Cambridge: Cambridge University Press, 2008.

———. *The Secular Commedia: Comic Mimesis in Late Eighteenth-Century Music*. Edited by Mary Ann Smart and Richard Taruskin. Berkeley: University of California Press, 2014.

Allewaert, Monique. "Toward a Materialist Configuration: A Slight Manifesto." *English Language Notes* 51, no. 2 (2013): 61–77.

Alpers, Edward A. *Ivory and Slaves in East Central Africa*. Berkeley: University of California Press, 1975.

Angelo, Henry. *Reminiscences of Henry Angelo, with Memoirs of his Late Father and Friends*. Vol. 2. London: Henry Colburn and Richard Bentley, 1830.

Appadurai, Arjun. "Disjuncture and Difference in the Global Cultural Economy." *Theory, Culture and Society* 7, no. 2–3 (1990): 295–310.

———. "Introduction: Commodities and the Politics of Value." In *The Social Life of Things: Commodities in Cultural Perspective*, edited by Arjun Appadurai, 3–63. Cambridge: Cambridge University Press, 1986.

Apter, Emily. *Against World Literature: On the Politics of Untranslatability*. New York: Verso, 2013.

Aravamudan, Srinivas. *Tropicopolitans: Colonialism and Agency, 1688–1804*. Durham, NC: Duke University Press, 1999.

Arendt, Hannah. *The Human Condition*. New York: Doubleday Anchor, 1958.

Attali, Jacques. *Noise: A Political Economy of Music*. Translated by Brian Massumi. Minneapolis: University of Minnesota Press, 1991.

Bannet, Eve Tavor. *Eighteenth-Century Manners of Reading: Print Culture and Popular Instruction in the Anglophone Atlantic World*. Cambridge: Cambridge University Press, 2017.

Barbauld, Anna Letitia. *Selected Poetry and Prose*. Peterborough, Canada: Broadview, 2002.

Barlow, Jeremy. *The Enraged Musician: Hogarth's Musical Imagery*. Aldershot, UK: Ashgate, 2005.

Barney, Richard, and Warren Montag, eds. *Systems of Life: Biopolitics, Economics, and Literature on the Cusp of Modernity*. New York: Fordham University Press, 2018.

Barrett, Lindon. *Blackness and Value: Seeing Double*. Cambridge: Cambridge University Press, 1999.

Barron, Anne. "Copyright Law's Musical Work." *Social and Legal Studies* 15, no. 101 (2006): 101–27.

Barry, Anna Maria. "Charles Incledon: A Singing Sailor on the Georgian Stage." In *Martial Masculinities: Experiencing and Imagining the Military in the Long Nineteenth Century*, edited by Anna Maria Barry, Joanne Begiato, and Michael Brown, 82–101. Manchester: Manchester University Press, 2019.

Barthes, Roland. "The Structuralist Activity." In *Critical Essays*, translated by Richard Howard, 213–20. Evanston, IL: Northwestern University Press, 1972.

———. "The Reality Effect." In *The Rustle of Language*, translated by Richard Howard, 141–48. Berkeley: University of California Press, 1989.

Bates, Eliot. *Digital Tradition: Arrangement and Labor in Istanbul's Recording Studio Culture*. New York: Oxford University Press, 2016.

Battistoni, Alyssa. "Bringing in the Work of Nature: From Natural Capital to Hybrid Labor." *Political Theory* 45, no. 1 (2017): 5–31.

Baudrillard, Jean. *For a Critique of the Political Economy of the Sign*. Translated by Charles Levin. New York: Telos Candor, 1981.

Beauvoir, Simone de. *The Second Sex*. Translated by H. M. Parshley. New York: Vintage, 1989.

Becker, Howard. *Art Worlds*. Berkeley: University of California Press, 1982.

Beethoven, Ludwig van. *The Letters of Beethoven*. Edited and translated by Emily Anderson. 3 vols. London: Macmillan, 1961.

Beghin, Tom. *The Virtual Haydn: Paradox of a Twenty-First Century Keyboardist*. Chicago: University of Chicago Press, 2015.

Bellamy, Liz. *Commerce, Morality and the Eighteenth-Century Novel*. Cambridge: Cambridge University Press, 1998.

Benedict, Barbara M. *Curiosity: A Cultural History of Early Modern Inquiry*. Chicago: University of Chicago Press, 2001.

Benjamin, Walter. *The Arcades Project*. Edited by Rolf Tiedemann. Translated by Howard Eiland and Kevin McLaughlin. Cambridge, MA: Harvard University Press, 1999.

Bennett, Jane. *Vibrant Matter: A Political Ecology of Things*. Durham, NC: Duke University Press, 2010.

Benton, Rita. "Pleyel as Music Publisher." *Journal of the American Musicological Society* 32, no. 1 (1979): 125–40.

Berg, Maxine. *Luxury and Pleasure in Eighteenth-Century Britain*. New York: Oxford University Press, 2005.

Best, Stephen. *None Like Us: Blackness, Belonging, Aesthetic Life*. Durham, NC: Duke University Press, 2018.

Best, Stephen, and Sharon Marcus. "Surface Reading: An Introduction." *Representations* 108 (2009): 1–21.

Bijsterveld, Karin, ed. *Soundscapes of the Urban Past: Staged Sound as Mediated Cultural Heritage*. Bielefeld, Germany: Transcript, 2013.

Bhattacharya, Nandini. "Family Jewels: George Colman's *Inkle and Yarico* and Connoisseurship." *Eighteenth-Century Studies* 34, no. 2 (2001): 206–26.

Blackwell, Mark, ed. *The Secret Life of Things: Animals, Objects, and It-Narratives in Eighteenth-Century England*. Lewisburg, PA: Bucknell University Press, 2007.

Bloechl, Olivia. *Native American Song at the Frontiers of Early Modern Music*. Cambridge: Cambridge University Press, 2008.

Bogost, Ian. *Alien Phenomenology, or What It's Like to Be a Thing*. Minneapolis: University of Minnesota Press, 2012.

Bohlman, Philip. "Ontologies of Music." In *Rethinking Music*, edited by Nicholas Cook and Mark Everist, 17–34. Oxford: Oxford University Press, 1999.

Bohrer, Karl Heinz. *Suddenness: On the Moment of Aesthetic Appearance*. Translated by Ruth Crowley. New York: Columbia University Press, 1994.

Boltanski, Luc, and Eve Chiapello. *The New Spirit of Capitalism*. Translated by Gregory Elliot. New York: Verso, 2005.

Bonds, Mark Evan. *Music as Thought: Listening to the Symphony in the Age of Beethoven*. Princeton, NJ: Princeton University Press, 2006.

———. "Symphonic Politics: Haydn's 'National Symphony' for France." *Eighteenth-Century Music* 8, no. 1 (2011): 9–19.

Borg, Alan, and David Coke. *Vauxhall Gardens: A History*. New Haven, CT: Yale University Press, 2011.

Borthwick, E. Kerr. "The Latin Quotations in Haydn's London Notebooks." *Music and Letters* 71 (1990): 505–10.

———. "Haydn's Latin Quotations: A Postscript." *Music and Letters* 75 (1994): 576–79.

Boswell, James. *Boswell's London Journal, 1762–1763*. Edited by Frederick A. Pottle and Christopher Morley. New York: McGraw-Hill, 1950.

———. *The Life of Samuel Johnson*. Ware, UK: Wordsworth Classics, 1999.

Boulukos, George. *The Grateful Slave: The Emergence of Race in Eighteenth-Century British and American Culture*. Cambridge: Cambridge University Press, 2008.

———. "Capitalism and Slavery: Once Again with Feeling." In *Affect and Abolition in the Anglo-Atlantic, 1770–1830*, edited by Stephen Ahern, 23–43. Farnham, UK: Ashgate, 2013.

Bourdieu, Pierre. *Distinction: A Social Critique of the Judgement of Taste*. Translated by Richard Nice. Cambridge, MA: Harvard University Press, 1984.

———. *The Rules of Art: Genesis and Structure of the Literary Field*. Translated by Susan Emanuel. Stanford, CA: Stanford University Press, 1996.

Brittan, Francesca, and Carmel Raz, eds. "Colloquy: Attention, Anxiety, and Audition's Histories." *Journal of the American Musicological Society* 72, no. 2 (2019): 541–80.

Brown, A. Peter. *The Symphonic Repertoire.* 4 vols. Bloomington: Indiana University Press,
2002–12.

Brown, Bill, ed. *Things.* Chicago: University of Chicago Press, 2004.

Brown, Marshall. "Mozart and After: The Revolution in Musical Consciousness." *Critical Inquiry*
7 (1981): 689–706.

Brown, Wendy. "Freedom's Silences." In *Edgework: Critical Essays on Knowledge and Politics*, 83–
97. Princeton, NJ: Princeton University Press, 2005.

Burgess, Miranda. "Mobility, Anxiety, and the Romantic Poetics of Feeling." *Studies in Romanticism* 49, no. 2 (2010): 229–60.

———. "On Being Moved: Sympathy, Mobility, and Narrative Form." *Poetics Today* 32, no. 2
(2011): 289–321.

Burke, Edmund. *A Philosophical Enquiry into the Origin of Our Ideas of the Sublime and Beautiful.* Edited and with an introduction by Adam Phillips. New York: Oxford University Press,
1990. [Based on the 2nd ed. of 1759.]

———. "Thoughts and Details on Scarcity." In *The Writings and Speeches of Edmund Burke*,
vol. 9, edited by R. B. McDowell. Oxford: Clarendon, 1991.

Burney, Charles. *The Present State of Music in France and Italy.* London: G. Robinson, 1773.

———. *The Present State of Music in Germany, the Netherlands, and United Provinces.* Vol. 1.
London: T. Becket and Co., 1773.

———. *A General History of Music from the Earliest Ages to the Present* [1776–1789]. 2 vols. Edited
by Frank Mercer. New York: Dover, 1957.

Burney, Frances. *Evelina.* New York: Oxford University Press, 2002.

Burney, Susan. *The Letters and Journals of Susan Burney.* Edited by Edward Olleson. Farnham,
UK: Ashgate, 2012.

Busby, Thomas. *Concert Room and Orchestra: Anecdotes of Music and Musicians, Ancient and
Modern.* 2 vols. London: Clementi, 1825.

Cabranes-Grant, Leo. *From Scenarios to Networks: Performing the Intercultural in Colonial Mex-
ico.* Evanston, IL: Northwestern University Press, 2016.

Campbell, Colin. *The Romantic Ethic and the Spirit of Modern Consumerism.* Oxford: Blackwell,
1987.

Cannon, Beekman C. *Johann Mattheson: Spectator in Music.* New Haven, CT: Yale University
Press, 1947.

Carey, Brycchan. *British Abolitionism and the Rhetoric of Sensibility: Writing, Sentiment, and
Slavery, 1760–1807.* New York: Palgrave MacMillan, 2005.

———. "To Force a Tear: British Abolitionism and the Eighteenth-Century London Stage." In *Affect and Abolition in the Anglo-Atlantic, 1770–1830*, edited by Stephen Ahern, 109–28. Farnham, UK: Ashgate, 2013.

Carnall, Geoffrey, and Colin Nicholson, eds. *The Impeachment of Warren Hastings: Papers from
a Bicentenary Commemoration.* Edinburgh: Edinburgh University Press, 1989.

Carpani, Giuseppe. *Le Haydine.* Milan: Buccinelli, 1812.

Carroll, Michael. "The Struggle for Music Copyright." *Florida Law Review* 57 (2005): 905–61.

Cartwright, George. *A Journal of Transactions and Events During a Residence of Nearly Sixteen
Years on the Coast of Labrador.* Vol. 1. Facsimile reprint [1792]. Cambridge: Cambridge University Press, 2012.

Caygill, Howard. *Art of Judgement*. Oxford: Blackwell, 1989.

Certeau, Michel de. *The Practice of Everyday Life*. Translated by Steven F. Rendall. Berkeley: University of California Press, 1984.

Chakrabarty, Dipesh. *Provincializing Europe: Postcolonial Thought and Historical Difference*. Princeton, NJ: Princeton University Press, 2000.

Chandler, James. *An Archaeology of Sympathy: The Sentimental Mode in Literature and Cinema*. Chicago: University of Chicago Press, 2013.

Chandler, James, and Kevin Gilmartin, eds. *Romantic Metropolis: The Urban Scene of British Culture, 1780–1840*. Cambridge: Cambridge University Press, 2005.

Chaplin, Simon. "Nature Dissected or Dissection Naturalized: The Case of John Hunter's Museum." *Museum and Society* 6, no. 2 (2008): 135–51.

Chapman, Dale. *The Jazz Bubble: Neoclassical Jazz in Neoliberal Culture*. Oakland: University of California Press, 2018.

Chen, Jen-yen. "Musical Culture and Social Ideology in Vienna *circa* 1800: Aristocratic Patronage and Bourgeois Reception of Joseph Haydn's Oratorios." *Concentric: Literary and Cultural Studies* 36, no. 1 (2010): 189–215.

Cheng, Anne. *Ornamentalism*. New York: Oxford University Press, 2019.

Cheng, William. *Just Vibrations: The Purpose of Sounding Good*. Ann Arbor: University of Michigan Press, 2016.

Chua, Daniel. "Myth: Mozart, Money, Music." In *Mozart Studies*, edited by Simon P. Keefe, 193–213. Cambridge: Cambridge University Press, 2006.

Clark, Caryl. "Haydn in the Theater: The Operas." In *The Cambridge Companion to Haydn*, edited by Caryl Clark, 176–99. Cambridge: Cambridge University Press, 2005.

———, ed. *The Cambridge Companion to Haydn*. Cambridge: Cambridge University Press, 2005.

Clark, Andy, and David Chalmers. "The Extended Mind." *Analysis* 58 (1998): 7–19.

Clarke, Thomas B. *A Statistical View of Germany*. London: C. Dilly, 1790.

Clarkson, Thomas. *History of the Rise, Progress, and Accomplishment of the Abolition of the African Slave Trade by the British Parliament*. Vol. 1. London: R. Taylor, 1808.

Clery, E. J. *The Feminization Debate in Eighteenth-Century England: Literature, Commerce, and Luxury*. London: Palgrave MacMillan, 2004.

Clune, Michael W. *Writing against Time*. Stanford, CA: Stanford University Press, 2013.

Cobbett, William, ed. "Debate on Mr. Wilberforce's Resolutions respecting the Slave Trade." In *The Parliamentary History of England. From the Norman Conquest in 1066 to the Year 1803*. Vol. 28, cols. 42–68. London: T. Curson Hansard, 1789–91.

Cockayne, Emily. *Hubbub: Filth, Noise, and Stench in England, 1600–1770*. New Haven, CT: Yale University Press, 2007.

Coleman, Deirdre. "Firebrands, Letters, and Flowers: Mrs. Barbauld and the Priestleys." In *Romantic Sociability: Social Networks and Literary Culture in Britain, 1770–1840*, edited by Gillian Russell and Clara Tuite, 82–103. Cambridge: Cambridge University Press, 2002.

Collin, Heinrich Joseph von. "An Joseph Haydn." In *Sämmtliche Werke*, 3:125–26. Vienna: Anton Struß, 1812.

———. "Haydn's Jubelfeyer." In *Sämmtliche Werke*, 3:128–29. Vienna: Anton Struß, 1812.

A Complete Register of all the New Musical Publications imported from Different Parts of Europe by Longman and Broderip. London: Longman & Broderip, 1786.

Cox Jensen, Oskar. *The Ballad-Singer in Georgian and Victorian London*. Cambridge: Cambridge University Press, 2021.

Crary, Jonathan. *Techniques of the Observer: On Vision and Modernity in the Nineteenth Century.* Cambridge, MA: MIT Press, 1990.

———. *Suspensions of Perception: Attention, Spectacle, and Modern Culture.* Cambridge, MA: MIT Press, 1999.

Crotch, William. *Specimens of Various Styles of Music Referred to in a Course of Lectures Read at Oxford and London and Adapted to Keyed Instruments.* Vol. 1. London: Robert Birchall, 1807.

Cudworth, Charles. "The Vauxhall 'Lists.'" *Galpin Society Journal* 20 (1967): 24–42.

Cuming, H. Syer. "On Phonic Horns." *Journal of the British Archaeological Association* 5 (1850): 119–33.

Currie, James R. *Music and the Politics of Negation.* Bloomington: Indiana University Press, 2012.

Dalla Costa, Mariarosa. *The Power of Women and the Subversion of the Community.* Bristol, UK: Falling Wall, 1973.

Daston, Lorraine. "Taking Note(s)." *Isis* 95 (2004): 443–48.

Daston, Lorraine, and Katharine Park. *Wonders and the Order of Nature, 1150–1750.* New York: Zone Books, 2001.

Davies, James. "On Being Moved/Against Objectivity." *Representations* 132 (2015): 79–87.

———. "'I Am an Essentialist': Against the Voice Itself." In *The Voice as Something More: Essays toward Materiality,* edited by Martha Feldman and Judith Zeitlin, 142–68. Chicago: University of Chicago Press, 2019.

Davison, Alan. "The Face of a Musical Genius: Thomas Hardy's Portrait of Joseph Haydn." *Eighteenth-Century Music* 6 (2009): 209–27.

Dawe, Kevin. "Materials Matter: Towards a Political Ecology of Musical Instrument Making." In *Current Directions in Ecomusicology: Music, Nature, Environment,* 109–21. New York: Routledge, 2015.

Day-O'Connell, Sarah. "Anatomy, Industry, and the English Canzonet (1770–1820): Placing Women in the Private Sphere." PhD diss., Cornell University, 2004.

———. "The Composer, the Surgeon, His Wife and Her Poems: Haydn and the Anatomy of the English Canzonetta." *Eighteenth-Century Music* 6, no. 1 (2009): 77–112.

———. "'The Clock Points Its Moral to the Heart': Time and Memory in Haydn's English Canzonettas." In *Zyklus und Prozess: Joseph Haydn und die Zeit,* edited by Marie-Agnes Dittrich, Marin Eybl, and Reinhard Kapp, 153–78. Vienna: Böhlau Verlag, 2012.

Dayan, Joan. "Amorous Bondage: Poe, Ladies, and Slaves." *American Literature* 66, no. 2 (1994): 239–73.

Denning, Michael. *Noise Uprising: The Audiopolitics of a World Musical Revolution.* London: Verso, 2015.

De Nora, Tia. *Beethoven and the Construction of Genius: Musical Politics in Vienna, 1792–1803.* Berkeley: University of California Press, 1997.

Derrida, Jacques. *Of Grammatology.* Translated by Gayatri Chakravorty Spivak. Baltimore: Johns Hopkins University Press, 1974.

———. "Economimesis." *Diacritics* 11, no. 2 (1981): 2–25.

———. "Signature Event Context." In *Margins of Philosophy,* translated by Alan Bass, 309–30. Chicago: University of Chicago Press, 1982.

———. *Given Time I: Counterfeit Money.* Translated by Peggy Kamuf. Chicago: University of Chicago Press, 1992.

Devine, Kyle. *Decomposed: The Political Ecology of Music.* Cambridge, MA: MIT Press, 2019.

Devine, Kyle, and Alexandrine Boudreault-Fournier, eds. *Audible Infrastructures: Music, Sound, Media*. New York: Oxford University Press, 2021.

Devriès-Lesure, Anik. "Technological Aspects." In *The Circulation of Music in Europe, 1600–1900*, edited by Rudolf Rasch, 63–88. Berlin: BWV, 2008.

Diderot, Denis. "Rameau's Nephew." In *"Rameau's Nephew" and Other Works*, translated by Jacques Barzun, 8–91. Indianapolis: Hackett, 2001.

Diergarten, Felix. "'The True Fundamentals of Composition': Haydn's Partimento Counterpoint." *Eighteenth-Century Music* 8, no. 1 (2011): 53–75.

Dillon, Emma. *The Sense of Sound: Musical Meaning in France, 1260–1330*. New York: Oxford University Press, 2012.

Disney, Samuel. "Epilogue to *The Padlock*." *The Gentleman's Magazine*, June 1792, 557.

Dolan, Emily I. *The Orchestral Revolution: Haydn and the Technologies of Timbre*. Cambridge: Cambridge University Press, 2013.

Dolar, Mladen. *A Voice and Nothing More*. Cambridge, MA: MIT Press, 2006.

Domingo, Darryl P. *The Rhetoric of Diversion in English Literature and Culture, 1690–1760*. Cambridge: Cambridge University Press, 2016.

Douglas, Aileen. "Britannia's Rule and the It-Narrator." *Eighteenth-Century Fiction* 6, no. 1 (1993): 65–82.

Drott, Eric. "Rereading Jacques Attali's *Bruits*." *Critical Inquiry* 41, no. 4 (2015): 721–56.

Eagleton, Terry. *The Ideology of the Aesthetic*. Oxford: Blackwell, 1990.

———. *Ideology: An Introduction*. Rev. ed. New York: Verso, 2007.

———. *Faith, Reason, and Revolution: Reflections on the God Debate*. New Haven, CT: Yale University Press, 2009.

Eberle, Gottfried. *200 Jahre Sing-Akademie zu Berlin: "Ein Kunstverein für die heilge Musik."* Berlin: Nicolai, 1991.

Eckartshausen, Karl von. "Lehren eines Richters an seine Sohn." In *Sittenlehren für alle Stände der Menschen zur Bildung junger Hertzen*, 16–43. Salzburg: J. J. Mayer, 1784.

Edgeworth, Maria. *Tales of Fashionable Life*. 2nd ed. 3 vols. London: J. Johnson, 1809.

Eidsheim, Nina Sun. *Sensing Sound: Singing and Listening as Vibrational Practice*. Durham, NC: Duke University Press, 2015.

———. *The Race of Sound: Listening, Timbre, and Vocality in African-American Music*. Durham, NC: Duke University Press, 2019.

Ellis, Markman. *The Politics of Sensibility: Race, Gender, and Commerce in the Sentimental Novel*. Cambridge: Cambridge University Press, 1996.

Enfield, William. *Observations on Literary Property*. London: Joseph Johnson, 1774.

Erwin, Timothy. "*Ut rhetorica artes*: The Rhetorical Theory of the Sister Arts." In *Haydn and the Performance of Rhetoric*, edited by Tom Beghin and Sander M. Goldberg, 61–79. Chicago: University of Chicago Press, 2007.

The European Magazine. March 1791.

Evans, R. J. W., and Alexander Marr, eds. *Curiosity and Wonder from the Renaissance to the Enlightenment*. New York: Routledge, 2016.

Fairclough, Mary. *The Romantic Crowd: Sympathy, Controversy, and Print Culture*. Cambridge: Cambridge University Press, 2013.

Fanon, Frantz. *Black Skin, White Masks*. Translated by Charles Lam Markmann. New York: Grove Press, 1967.

Federici, Silvia. *The Revolution at Point Zero: Housework, Reproduction, and Feminist Struggle.* Oakland: PM Press, 2012.

Feinberg, H. M., and M. Johnson. "The West African Ivory Trade during the Eighteenth Century: The '. . . and Ivory' Complex." *International Journal of Historical African Studies* 15 (1982): 435–53.

Feld, Steven. "Pygmy POP: A Genealogy of Schizophonic Mimesis." *Yearbook for Traditional Music* 28 (1996): 1–35.

Feldman, Martha. "The Interstitial Voice: An Opening." *Journal of the American Musicological Society* 68, no. 3 (2015): 653–59.

Feldman, Martha, and Judith Zeitlin, eds. *The Voice as Something More: Essays Toward Materiality.* Chicago: University of Chicago Press, 2019.

Felsenstein, Frank ed. *English Trader, Indian Maid: Representing Gender, Race, and Slavery in the New World.* Baltimore: Johns Hopkins University Press, 1999.

Felski, Rita. *The Limits of Critique.* Chicago: University of Chicago Press, 2015.

———. *Hooked: Art and Attachment.* Chicago: University of Chicago Press, 2020.

Ferguson, Mary. "Mary Wollstonecraft and the Problematic of Slavery." *Feminist Review* 42 (1992): 82–102.

Ferraguto, Mark. *Beethoven 1806.* New York: Oxford University Press, 2019.

Ferry, Luc. *Homo Aestheticus: The Invention of Taste in the Democratic Age.* Translated by Robert de Loaiza. Chicago: University of Chicago Press, 1993.

Festa, Lynn. *Sentimental Figures of Empire in Eighteenth-Century Britain and France.* Baltimore: Johns Hopkins University Press, 2006.

Fineman, Joel. "The History of the Anecdote: Fiction and Fiction." In *The New Historicism*, edited by H. Aram Veeser, 49–76. New York: Routledge, 1989.

Fink, George, ed. *Stress: Concepts, Cognition, Emotion, and Behavior.* London: Academic, 2016.

Finn, Margot. *The Character of Credit: Personal Debt in English Culture, 1740–1914.* Cambridge: Cambridge University Press, 2003.

Fischer, Wilhelm. "Zur Entwicklungsgeschichte des Wiener klassischen Stils." *Studien zur Musikwissenschaft* 3 (1915): 24–84.

Florida, Richard. *The Rise of the Creative Class.* New York: Basic Books, 2002.

———. *Cities and the Creative Class.* New York: Routledge, 2005.

Forman-Barzilai, Fonna. "Sympathy in Space(s): Adam Smith on Proximity." *Political Theory* 33, no. 2 (2005): 189–217.

Foucault, Michel. *The Order of Things: An Archaeology of the Human Sciences.* New York: Vintage Books, 1994.

Franzel, Sean. "Metaphors of Spatial Storage in Enlightenment Historiography and the Eighteenth-Century 'Magazine.'" In *The Radical Enlightenment in Germany: A Cultural Perspective*, edited by Carl Niekerk, 328–52. Boston: Brill-Rodopi, 2018.

Frazer, Michael. *The Enlightenment of Sympathy: Justice and the Moral Sentiments in the Eighteenth Century and Today.* New York: Oxford University Press, 2010.

Fuhrmann, Wolfgang. *Haydn und sein Publikum. Die Veröffentlichung eines Komponisten, ca. 1750–1815.* Bern: University of Bern, 2010.

———. "Originality as Market-Value: Remarks on the Fantasia in C Hob. XVII:4 and Haydn as Musical Entrepreneur." *Studia Musicologica* 51 (2010): 303–16.

Gallagher, Catherine. *The Body Economic.* Princeton, NJ: Princeton University Press, 2006.

Gallagher, Catherine, and Stephen Greenblatt. *Practicing New Historicism*. Chicago: University of Chicago Press, 2000.

Garratt, James. "Haydn and Posterity: The Long Nineteenth Century." In *The Cambridge Companion to Haydn*, edited by Caryl Clark, 226–38. Cambridge: Cambridge University Press, 2005.

Geiringer, Karl. *Haydn: A Creative Life in Music*. 3rd rev. ed. Berkeley: University of California Press, 1987.

The Gentleman's Magazine. 53, no. 1 (1783).

Gerber, Ernst Ludwig. *Historisch-Biographisches Lexicon der Tonkünstler*. Leipzig: Breitkopf, 1790.

Gerzina, Gretchen. *Black London: Life before Emancipation*. New Brunswick, NJ: Rutgers University Press, 1995.

Gikandi, Simon. *Slavery and the Culture of Taste*. Princeton, NJ: Princeton University Press, 2011.

Gilroy, Paul. *The Black Atlantic: Modernity and Double Consciousness*. London: Verso, 1993.

Gitelman, Lisa. *Always Already New: Media, History, and the Data of Culture*. Cambridge, MA: MIT Press, 2006.

Gjerdingen, Robert O. *Music in the Galant Style*. New York: Oxford University Press, 2007.

———. "Partimento, que me veux-tu?" *Journal of Music Theory* 51, no. 1 (2007): 85–135.

Goehr, Lydia. *The Imaginary Museum of Musical Works*. Oxford: Clarendon, 1992.

Goldsmith, Oliver. *The Citizen of the World, or Letters from a Chinese Philosopher, Residing in London, to his Friends in the East*. Vol. 2. London: J. Parsons, 1794.

Goldstein, Amanda Jo. *Sweet Science: Romantic Materialism and the New Logics of Life*. Chicago: University of Chicago Press, 2017.

Goodman, Glenda. "Sounds Heard, Meaning Deferred: Music Transcription as Imperial Technology." *Eighteenth-Century Studies* 51, no. 1 (2018): 39–45.

———. *Cultivated by Hand: Amateur Musicians in the Early American Republic*. New York: Oxford University Press, 2020.

Goodman, Kevis. *Georgic Modernity and British Romanticism: Poetry and the Mediation of History*. Cambridge: Cambridge University Press, 2004.

Gopinath, Sumanth, and Jason Stanyek, eds. *The Oxford Handbook of Mobile Music Studies*. 2 vols. New York: Oxford University Press, 2014.

Gotwals, Vernon, ed. and trans. *Haydn: Two Contemporary Portraits*. Madison: University of Wisconsin Press, 1968.

Goux, Jean-Joseph. *Symbolic Economies: After Marx and Freud*. Translated by Jennifer Curtiss Gage. Ithaca, NY: Cornell University Press, 1990.

Graeber, David. *Toward an Anthropological Theory of Value: The False Coin of Our Own Dreams*. New York: Palgrave, 2001.

———. *Debt: The First 5,000 Years*. Brooklyn: Melville House, 2011.

———. "Radical Alterity Is Just Another Way of Saying 'Reality': A Reply to Eduardo Viveiros de Castro." *Journal of Ethnographic Theory* 5, no. 2 (2015): 1–41.

Gramit, David. *Cultivating Music: The Aspirations, Interests, and Limits of German Musical Culture, 1770–1848*. Berkeley: University of California Press, 2002.

Grant, Roger. *Peculiar Attunements: How Affect Theory Turned Musical*. New York: Fordham University Press, 2020.

Green, Emily. "Memoirs of a Musical Object, Supposedly Written by Itself: It-Narrative and Eighteenth-Century Marketing." *Current Musicology* 95 (2013): 193–213.

———. *Dedicating Music, 1785–1850.* Rochester, NY: University of Rochester Press, 2019.

———. "How to Read a Rondeau: On Pleasure, Analysis, and the Desultory in Amateur Performance Practice of the Eighteenth Century." *Journal of the American Musicological Society* 73, no. 2 (2020): 267–325.

Green, Emily, and Catherine Mayes, eds. *Consuming Music: Individuals, Institutions, Communities, 1730–1830.* Rochester, NY: University of Rochester Press, 2017.

Green, Henry, and James Hook. *The Wooden Walls of Old England. An Ode, Written by H. Green.* London: A. and P. Thompson, 1790.

Greenblatt, Stephen. "A Mobility Studies Manifesto." In *Cultural Mobility: A Manifesto*, edited by Ine G. Zupanov, Reinhard Meyer-Klkus, Heike Paul, Pál Nyíri, and Friederike Pannewick, 250–53. Cambridge: Cambridge University Press, 2010.

Greig, Hannah. *The Beau Monde: Fashionable Society in Georgian London.* New York: Oxford University Press, 2013.

Grigson, Caroline. *The Life and Poems of Anne Hunter: Haydn's Tuneful Voice.* Liverpool: Liverpool University Press, 2009.

Guilbault, Jocelyne. "Roy Cape's Labour of Love: Theorising Work Ethics through Musical Biography." *Popular Music* 36, no. 2 (2017): 353–69.

Guilbault, Jocelyne, and Timothy Rommen, eds. *Sounds of Vacation: Political Economies of Caribbean Tourism.* Durham, NC: Duke University Press, 2019.

Guillory, John. *Cultural Capital: The Problem of Literary Canon Formation.* Chicago: University of Chicago Press, 1993.

———. "Genesis of the Media Concept." *Critical Inquiry* 36, no. 2 (2010): 321–62.

Habermas, Jürgen. *Erkenntnis und Interesse.* Frankfurt: Suhrkamp, 1968.

Håkansson, N. Thomas. "The Human Ecology of World Systems in East Africa: The Impact of the Ivory Trade." *Human Ecology* 32, no. 5 (2004): 561–91.

Hamilton, Julia. "'African' Songs and Women's Abolitionism in the Home, 1787–1807." *Studies in Eighteenth-Century Culture* 50 (2021): 153–68.

Harding, Anthony John. "Commerce, Sentiment, and Free Air: Contradictions of Abolitionist Rhetoric." In *Affect and Abolition in the Anglo-Atlantic, 1770–1830*, edited by Stephen Ahern, 71–88. Farnham, UK: Ashgate, 2013.

Hardt, Michael. "Affective Labor." *boundary 2* 26, no. 2 (1999): 89–100.

Hardt, Michael, and Antonio Negri. *Empire.* Cambridge, MA: Harvard University Press, 2000.

Harris, Daniel. *Cute, Quaint, Hungry, and Romantic: The Aesthetics of Consumerism.* New York: Basic Books, 2000.

Hart, William. "New Light on George Bridgetower." *Musical Times*, Autumn 2017, 95–106.

Hartman, Saidiya. *Scenes of Subjection: Terror, Slavery, and Self-Making in Nineteenth-Century America.* New York: Oxford University Press, 1997.

Harvey, David. *Rebel Cities: From the Right to the City to the Urban Revolution.* London: Verso, 2013.

Hawkins, John. *A General History of the Science and Practice of Music* [1776]. 2 vols. New York: Dover, 1963.

Haydn, Joseph. *The Collected Correspondence and London Notebooks of Joseph Haydn [CC].* Edited and translated by H. C. Robbins Landon. London: Barrie and Rockliff, 1959.

———. *Gesammelte Briefe und Aufzeichnungen [GB]*. Edited by Dénes Bartha. Kassel: Bärenreiter, 1965.

———. *Haydn's Celebrated Grand Military Symphony, Composed for and Performed at Mr. Salomon's and the Opera Concerts*. London: Salomon, 1797.

Head, Matthew. "Music with 'No Past'? Archaeologies of Joseph Haydn and *The Creation*." *Nineteenth-Century Music* 23, no. 3 (2000): 191–217.

———. "Haydn's Exoticisms: 'Difference' and the Enlightenment." In *The Cambridge Companion to Haydn*, edited by Caryl Clark, 77–92. Cambridge: Cambridge University Press, 2005.

———. *Sovereign Feminine: Music and Gender in Eighteenth-Century Germany*. Berkeley: University of California Press, 2013.

Head, Raymond. "Corelli in Calcutta: Colonial Music Making in India during the Seventeenth and Eighteenth Centuries." *Early Music* 13, no. 4 (1985): 548–53.

Heartz, Daniel. *Mozart, Haydn and Early Beethoven, 1780–1802*. New York: W. W. Norton, 2009.

Herder, Johann Gottfried. "Essay on the Origin of Language." In *On the Origin of Language: Jean-Jacques Rousseau, "Essay on the Origin of Languages"; Johann Gottfried Herder, "Essay on the Origin of Language,"* edited and translated by John H. Moran and Alexander Gode, 85–166. Chicago: University of Chicago Press, 1966.

Hinton, Laura. *The Perverse Gaze of Sympathy: Sadomasochistic Sentiments from Clarissa to Rescue 911*. Albany: State University of New York Press, 1999.

Hirschman, Albert O. *The Passions and the Interests: Political Arguments for Capitalism before Its Triumph*. Princeton, NJ: Princeton University Press, 1977.

Hitchcock, Tim. *Down and Out in Eighteenth-Century London*. London: Hambledon and London, 2004.

Hochman, Brian. *Savage Preservation: The Ethnographic Origins of Modern Media Technology*. Minneapolis: University of Minnesota Press, 2014.

Hochschild, Arlie, with Anne Machung. *The Second Shift: Working Parents and the Revolution at Home*. New York: Viking, 1989.

Hofmeyr, Isabel, and Sarah Nuttall. "The Book in Africa." *Current Writing* 13, no. 2 (2001): 1–8.

Hogarth, William. *The Analysis of Beauty, Written with a View to Fixing the Fluctuating Ideas of Taste*. London: W. Strahan, 1772.

Homer, Sidney, and Richard Sylla. *A History of Interest Rates*. New Brunswick, NJ: Rutgers University Press, 1963.

Hook, James. *A Third Collection of Songs Sung by Miss Milne, Mrs. Addison, Mr. Darley, & Mr. Duffey at Vauxhall*. London: Harrison, 1791.

———. *A Collection of Favorite Songs sung by Mr. Darly, Mr. Clifford, Mrs. Franklin, Miss Milne, Mrs. Addison, & Mrs. Mountain at Vauxhall Gardens*. London: A. Bland & Weller, 1793.

———. *A Collection of Favorite Songs sung by Mr. Dignum, Mr. Denman, Mrs. Franklin, Master Welsh, & Mrs. Mountain at Vauxhall Gardens*. London: A. Bland & Weller, 1796.

Horwärthner, Maria. "Joseph Haydn's Library: An Attempt at Literary-Historical Reconstruction." In *Haydn and His World*, edited by Elaine Sisman, 395–461. Princeton, NJ: Princeton University Press, 1997.

Hoyt, Peter. "Haydn's Rowdy Fellows and the Music of English Religious Intolerance." Paper presented at the annual conference of the Society for Eighteenth-Century Music, Charleston, SC, April 2012.

Hudson, Nicholas. "From 'Nation' to 'Race': The Origin of Racial Classification in Eighteenth-Century Thought." *Eighteenth-Century Studies* 29, no. 3 (1996): 247–64.

Huhn, Thomas. *Imitation and Society: The Persistence of Mimesis in the Aesthetics of Burke, Hogarth, and Kant.* University Park: Pennsylvania State University Press, 2004.

Hume, David. *A Treatise of Human Nature.* Edited by Ernest C. Mossner. London: Penguin, 1969.

———. *Political Essays.* Edited by Knud Haakonnsen. Cambridge: Cambridge University Press, 1994.

Hunter, David. "Music Copyright in Britain to 1800." *Music and Letters* 67 (1986): 269–82.

Hunter, John. *Essays and Observations on Natural History, Anatomy, Physiology, Psychology, and Geology, by John Hunter, Being His Posthumous Papers.* Vol. 1. London: John van Voorst, 1861.

Hunter, Mary. "'The Most Interesting Genre of Music': Performance, Sociability and Meaning in the Classical String Quartet, 1800–1830." *Nineteenth-Century Music Review* 9 (2012): 53–74.

Huyssen, Andreas. *After the Great Divide: Modernism, Mass Culture, Postmodernism.* Bloomington: Indiana University Press, 1986.

Ingold, Tim. "The Temporality of the Landscape." *World Archaeology* 25 (1993): 152–74.

Innis, Harold A. *The Bias of Communication.* Toronto: University of Toronto Press, 1951. Reprint, 1995.

Irvine, Thomas. *Listening to China: Sound and the Sino-Western Encounter, 1770–1839.* Chicago: University of Chicago Press, 2019.

Irving, Howard. *Ancients and Moderns: William Crotch and the Development of Classical Music.* Aldershot: Ashgate, 1999.

———. "Empiricism, Ideology, and William Crotch's Specimens." *Nineteenth-Century Music Review* 9, no. 2 (2012): 237–53.

Jacobs, Jane. *Cities and the Wealth of Nations: Principles of Economic Life.* New York: Vintage, 1985.

James, William. *The Principles of Psychology.* 2 vols. New York: Dover, 1950.

Jameson, Fredric. *Postmodernism, or The Cultural Logic of Late Capitalism.* Durham, NC: Duke University Press, 1991.

Janowitz, Anne. "The Artifactual Sublime: Making London Poetry." In *Romantic Metropolis: The Urban Scene of British Culture, 1780–1840,* edited by James Chandler and Kevin Gilmartin, 246–60. Cambridge: Cambridge University Press, 2005.

Johns, Adrian. *The Nature of the Book: Print and Knowledge in the Making.* Chicago: University of Chicago Press, 1998.

———. "The Piratical Enlightenment." In *This Is Enlightenment,* edited by Clifford Siskin and William Warner, 301–20. Chicago: University of Chicago Press, 2010.

Johns, Donald C. "In Defence of Haydn: The 'Surprise' Symphony Revisited." *Music Review* 24 (1963): 305–12.

Johnson, Barbara. *The Critical Difference: Essays in the Contemporary Rhetoric of Reading.* Baltimore: Johns Hopkins University Press, 1980.

———. *Persons and Things.* Cambridge, MA: Harvard University Press, 2008.

Johnson, Samuel. *A Dictionary of the English Language.* 2 vols. London: J. and P. Knapton, T. and T. Longman, C. Hitch and L. Hawes, A. Millar, and R. and J. Dodsley, 1755.

———. *"The Idler" and "The Adventurer."* Vol. 2 of *The Yale Edition of the Works of Samuel Johnson.* Edited by W. J. Bate, J. M. Bullitt, and L. F. Powell. New Haven, CT: Yale University Press, 1958.

———. *The Rambler*. Vol. 3 of *The Yale Edition of the Works of Samuel Johnson*. Edited by W. J. Bate and Albrecht B. Strauss. New Haven, CT: Yale University Press, 1969.

Jordan, Sarah. "From Grotesque Bodies to Useful Hands: Idleness, Industry, and the Laboring Class." *Eighteenth-Century Life* 25, no. 3 (2001): 62–79.

Jost, Jacob Sider. *Interest and Connection in the Eighteenth Century: Hervey, Johnson, Smith, Equiano*. Charlottesville: University of Virginia Press, 2020.

Junker, Carl Ludwig. *Zwanzig Componisten: Eine Skizze*. Bern: Typographischen Gesellschaft, 1776.

Kames, Lord Henry Home. *Loose Hints upon Education, Chiefly Concerning the Culture of the Heart*. 2nd ed. London: John Murray, 1782.

Kane, Brian. *Sound Unseen: Acousmatic Sound in Theory and Practice*. New York: Oxford University Press, 2014.

Kant, Immanuel. *Critique of Judgment*. Translated by Werner S. Pluhar. Indianapolis: Hackett, 1987.

Karamzin, Nikolai. *Letters of a Russian Traveler, 1789-90*. Translated by Andrew Kahn. Oxford: Voltaire Foundation, 2003.

Kassler, Michael, ed. *The Music Trade in Georgian England*. Aldershot, UK: Ashgate, 2011.

Kelly, Isabella. *Joscelina, or The Rewards of Benevolence*. Vol 1. London: T. N. Longman, 1797.

King, Alec Hyatt. "Music Circulating Libraries in Britain." *Musical Times* 119 (1978): 134–38.

Kittler, Friedrich. "The City Is a Medium." Translated by Matthew Griffin. *New Literary History* 27, no. 4 (1996): 717–29.

Kivy, Peter. *Authenticities: Philosophical Reflections on Musical Performance*. Ithaca, NY: Cornell University Press, 1995.

Knapp, Raymond. *Making Light: Haydn, Musical Camp, and the Long Shadow of German Idealism*. Durham, NC: Duke University Press, 2018.

Knight, Richard Payne. *The Progress of Civil Society: A Didactic Poem in Six Books*. London: G. Nicol, 1796.

Komlós, Katalin. "Miscellaneous Vocal Genres." In *The Cambridge Companion to Haydn*, edited by Caryl Clark, 164–75. Cambridge: Cambridge University Press, 2005.

———. "Haydn's English Canzonettas in Their Local Context." In *Engaging Haydn: Culture, Context, and Criticism*, edited by Mary Hunter and Richard Will, 75–99. Cambridge: Cambridge University Press, 2012.

Kramer, Lawrence. "The Kitten and the Tiger: Tovey's Haydn." In *The Cambridge Companion to Haydn*, edited by Caryl Clark, 239–48. Cambridge: Cambridge University Press, 2005.

———. "Recalling the Sublime: The Logic of Creation in Haydn's *Creation*." *Eighteenth-Century Music* 6, no. 1 (2009): 41–57.

Kramer, Richard. *Cherubino's Leap: In Search of the Enlightenment Moment*. Chicago: University of Chicago Press, 2016.

Kubler, George A. *A New History of Stereotyping*. New York: J. J. Little & Ives, 1941.

Lamb, Jonathan. *The Things Things Say*. Princeton, NJ: Princeton University Press, 2011.

Larkin, Brian. "The Poetics and Politics of Infrastructure." *Annual Review of Anthropology* 42 (2013): 327–43.

Latour, Bruno. *Pandora's Hope: Essays on the Reality of Science Studies*. Cambridge, MA: Harvard University Press, 1999.

———. "Why Has Critique Run Out of Steam? From Matters of Fact to Matters of Concern." *Critical Inquiry* 30 (2004): 225–48.

————. *Reassembling the Social: An Introduction to Actor-Network-Theory.* New York: Oxford University Press, 2005.

Levine, Caroline. *Forms: Whole, Rhythm, Network, Hierarchy.* Princeton, NJ: Princeton University Press, 2015.

Lindorff, Joyce. "Burney, Macartney and the Qianlong Emperor: The Role of Music in the British Embassy to China, 1792–1794." *Early Music* 40, no. 3 (2012): 441–53.

Locke, John. *An Essay concerning Human Understanding.* Edited by Peter H. Nidditch. Oxford: Clarendon, 1975.

————. *Second Treatise of Government.* Indianapolis: Hackett, 1980.

————. "Some Thoughts on Education." In *"Some Thoughts on Education" and "Of the Conduct of the Understanding,"* edited by Ruth W. Grant and Nathan Tarcov, 1–162. Indianapolis: Hackett, 1996.

Lockhart, Ellen. "Pygmalion and the Music of Mere Interest." *Representations* 132 (2015): 95–103.

————. "Voice Boxes." In *London Voices 1820–1840: Performers, Practices, Histories,* edited by Roger Parker and Susan Rutherford, 261–79. Chicago: University of Chicago Press, 2019.

Lodes, Birgit, Elisabeth Reisinger, and John Wilson, eds. *Beethoven und andere Hofmusiker seiner Generation.* Bonn: Beethoven-Haus Bonn, 2018.

Loughridge, Deirdre. *Haydn's Sunrise, Beethoven's Shadow: Audiovisual Culture and the Emergence of Musical Romanticism.* Chicago: University of Chicago Press, 2016.

Lynch, Deidre. *The Economy of Character: Novels, Market Culture, and the Business of Inner Meaning.* Chicago: University of Chicago Press, 1998.

————. "Personal Effects and Sentimental Fictions." *Eighteenth-Century Fiction* 12, no. 2–3 (2000): 345–68.

————. "Counterpublics: Shopping and Women's Sociability." In *Romantic Sociability: Social Networks and Literary Culture in Britain, 1770–1840,* edited by Gillian Russell and Clara Tuite, 211–36. Cambridge: Cambridge University Press, 2002.

————. *Loving Literature: A Cultural History.* Chicago: University of Chicago Press, 2015.

Mace, Nancy. "Haydn and the London Music Sellers: Forster v. Longman & Broderip." *Music and Letters* 77, no. 4 (1996): 527–41.

————. "Litigating the 'Musical Magazine': The Definition of British Music Copyright in the 1780s." *Book History* 2 (1999): 122–45.

————. "Charles Rennett and the London Music-Sellers in the 1780s: Testing the Ownership of Reversionary Copyrights." *Journal of the Royal Musical Association* 129, no. 1 (2004): 1–23.

Madrid, Alejandro. "Diversity, Tokenism, Non-Canonical Musics, and the Crisis of the Humanities in US Academia." *Journal of Music History Pedagogy* 7, no. 2 (2017): 124–30.

Mainwaring, John. *Memoirs of the Life of the late George Frederic Handel.* London: R and J. Dodsley, 1760.

Mann, Friedrich Theodor. "Extraconcerte." In *Musikalisches Taschenbuch auf das Jahr 1805,* 62–63. Penig: F. Dienemann, 1805.

March, James, and Johan Olsen. "Elaborating the 'New Institutionalism.'" In *The Oxford Handbook of Political Institutions,* edited by Sarah Binder, R. A. W. Rhodes, and Bert Rockman, 3–22. New York: Oxford University Press, 2006.

Marshall, David. *The Figure of Theater: Shaftesbury, Defoe, Adam Smith, and George Eliot.* New York: Columbia University Press, 1986.

Marx, Karl. *Grundrisse: Foundations of the Critique of Political Economy.* Translated by Martin Nicolaus. London: Penguin, 1973.

———. *Capital: A Critique of Political Economy.* Vol. 1. Translated by Ben Fowkes. London: Penguin, 1990.

Mathew, Nicholas. "Heroic Haydn, the Occasional Work, and 'Modern' Political Music." *Eighteenth-Century Music* 4 (2007): 7–25.

———. "'Achieved Is the Glorious Work': *The Creation* and the Choral Work Concept." In *Engaging Haydn: Culture, Context, and Criticism,* edited by Mary Hunter and Richard Will, 124–42. Cambridge: Cambridge University Press, 2012.

———. *Political Beethoven.* Cambridge: Cambridge University Press, 2013.

———. "Out of Circulation: Beethoven, 'Hat man nicht auch Gold beineben' (Rocco), *Fidelio,* Act I." *Cambridge Opera Journal* 28, no. 2 (2016): 145–48.

———. "Vienna, 18 October 1814: Urban Space and Public Memory in the Napoleonic 'Occasional Melodrama.'" In *The Melodramatic Moment: Music and Theatrical Culture, 1790–1820,* edited by Katherine Hambridge and Jonathan Hicks, 171–89. Chicago: University of Chicago Press, 2018.

———. "Interest and the Musical History of the Attention Economy." *Journal of the American Musicological Society* 72, no. 2 (2019): 547–52.

———. "Listening(s) Past: History and the Mediatic Musicology." *Representations* 154 (2021): 143–55.

Mathew, Nicholas, and Mary Ann Smart. "Elephants in the Music Room: The Future of Quirk Historicism." *Representations* 132 (2015): 61–78.

Mattheson, Johann. *Der vollkommene Capellmeister* [1739]. Facsimile ed., edited by Margarete Reimann. Kassel: Bärenreiter, 1954.

Mauss, Marcel. *The Gift: The Form and Reason for Exchange in Archaic Societies.* Translated by W. D. Halls. New York: W. W. Norton, 1990.

Mayes, Catherine. "Reconsidering an Early Exoticism: Viennese Adaptations of Hungarian-Gypsy Music around 1800." *Eighteenth-Century Music* 6, no. 2 (2009): 161–81.

———. "Eastern European National Music as Concept and Commodity at the Turn of the Nineteenth Century." *Music and Letters* 95, no. 1 (2014): 70–91.

McDonald, Rónán, ed. *The Values of Literary Studies: Critical Institutions, Scholarly Agendas.* Cambridge: Cambridge University Press, 2015.

McDowell, Paula. *The Invention of the Oral: Print Commerce and Fugitive Voices in Eighteenth-Century Britain.* Chicago: University of Chicago Press, 2017.

McEnaney, Tom. *Acoustic Properties: Radio, Narrative, and the New Neighborhood of the Americas.* Evanston, IL: Northwestern University Press, 2017.

McKendrick, Neil. "George Packwood and the Commercialization of Shaving: The Art of Eighteenth-Century Advertising, or 'The Way to Get Money and Be Happy.'" In *The Birth of a Consumer Society: The Commercialization of Eighteenth-Century England,* edited by John Brewer, Neil McKendrick, and J. H. Plumb, 146–96. London: Europa, 1982.

McVeigh, Simon. *Concert Life in London from Mozart to Haydn.* Cambridge: Cambridge University Press, 1993.

Mears, Helen. "Silver Service Slavery: The Black Presence in the White Home." In *(Re)Figuring Human Enslavement: Images of Power, Violence, and Resistance,* edited by Andreas Exenberger, Adrian Knapp, and Ulrich Pallua, 45–66. Innsbruck, Austria: Innsbruck University Press, 2009.

Meci, Jonathan. "The Afterlives of Pergolesi's *Stabat Mater.*" PhD diss., University of California, Berkeley, 2019.

Mehta, Uday Singh. *Liberalism and Empire: A Study in Nineteenth-Century British Liberal Thought.* Chicago: University of Chicago Press, 1999.

Meneley, Tobias. "Acts of Sympathy: Abolitionist Poetry and Transatlantic identification." In *Affect and Abolition in the Anglo-Atlantic, 1770-1830*, edited by Stephen Ahern, 45–67. Farnham, UK: Ashgate, 2013.

Mieszkowski, Jan. *Labors of Imagination: Aesthetics and Political Economy from Kant to Althusser.* New York: Fordham University Press, 2006.

Mikusi, Balázs. "New Light on Haydn's 'Invocation of Neptune.'" *Studia Musicologica* 3, no. 4 (2005): 237–55.

Miller, Christopher. *Surprise: The Poetics of the Unexpected from Milton to Austen.* Ithaca, NY: Cornell University Press, 2015.

Mirka, Danuta. "Introduction." In *The Oxford Handbook of Topic Theory*, edited by Danuta Mirka, 1–60. New York: Oxford University Press, 2014.

———. "Topics and Meter." In *The Oxford Handbook of Topic Theory*, edited by Danuta Mirka, 357–80. New York: Oxford University Press, 2014.

Mitchell, W. J. T., ed. *Landscape and Power.* Chicago: University of Chicago Press, 1994.

Monelle, Raymond. *The Musical Topic: Hunt, Military and Pastoral.* Bloomington: Indiana University Press, 2006.

Moreno, Jairo, and Gavin Steingo. "Introduction." In "Econophonia: Music, Value, and Forms of Life." Special issue, *boundary 2* 43, no. 1 (2016): 1–3.

Morley, Henry, ed. *The Spectator: A New Edition.* 3 vols. London: Routledge, 1891.

Morrison, Matthew. "Race, Blacksound, and the (Re)Making of Musicological Discourse." *Journal of the American Musicological Society* 72, no. 3 (2019): 781–823.

Morrow, Mary Sue. *Concert Life in Haydn's Vienna: Aspects of a Developing Musical and Social Institution.* Stuyvesant, NY: Pendragon, 1989.

Moseley, Roger. *Keys to Play: Music as a Ludic Medium from Apollo to Nintendo.* Oakland: University of California Press, 2016.

Moten, Fred. *In the Break: The Aesthetics of the Black Radical Tradition.* Minneapolis: University of Minnesota Press, 2003.

Multigraph Collective. *Interacting with Print: Elements of Reading in the Era of Print Saturation.* Chicago: University of Chicago Press, 2018.

Mundy, Rachel. "Evolutionary Categories and Musical Style, from Adler to America." *Journal of the American Musicological Society* 67, no. 3 (2014): 735–68.

Murdoch, John. "The Landscape of Labor: Transformations of the Georgic." In *Romantic Revolutions: Criticism and Theory*, edited by Kenneth R. Johnston, Gilbert Chaitin, Karen Hanson, and Herbert Marks, 176–93. Bloomington: Indiana University Press, 1990.

Musselwhite, David. "The Trial of Warren Hastings." In *Literature, Politics, Theory*, edited by Francis Barker, Peter Hulme, Margaret Iversen, and Diana Loxley, 77–103. New York: Methuen, 1986.

Nash, Richard. "Animal Nomenclature: Facing Other Animals." In *Humans and Other Animals in Eighteenth-Century British Culture: Representation, Hybridity, Ethics*, edited by Frank Palmeri, 101–18. Aldershot, UK: Ashgate, 2006.

Nathan, Hans. "Negro Impersonation in Eighteenth-Century England." *Notes* 2, no. 4 (1945): 245–54.

The New Cries of London, with Characteristic Engravings. London: Darton & Harvey, 1803.

New Music Published in London, and imported from different Parts of Europe, in the Year, 1781. London: Longman & Broderip, 1781.

Nex, Jenny. "Longman & Broderip." In *The Music Trade in Georgian England*, edited by Michael Kassler, 9–93. Aldershot, UK: Ashgate, 2011.

Ngai, Sianne. *Our Aesthetic Categories: Zany, Cute, Interesting*. Cambridge, MA: Harvard University Press, 2012.

Nugent, Thomas. *The Grand Tour. Containing an Exact Description of Most of the Cities, Towns, and Remarkable Places of Europe*. Vol. 3. London: Birt, Browne, Millar, and Hawkins, 1749.

Nussbaum, Felicity. *The Limits of the Human: Fictions of Anomaly, Race, and Gender in the Long Eighteenth Century*. Cambridge: Cambridge University Press, 2003.

———. "'Mungo here, Mungo there': Charles Dibdin and Racial Performance." In *Charles Dibdin and Late Georgian Culture*, edited by Oskar Cox Jensen, David Kennerley, and Ian Newman, 23–42. New York: Oxford University Press, 2018.

Nussbaum, Martha. *Upheavals of Thought: The Intelligence of Emotions*. Cambridge: Cambridge University Press, 2001.

———. *Political Emotions: Why Love Matters for Justice*. Cambridge, MA: Harvard University Press, 2013.

Oakleaf, David. "Marks, Stamps, and Representations: Character in Eighteenth-Century Fiction." *Studies of the Novel* 23 (1991): 295–311.

Ochoa Gautier, Ana Maria. *Aurality: Listening and Knowledge in Nineteenth-Century Columbia*. Durham, NC: Duke University Press, 2014.

———. "Acoustic Multinaturalism, the Value of Nature, and the Nature of Music in Ecomusicology." *boundary 2* 43, no. 1 (2016): 107–41.

Olleson, Edward. "The Origin and Libretto of Haydn's *Creation*." *Haydn Yearbook* 4 (1968): 148–66.

O'Quinn, Daniel. "George Colman's *Inkle and Yarico* and the Racialization of Class Relations." *Theater Journal* 54, no. 3 (2002): 389–409.

"Oratorium." *Wiener allgemeine musikalische Zeitung* 5 (January 30, 1813): cols. 66–75.

Osteen, Mark, and Martha Woodmansee. *The New Economic Criticism*. New York: Routledge, 1999.

Packham, Catherine. *Eighteenth-Century Vitalism: Bodies, Culture, Politics*. New York: Palgrave Macmillan, 2012.

———. "System and Subject in Adam Smith's Political Economy: Nature, Vitalism, and Bioeconomic Life." In *Systems of Life: Biopolitics, Economics, and Literature on the Cusp of Modernity*, edited by Richard Barney and Warren Montag, 93–113. New York: Fordham University Press, 2018.

Paganelli, Maria Pia. "The Moralizing Role of Distance in Adam Smith: *The Theory of Moral Sentiments* as Possible Praise of Commerce." *History of Political Economy* 42, no. 3 (2010): 425–41.

Pandi, Marianne, and Fritz Schmidt. "Musik zur Zeit Haydns und Beethovens in der Pressburger Zeitung." *Haydn Jahrbuch* 8 (1971): 165–265.

Parke, William. *Musical Memoirs, Comprising an Account of the General State of Music in England, from the First Commemoration of Handel in 1784, to the Year 1830*. Vol. 1. London: Henry Colburn and Richard Bentley, 1830.

Parker, Roger. "Two Styles in 1830s London: 'The Form and Order of a Perspicuous Unity.'" In *The Invention of Beethoven and Rossini: Historiography, Analysis, Criticism*, edited by Nicholas Mathew and Benjamin Walton, 123–38. Cambridge: Cambridge University Press, 2013.

Paulson, Ronald. *The Beautiful, Novel, and Strange: Aesthetics and Heterodoxy*. Baltimore: Johns Hopkins University Press, 1996.

Perec, Georges. *Species of Spaces and Other Pieces*. Edited and translated by John Sturrock. London: Penguin, 1997.

Phillips, Adam. "On Being Bored." In *On Kissing, Tickling, and Being Bored: Psychoanalytic Essays on the Unexamined Life*, 68–78. Cambridge, MA: Harvard University Press, 1993.

——. *Attention Seeking*. London: Penguin, 2019.

Phillips, Natalie M. *Distraction: Problems of Attention in Eighteenth-Century Literature*. Baltimore: Johns Hopkins University Press, 2016.

Piekut, Benjamin. *Experimentalism Otherwise: The New York Avant-Garde and Its Limits*. Berkeley: University of California Press, 2011.

——. "Actor-Networks in Music History: Clarifications and Critiques." *Twentieth-Century Music* 11 (2014): 191–215.

Piekut, Benjamin, and Jason Stanyek. "Deadness: Technologies of the Intermundane." *Drama Review* 54, no. 1 (2010): 14–38.

Pikulik, Lothar. *Ästhetik des Interessanten: Zum Wandel der Kunst- und Lebensanschauung in der Moderne*. Hildesheim, Germany: Olms, 2014.

Pisani, Michael. *Imagining Native America in Music*. New Haven, CT: Yale University Press, 2006.

Pitts, Jennifer. *A Turn to Empire: The Rise of Imperial Liberalism in Britain and France*. Princeton, NJ: Princeton University Press, 2006.

Pocock, J. G. A. "The Mobility of Property and the Rise of Eighteenth-Century Sociology." In *Virtue, Commerce, and History: Essays on Political Thought and History, Chiefly in the Eighteenth Century*, 103–24. Cambridge: Cambridge University Press, 1985.

Pohl, Carl Ferdinand. *Mozart und Haydn in London*. Vienna: C. Gerold's Sohn, 1867.

Polanyi, Karl. *The Great Transformation: The Political and Economic Origins of Our Time* [1945]. Boston: Beacon Press, 2011.

Pomian, Krzysztof. *Collectors and Curiosities: Paris and Venice, 1500–1800*. Translated by Elizabeth Wiles-Portier. Cambridge: Polity, 1990.

Poovey, Mary. "Aesthetics and Political Economy in the Eighteenth Century: The Place of Gender in the Social Constitution of Knowledge." In *Aesthetics and Ideology*, edited by George Levine, 79–105. New Brunswick, NJ: Rutgers University Press, 1994.

——. *Genres of the Credit Economy: Mediating Value in Eighteenth- and Nineteenth-Century Britain*. Chicago: University of Chicago Press, 2008.

Poriss, Hilary. *Changing the Score: Arias, Prima Donnas, and the Authority of Performance*. New York: Oxford University Press, 2009.

Porter, David. "Monstrous Beauty: Eighteenth-Century Fashion and the Aesthetics of Chinese Taste." *Eighteenth-Century Studies* 35, no. 3 (2002): 395–411.

Power, Susan C. *Art of the Cherokee: Prehistory to the Present*. Athens: University of Georgia Press, 2007.

Pratt, Mary Louise. *Imperial Eyes: Travel Writing and Transculturation*. New York: Routledge, 1992.

Price, F. G. Hilton. *A Handbook of London Bankers, with Some Account of Their Predecessors, the Early Goldsmiths*. London: Chatto and Windus, 1876.

Price, Leah. *The Anthology and the Rise of the Novel: From Richardson to George Eliot*. Cambridge: Cambridge University Press, 2000.

——. "From *The History of a Book* to a 'History of the Book.'" *Representations* 108 (2009): 120–38.

Price, Uvedale. *An Essay on the Picturesque as Compared with the Sublime and the Beautiful.* London: J. Robson, 1794.

Rabin, Ronald, and Steven Zohn. "Arne, Handel, Walsh, and Music as Intellectual Property: Two Eighteenth-Century Lawsuits." *Journal of the Royal Musical Association* 120, no. 1 (1995): 112–45.

Rasch, Rudolf, ed. *Music Publishing in Europe, 1600–1900.* Berlin: BWV, 2005.

———, ed. *The Circulation of Music in Europe, 1600–1900.* Berlin: BWV, 2008.

Ratner, Leonard. *Classic Music: Expression, Form, Style.* New York: Schirmer, 1980.

Raynal, Guillaume Thomas. *A Philosophical and Political History of the Settlements and Trade of the Europeans in the East and West Indies.* 2nd ed., vol. 6. Translated by J. O. Justamond. London: Strahan, Cadell, and Davies, 1798.

Raz, Carmel. "An Eighteenth-Century Theory of Musical Cognition? John Holden's *Essay toward a Rational System of Music* (1770)." *Journal of Music Theory* 62.2 (2018): 205–48.

Reichardt, Johann Friedrich. *Musikalisches Kunstmagazin* 1 (1782).

———. *Berlinische musikalische Zeitung* 1 (1805).

Rice, John. "*Montezuma* at Eszterház: A Pasticcio on a New World Theme." Paper presented at the conference Joseph Haydn und die Neue Welt: Musik- und Kulturgeschichtliche Perspektiven, Eisenstadt, April 2011.

———. "Did Haydn Attend the Handel Commemoration in Westminster Abbey?" *Early Music* 40, no. 1 (2012): 73–80.

Richards, Annette. *The Free Fantasia and the Musical Picturesque.* Cambridge: Cambridge University Press, 2001.

———. "Carl Philipp Emanuel Bach, Portraits, and the Physiognomy of Music History." *Journal of the American Musicological Society* 66 (2013): 337–96.

Ridgewell, Rupert. "Mozart's Publishing Plans with Artaria in 1787: New Archival Evidence." *Music and Letters* 83, no. 1 (2002): 30–74.

———. "Artaria's Music Shop and Boccherini's Music in Viennese Musical Life." *Early Music* 33, no. 2 (2005): 179–89.

———. "Economic Aspects: The Artaria Case." In *The Circulation of Music in Europe, 1600–1900*, edited by Rudolf Rasch, 89–113. Berlin: BWV, 2008.

———. "Inside a Viennese *Kunsthandlung*: Artaria in 1784." In *Consuming Music: Individuals, Institutions, Communities, 1730–1830*, edited by Emily Green and Catherine Mayes, 29–61. Rochester, NY: University of Rochester Press, 2017.

Riley, Matthew. *Musical Listening in the German Enlightenment: Attention, Wonder, and Astonishment.* Aldershot, UK: Ashgate, 2004.

Rind, Miles. "The Concept of Disinterestedness in Eighteenth-Century British Aesthetics." *Journal of the History of Philosophy* 40 (2002): 67–87.

Roach, Joseph. *The Player's Passion: Studies in the Science of Acting.* Ann Arbor: University of Michigan Press, 1993.

———. *Cities of the Dead: Circum-Atlantic Performance.* New York: Columbia University Press, 1996.

———. *It.* Ann Arbor: University of Michigan Press, 2007.

Robbins Landon, H. C. *Haydn: Chronicle and Works.* 5 vols. Bloomington: Indiana University Press, 1976–80.

———. "Four New Haydn Letters." *Haydn Yearbook* 13 (1982): 213–19.

Robinson, Dylan. *Hungry Listening: Resonant Theory for Indigenous Sound Studies.* Minneapolis: University of Minnesota Press, 2020.

Roscoe, Christopher. "Haydn and London in the 1780s." *Music and Letters* 49, no. 3 (1968): 203–12.

Rose, Mark. *Authors and Owners: The Invention of Copyright.* Cambridge, MA: Harvard University Press, 1993.

Rose, Stephen. *Musical Authorship from Schütz to Bach.* Cambridge: Cambridge University Press, 2019.

Rosenthal, Albi. "The Contract between Joseph Haydn and Frederick Augustus Hyde." In *Studies in Music History Presented to H. C. Robbins Landon on His Seventieth Birthday,* edited by Otto Biba and David Wyn Jones, 72–111. London: Thames and Hudson, 1996.

Rosenthal, Jamie. "The Contradictions of Racialized Sensibility: Gender, Slavery, and the Limits of Sympathy." In *Affect and Abolition in the Anglo-Atlantic, 1770–1830,* edited by Stephen Ahern, 172–88. Farnham, UK: Ashgate, 2013.

Rowland, David. "Clementi as Publisher." In *The Music Trade in Georgian England,* edited by Michael Kassler, 159–91. Aldershot, UK: Ashgate, 2011.

Rowlinson, Matthew. *Real Money and Romanticism.* Cambridge: Cambridge University Press, 2010.

Rumph, Stephen. *Mozart and Enlightenment Semiotics.* Berkeley: University of California Press, 2012.

Salmen, Walter. "Johann Friedrich Reichardt in Berlin." *Jahrbuch des Staatlichen Instituts für Musikforschung Preußischer Kulturbesitz* (2001): 27–44.

Sanguinetti, Giorgio. *The Art of Partimento: History, Theory, and Practice.* New York: Oxford University Press, 2012.

Sauberlich, Kim. "Haydn's Spirits: Genealogies of Black Performance in Nineteenth-Century Brazil." Paper presented at the Annual Meeting of the American Musicological Society, Boston, 2019.

Scarry, Elaine. *The Body in Pain: The Making and Unmaking of the World.* New York: Oxford University Press, 1985.

Scarry, Richard. *What Do People Do All Day?* New York: Random House, 1968.

Schabas, Margaret. *The Natural Origins of Economics.* Chicago: University of Chicago Press, 2005.

Schafer, R. Murray. *The Soundscape: Our Sonic Environment and the Tuning of the World.* Rochester, VT: Destiny Books, 1977. Reprint, 1994.

Schlegel, Friedrich. *On the Study of Greek Poetry.* Edited and translated by Stuart Barnett. Albany: State University of New York Press, 2001.

Schönfeld, Johann Ferdinand Ritter von. "A Yearbook of the Music of Vienna and Prague, 1796," translated by Kathrine Talbot. In *Haydn and His World,* edited by Elaine Sisman, 289–320. Princeton, NJ: Princeton University Press, 1997.

Schroeder, David P. *Haydn and the Enlightenment: The Late Symphonies and Their Audience.* Oxford: Clarendon, 1998.

Searle, Arthur. "Pleyel's 'London' Symphonies." *Early Music* 36 (2008): 231–42.

Senici, Emanuele. "Rossinian Repetitions." In *The Invention of Beethoven and Rossini: Historiography, Analysis, Criticism,* edited by Nicholas Mathew and Benjamin Walton, 236–62. Cambridge: Cambridge University Press, 2013.

———. *Music in the Present Tense: Rossini's Italian Operas in Their Time.* Chicago: University of Chicago Press, 2019.

Shaftesbury, 3rd Earl of [Anthony Ashley Cooper]. *Characteristics of Men, Manners, Opinions, Times.* Edited by Lawrence E. Klein. Cambridge: Cambridge University Press, 1999.

Sheehan, Jonathan, and Dror Wahrman. *Invisible Hands: Self-Organization and the Eighteenth Century*. Chicago: University of Chicago Press, 2015.

Shell, Marc. *Money, Language, and Thought: Literary and Philosophic Economies from the Medieval to the Modern Era*. Baltimore: Johns Hopkins University Press, 1982.

Shesgreen, Sean. *Images of the Outcast: The Urban Poor in the Cries of London*. New Brunswick, NJ: Rutgers University Press, 2002.

Simmel, Georg. "The Metropolis and Mental Life" (1903). Translated by Edward Shils. In *The Blackwell City Reader*, 2nd ed., edited by Gary Bridge and Sophie Watson, 103–10. Chichester, UK: Wiley-Blackwell, 2010.

Siskin, Clifford. *The Work of Writing: Literature and Social Change in Britain, 1700–1830*. Baltimore: Johns Hopkins University Press, 1998.

Siskin, Clifford, and William Warner, eds. *This Is Enlightenment*. Chicago: University of Chicago Press, 2010.

———. "If This Is Enlightenment then What Is Romanticism?" *European Romantic Review* 22, no. 3 (2011): 281–91.

Sisman, Elaine R. "Haydn's Theater Symphonies." *Journal of the American Musicological Society* 43, no. 2 (1990): 292–352.

———. *Haydn and the Classical Variation*. Cambridge, MA: Harvard University Press, 1993.

———. "Haydn, Shakespeare, and the Rules of Originality." In *Haydn and His World*, edited by Elaine Sisman, 3–56. Princeton, NJ: Princeton University Press, 1997.

———. "Haydn's Career and the Idea of the Multiple Audience." In *The Cambridge Companion to Haydn*, edited by Caryl Clark, 3–16. Cambridge: Cambridge University Press, 2005.

———. "The Voice of God in Haydn's *Creation*." In *Essays in Honor of László Somfai on His 70th Birthday: Studies in the Sources and the Interpretation of Music*, edited by László Vikárius and Vera Lampert, 139–53. Lanham, MD: Scarecrow, 2005.

Sloterdijk, Peter. *In the World Interior of Capital: For a Philosophical Theory of Globalization*. Translated by Wieland Hoban. Cambridge: Polity, 2013.

Small, John. "The Development of Musical Copyright." In *The Music Trade in Georgian England*, edited by Michael Kassler, 233–86. Aldershot, UK: Ashgate, 2011.

Smith, Adam. *The Theory of Moral Sentiments*. Edited by Knud Haakonssen. Cambridge: Cambridge University Press, 2002.

———. *The Wealth of Nations, Books I–III*. London: Penguin, 1986.

Smith, Jacob. *Eco-Sonic Media*. Oakland: University of California Press, 2015.

Smith, John Thomas. *Vagabondiana, or Anecdotes of Mendicant Wanderers through the Streets of London, with Portraits of the Most Remarkable Drawn from the Life*. London: J. & A. Arch, Hatchard & Clarke, 1817.

Smith, Ruth. *Handel's Oratorios and Eighteenth-Century Thought*. Cambridge: Cambridge University Press, 1995.

Solomon, Maynard. "Beethoven's *Magazin der Kunst*." In *Beethoven Essays*, 193–204. Cambridge, MA: Harvard University Press, 1988.

———. "The Nobility Pretense." In *Beethoven Essays*, 43–55. Cambridge, MA: Harvard University Press, 1988.

———. "Some Images of Creation in Music of the Viennese Classical School." *Musical Quarterly* 89, no. 1 (2006): 121–135.

Somfai, László. "The London Revision of Haydn's Instrumental Style." *Proceedings of the Royal Musical Association* 100 (1973): 159–74.

South, Robert. *Twelve Sermons Preached Upon Several Occasions*. 6th ed. Vol. 1. London: Bowyer, 1727.

Spacks, Patricia Meyer. *Boredom: The Literary History of a State of Mind*. Chicago: University of Chicago Press, 1995.

Spazier, Johann Gottlieb Karl. "Die Jahreszeiten von Haydn, in Leipzig." *Zeitung für die elegante Welt* 157 (December 31, 1801): cols. 1261–63.

Spillers, Hortense. "Mama's Baby, Papa's Maybe: An American Grammar Book." *Diacritics* 17, no. 2 (1987): 64–81.

Spivak, Gayatri Chakravorty. "Scattered Speculations on the Question of Value." *Diacritics* 15 (1985): 73–93.

———. "Can the Subaltern Speak?" In *Marxism and the Interpretation of Culture*, edited by Cary Nelson and Lawrence Grossberg, 271–313. Urbana: University of Illinois Press, 1988.

Stahl, Matt. *Unfree Masters: Recording Artists and the Politics of Work*. Durham, NC: Duke University Press, 2013.

Steege, Benjamin. *Helmholtz and the Modern Listener*. Cambridge: Cambridge University Press, 2012.

Steingo, Gavin. *Kwaito's Promise: Music and the Aesthetics of Freedom in South Africa*. Chicago: University of Chicago Press, 2016.

———. "Musical Economies of the Elusive Metropolis." In *Audible Empire: Music, Global Politics, Critique*, edited by Tejumola Olaniyan and Ronald Radano, 246–66. Durham, NC: Duke University Press, 2016.

———. "Actors and Accidents in South African Electronic Music: An Essay on Multiple Ontologies." *Contemporary Music Review* 37, no. 5–6 (2018): 554–74.

Steingo, Gavin, and Jim Sykes, eds. *Remapping Sound Studies*. Durham, NC: Duke University Press, 2019.

[Stendhal] Bombet, L. A. C. *Life of Haydn, in a Series of Letters Written at Vienna, followed by the Life of Mozart with Observations on Metastasio*. [Edited by William Gardiner]. London: John Murray, 1817.

Stengers, Isabelle. *Power and Invention: Situating Science*. Translated by Paul Bains. With a foreword by Bruno Latour. Minneapolis: University of Minnesota Press, 1997.

Sterne, Jonathan. *The Audible Past: The Cultural Origins of Sound Reproduction*. Durham, NC: Duke University Press, 2003.

———. "'What Do We Want?' 'Materiality!' 'When Do We Want It?' 'Now!'" In *Media Technologies: Essays on Communication, Materiality, and Society*, edited by Tarleton Gillespie, Pablo J. Boczkowski, and Kirsten A. Foot, 119–28. Cambridge, MA: MIT Press, 2014.

Sterne, Laurence. *A Sentimental Journey and Other Writings*. New York: Oxford University Press, 2003.

Stevens, Jane. "The Meanings and Uses of *Caractère* in Eighteenth-Century France." In *French Musical Thought, 1600–1800*, edited by Georgia Cowart, 23–53. Ann Arbor: University of Michigan Research Press, 1989.

Stewart, Susan. *On Longing: Narratives of the Miniature, the Gigantic, the Souvenir, the Collection*. Durham, NC: Duke University Press, 1993.

Stokes, Martin. "Marx, Money, and Musicians." In *Marx and Music: Ideas, Practice, Politics*, edited by Regula Burckhardt Qureshi, 139–66. London: Routledge, 2002.

Stolnitz, Jerome. "On the Origins of 'Aesthetic Disinterestedness.'" *Journal of Aesthetics and Art Criticism* 20 (1961): 131–43.

Straw, Will. "Some Things a Scene Might Be." *Cultural Studies* 29, no. 3 (2015): 476–85.

Strohm, Reinhard, ed. *The Eighteenth-Century Diaspora of Italian Music and Musicians*. Turnhout, Belgium: Brepols, 2001.

Sullivan, J. W. N. *Beethoven: His Spiritual Development* [1927]. London: Allen and Unwin, 1964.

Sulzer, Johann Georg. *Allgemeine Theorie der schönen Künste*. 2nd ed. 4 vols. Leipzig: Weidmann, 1792–94. Reprint, Hildesheim: Olms, 1967.

Sutcliffe, W. Dean. "Expressive Ambivalence in Haydn's Symphonic Slow Movements of the 1770s." *Journal of Musicology* 27 (2010): 84–134.

———. "Topics in Chamber Music." In *The Oxford Handbook of Topic Theory*, edited by Danuta Mirka, 118–40. New York: Oxford University Press, 2014.

———. *Instrumental Music in an Age of Sociability: Mozart, Haydn, and Friends*. New York: Cambridge University Press, 2020.

Swift, Jonathan. *A Letter of Advice to a Young Poet, together with a Proposal for the Encouragement of Poetry in This Kingdom*. London: W. Boreham, 1721.

Sykes, Jim. *The Musical Gift: Sonic Generosity in Post-War Sri Lanka*. New York: Oxford University Press, 2018.

———. "The Anthropocene and Music Studies." *Ethnomusicology Review* 22, no. 1 (2020): 4–21.

Sypher, Wylie. *Guinea's Captive Kings: British Anti-Slavery Literature of the Eighteenth-Century*. Chapel Hill: University of North Carolina Press, 1942.

Taylor, Ian. *Music in London and the Myth of Decline: From Haydn to the Philharmonic*. Cambridge: Cambridge University Press, 2010.

Taylor, Timothy. *Music and Capitalism: A History of the Present*. Chicago: University of Chicago Press, 2016.

Temperley, Nicholas. *Haydn: "The Creation."* Cambridge: Cambridge University Press, 1991.

Thayer, Alexander Wheelock. *Thayer's Life of Beethoven*. Edited and revised by Elliot Forbes. Princeton, NJ: Princeton University Press, 1967.

Thompson, E. P. *The Making of the English Working Class* [1963]. New York: Vintage Books, 1966.

———. "Time, Work-Discipline, and Industrial Capitalism." *Past and Present* 38 (1968): 56–97.

Thompson, Marie. "Whiteness and the Ontological Turn in Sound Studies." *Parallax* 23, no. 3 (2017): 266–82.

Thomson, James. *"The Seasons" and "The Castle of Indolence."* Edited by James Sambrook. Oxford: Clarendon, 1987.

Thormählen, Wiebke. "Playing with Art: Musical Arrangements as Educational Tools in van Swieten's Vienna." *Journal of Musicology* 27, no. 3 (2010): 342–76.

Tolley, Thomas. "Music in the Circle of Sir William Jones: A Contribution to the History of Haydn's Early Reputation." *Music and Letters* 73, no. 4 (1992): 525–50.

———. *Painting the Cannon's Roar: Music, the Visual Arts and the Rise of an Attentive Public in the Age of Haydn, c. 1750 to c. 1810*. Aldershot, UK: Ashgate, 2001.

———. *"Comic Readings* and *Tragic Readings:* Haydn's Observations on London Audience Responses in 1791." *Studia Musicologica* 51, no. 1–2 (2010): 153–78.

———. "Caricatures by Henry William Bunbury in the Collection of Joseph Haydn." In *The Land of Opportunity: Joseph Haydn and Britain*, edited by Richard Chesser and David Wyn Jones, 22–58. London: British Library, 2013.

Tong, Joanne. "Pity for the Poor Africans: William Cowper and the Limits of Abolitionist Affect." In *Affect and Abolition in the Anglo-Atlantic, 1770–1830*, edited by Stephen Ahern, 129–49. Farnham, UK: Ashgate, 2013.

Tovey, Donald Francis. *Essays in Musical Analysis: Symphonies and Other Orchestral Works.* New ed. London: Oxford University Press, 1981.

Triest, Johann Karl Friedrich. "Bermerkungen über die Ausbildung der Tonkunst in Deutschland im achtzehnten Jahrhundert." *Allgemeine musikalische Zeitung* 3 (1801): cols. 225–35, 241–49, 257–64, 273–86, 297–308, 321–32, 369–79, 389–401, 405–10, 421–32, 437–45.

Tsing, Anna. *The Mushroom at the End of the World: On the Possibility of Life in Capitalist Ruins.* Princeton, NJ: Princeton University Press, 2015.

Tuer, Andrew. *Bartolozzi and His Works.* 2 vols. London: Field & Tuer, 1882.

Twining, Thomas. "On the different Senses of the Word, Imitative, as applied to the Music by the Antients, and by the Moderns." In *Aristotle's Treatise on Poetry, translated: with notes on the translation, and the original; and two dissertations, on poetical, and musical, imitation* [1789], 2nd ed, vol. 1, 66–93. London: Luke Hansard & Sons, 1812.

Twyman, Michael. *Printing 1770–1970: An Illustrated History of Its Development and Uses in England.* London: Eyre and Spottiswoode, 1970.

van Oort, Bart. "Haydn and the English Classical Piano Style." *Early Music* 28, no. 1 (2000): 73–89.

van Orden, Kate, ed. *Music and the Cultures of Print.* New York: Garland, 2000.

———. *Music, Authorship, and the Book in the First Century of Print.* Berkeley: University of California Press, 2014.

———. *Materialities: Books, Readers, and the Chanson in Sixteenth-Century Europe.* New York: Oxford University Press, 2015.

Vogl, Joseph. *The Specter of Capital.* Translated by Joachim Redner and Robert Savage. Stanford, CA: Stanford University Press, 2015.

Wahrman, Dror. *The Making of the Modern Self: Identity and Culture in Eighteenth-Century England.* New Haven, CT: Yale University Press, 2004.

Wald, Gayle. "Soul Vibrations: Black Music and Black Freedom in Sound and Space." *American Quarterly* 63, no. 3 (2011): 673–96.

Wallerstein, Immanuel. *Historical Capitalism.* London: Verso, 1983.

Waltham-Smith, Naomi. *Music and Belonging between Revolution and Restoration.* New York: Oxford University Press, 2017.

Walton, Benjamin, "Quirk Shame." *Representations* 132 (2015): 121–29.

Waters, Mary. "Sympathy, Nerve Physiology, and National Degeneration in Anna Letitia Barbauld's *Epistle to William Wilberforce*." In *Affect and Abolition in the Anglo-Atlantic, 1770–1830,* edited by Stephen Ahern, 89–109. Farnham, UK: Ashgate, 2013.

Watkins, Holly. *Musical Vitalities: Ventures in a Biotic Aesthetics of Music.* Chicago: University of Chicago Press, 2018.

Weber, William. *The Rise of Musical Classics in Eighteenth-Century England: A Study in Canon, Ritual, and Ideology.* Oxford: Clarendon, 1992.

———, ed. *The Musician as Entrepreneur, 1700-1914.* Bloomington: Indiana University Press, 2004.

Webster, James. *Haydn's "Farewell" Symphony and the Idea of Classical Style: Through-Composition and Cyclic Integration in His Instrumental Music.* Cambridge: Cambridge University Press, 1991.

———. "*The Creation*, Haydn's Late Vocal Music, and the Musical Sublime." In *Haydn and His World,* edited by Elaine Sisman, 57–102. Princeton, NJ: Princeton University Press, 1997.

———. "The Sublime and the Pastoral in *The Creation* and *The Seasons*." In *The Cambridge Com-*

panion to Haydn, edited by Caryl Clark, 150–63. Cambridge: Cambridge University Press, 2005.

Weiss, Piero, and Richard Taruskin, eds. *Music in the Western World: A History in Documents.* 2nd ed. Belmont, CA: Thomson Schirmer, 2008.

Wendt, Amadeus. "Gedanken über die neuere Tonkunst, und van Beethoven's Music, namentlich dessen Fidelio." *Allgemeine musikalische Zeitung* 17 (June 21, 1815): cols. 400–415.

Wheatley, Phyllis. *Complete Writings.* London: Penguin, 2001.

Wheelock, Gretchen. "Marriage à la Mode: Haydn's Instrumental Works 'Englished' for Voice and Piano." *Journal of Musicology* 8, no. 3 (1990): 357–97.

———. *Haydn's "Ingenious Jesting with Art": Contexts of Musical Wit and Humor.* New York: Schirmer, 1992.

Whitaker, Katie. "The Culture of Curiosity." In *Cultures of Natural History*, edited by N. Jardine, J. A. Secord, and E. C. Spary, 75–90. Cambridge: Cambridge University Press, 1996.

Whiting, Steven Moore. "*Hört ihr wohl*: Zu Funktion und Programm von Beethovens Chorfantasie." *Archiv für Musikwissenschaft* 45 (1988): 132–47.

Will, Richard. *The Characteristic Symphony in the Age of Haydn and Beethoven.* Cambridge: Cambridge University Press, 2002.

Williams, Gavin. "A Voice of the Crowd: Futurism and the Politics of Noise." *Nineteenth-Century Music* 37 (2013): 113–29.

Williams, Raymond. *Culture and Society, 1780–1950.* New York: Columbia University Press, 1958.

———. *The Country and the City.* New York: Oxford University Press, 1973.

Wollstonecraft, Mary. "*A Vindication of the Rights of Men*" and "*A Vindication of the Rights of Woman*" and "*Hints*." Edited by Sylvana Tomaselli. Cambridge: Cambridge University Press, 1995.

Wood, Ellen Meiskins. *The Origin of Capitalism: A Longer View.* New York: Verso, 2002.

Woodfield, Ian. "Haydn Symphonies in Calcutta." *Music and Letters* 75, no. 1 (1994): 141–43.

———. "John Bland: London Retailer of the Music of Haydn and Mozart." *Music and Letters* 81 (2000): 210–44.

———. *Music of the Raj: A Social and Economic History of Music in Late Eighteenth-Century Anglo-Indian Society.* New York: Oxford University Press, 2000.

Woodmansee, Martha. *The Author, Art, and the Market: Rereading the History of Aesthetics.* New York: Columbia University Press, 1994.

Wordsworth, William. *William Wordsworth.* Selected by Seamus Heaney. London: Faber and Faber, 2011.

Wright, Josephine. "George Polgreen Bridgetower: An African Prodigy in England, 1789–99." *Musical Quarterly* 66, no. 1 (1980): 65–82.

Wu, Tim. *The Attention Merchants: The Epic Scramble to Get inside Our Heads.* New York: Vintage, 2017.

Wyn Jones, David. "From Artaria to Longman & Broderip: Mozart's Music on Sale in London." In *Studies in Music History Presented to H. C. Robbins Landon on His Seventieth Birthday*, edited by Otto Biba and David Wyn Jones, 105–11. London: Thames and Hudson, 1996.

———. *The Symphony in Beethoven's Vienna.* Cambridge: Cambridge University Press, 2006.

———. *The Life of Haydn.* Cambridge: Cambridge University Press, 2009.

———. "Haydn, Austria, and Britain: Music, Culture and Politics in the 1790s." In *The Land of Opportunity: Joseph Haydn and Britain*, edited by Richard Chesser and David Wyn Jones, 1–21. London: British Library, 2013.

————. *Music in Vienna: 1700, 1800, 1900.* Woodbridge, UK: Boydell, 2016.

Young, Edward. *Conjectures on Original Composition.* London: A. Millar, 1759.

Zaslaw, Neal. "Mozart as a Working Stiff." In *On Mozart*, edited by James Morris, 102–12. Cambridge: Cambridge University Press, 1994.

Zelter, Carl Friedrich. "Briefe an einen Freund über die Musik in Berlin." *Allgemeine musikalische Zeitung* 17 (January 21, 1801): cols. 289–96.

————. "Recension: Die Schöpfung. Ein Oratorium." *Allgemeine musikalische Zeitung* 24 (March 10, 1802): cols. 385–96.

————. "Recension: Die Jahreszeiten nach Thomson." *Allgemeine musikalische Zeitung* 31 (May 2, 1804): cols. 513–29.

Zerubavel, Eviatar. *Hidden in Plain Sight: The Social Structure of Irrelevance.* New York: Oxford University Press, 2015.

Index